Forwa

Dr. Brian Morley
Professor of Philosoph   ..geucs

I have always found the vast majority of Mormons to be very likable. Their emphasis on family, service, caring for each other, and traditional morality are also appealing. But of course what ultimately matters is whether their beliefs are true. It is just this question that my wife Donna faces head on. She has read thousands of pages of original Mormon documents, countless books by Mormon theologians on their church doctrine, and has talked with untold numbers of Latter-day Saints.

Over thirty years ago, Donna joined the Discipleship Evangelism outreach ministry (also known as Evangelism Explosion) at her former church, Grace Community, where John MacArthur pastors. As a trainee, and later a trainer, she had a lot of great opportunities to share with people, but realized that to be effective with people in a religion or sect she would have to learn a lot more about what they believed. She started her own study, and found that even basic words are understood differently. Words that seem straightforward, such as "grace," "salvation," "heaven," and "God," are defined differently, and will be misunderstood if we aren't aware of what the listener believes. Thus, much study led Donna to a more effective communication with people of different religious beliefs.

Donna soon found herself asked to friend's houses whenever people with different beliefs were due over, especially Mormon (or Jehovah's Witness) missionaries. Not being able to respond to every friend that asks her over, she has written this book, as a way of helping them and others, communicate effectively themselves. Donna has gotten a lot of encouraging emails about this book. One woman said,

> Donna, everything your wrote about what the
> Mormon missionaries would say– *they said.*
> This was so helpful to me, as I was readily able

to respond back, using your step-by-step approach. And, the Fact Sheet you provide is especially helpful in this endeavor. I wasn't intimidated at all! Best of all, because the Lord's Word doesn't come back void, I know I have given the missionaries much to think about. *Thank you!*"

A Mormon Bishop, who had held many positions in the Church and had been in meetings with the General Authorities, (members of the church's priesthood who are given administrative and ecclesiastical authority over the church) unintentionally complimented Donna on the earlier edition of this book when he wrote,

....be gentle with these young missionaries.
They generally have a simple but rock solid faith
in the message of the Church but they are not paid ministers,
and they are not trained to do battle with the likes of you.

For over ten years I have taught a class on Mormonism at a Christian college, and I know that it is difficult to find a resource that is well informed, biblical, and practical. I know of no book that does as much to prepare a person for real dialogue with their Mormon friend—using virtually all original Mormon sources along with relevant scriptural passages. And, while Donna didn't initially write this book for Mormons, many of them have contacted her expressing their deep gratitude that through this book they found Christ and His truth. *What Do I Say to Mormon Friends and Missionaries?* is indeed a valuable resource.

Those concerned about the biblical mandate regarding women teaching men can be assured that Donna is very sensitive to Paul's injunction (1 Timothy 2:12). She appeals *not to her own authority*, but refers to exegetes and scholars in all fields, such as F.F. Bruce, G. Abbott-Smith, Bruce Demarest, Alfred Plummer, H. E. Dana, Julius R. Manty, G.R. Beasley-Murray, Matthew George Easton, Robert Thomas, John MacArthur, Merrill C. Tenney, and Charles Ryre.

And wanting to be under my authority—myself a professor of biblical studies—I have gone over every line of the book. Her goal throughout is to equip for evangelism rather than to instruct in doctrine *per se*. She wants to help us understand what Mormons typically believe and say, and to equip us to carry on a constructive dialogue.

Throughout the writing of this book Donna has been a devoted wife and mother: cooking, cleaning, ironing, and schooling our children. It's all been a labor of love, for God, for her family, for the truth—and for going into the world to make disciples. Therefore I commend this book wholeheartedly to you. May you be a blessing in your endeavors.

In His Grace,

Brian Morley, Th.M., Ph.D.

Author of *God in the Shadows: Evil in God's World*, and,

Pathways to God: Comparing Apologetic Methods (forthcoming)

From the Desk of Duane Magnani Director, Witness Inc.

Greetings in Christ,

I have just finished reading *What Do I Say To Mormon Friends and Missionaries?* by Donna Morley. I greatly appreciate such efforts as they are far too few in number these days. I know this since I've been Director, since 1975 of Witness Inc., a comparative religion research organization.

As a writer of some thirty books and manuals (see John Ankerberg, *The Facts on Jehovah's Witnesses*, 1988: Harvest House), I can appreciate a good book on Mormonism. I think Donna's work is somewhat unique in the style of her presentation. As I was reading the book, I felt like I was in her home listening to her personally. Not many authors writing on counter-cult subjects accomplish that. This alone—the easy readability–is worth much more than the price of the book.

Donna spends her time explaining the key point in all counter-cult witnessing false spiritual authority. For years I have hoped that writings on cults would focus more adequately on the essentialness of this. For me, the key point was her stress on the cult's reliance on Smith. If he falls, so does Mormonism. I believe Donna knows how to prepare Christians to deal with cults. I especially write to you because Donna has informed us that she is writing a series on the cults with the same methodology that she has employed in the above work. I am greatly looking forward to reading her study on the Jehovah's Witnesses, even more so since our ministry specializes on that cult.... In this post-modern age in which we live and at the time when inclusivism is on the rise against the Gospel of Christ, the Christian public needs this book and a series of books that deal with the cults in the very style that Donna has employed. Finally, the most important point for me to make about the writing of Donna Morley is that the Christian message of Christ is explained in a way that will bolster the faith of Christian readers by encouraging them to be real "witnesses" for Jesus–even to the Jehovah's Witnesses....

Blessings in Christ,

Duane Magnani,

What Others Have Said:

Donna has combined her excellent writing ability with solid and extensive research on Mormonism. The result is a book that can be helpful to anyone trying to understand Latter Day Saints and what they really teach. It's all here in a brief, easy-to-read format. One of the most helpful features is 'Mormon Friend, Please Consider'–a section that appears in most of the chapters, which helps the reader compare Mormon teachings to what the Bible actually says. Donna gives many helpful ideas on how to gently confront Mormons, or people interested in Mormonism, with the truth: Mormonism claims to be Christian and uses all the familiar words in Christian vocabulary, but Mormonism is something vastly different than biblical Christianity. . . . This book has become a valuable addition to my library on Mormonism.

Fritz Ridenour
Author of the best seller,
So What's The Difference?

Many people today become confused when told by their Mormon acquaintances that the differences separating them from the Christian world are trivial or insignificant. Others find Mormon teachings and history to be daunting and somewhat of an enigma. Donna Morley helps cut through the complex and thorny issues, offering Christians a concise book that examines this fascinating religion without difficulty or intimidation.

Bill McKeever, Author of
In Their Own Words: A Collection of Mormon Quotations
Founder of *Mormonism Research Ministry*

Mormon missionaries call upon millions of homes annually. And there's a good chance that they've come to your door during the past 12 months. Have you ever faced the Mormon at your door (or perhaps a Mormon neighbor) and been uncertain about what to say to these sincere, but misguided people? For most Christians it can be seen as a frightening encounter. In *What Do I Say to Mormon Friends and Missionaries?* Author Donna Morley allays those fears....Morley has done an excellent study on Mormonism and not just for women—men will benefit equally from this important publication....

Angela Goedelman, *The Quarterly Journal*
Co-Founder of *Personal Freedom Outreach*

This book is good news for two reasons: first, it will help you witness with loving discernment to your Mormon friends and visitors. Just imagine not having to hide when the doorbell rings! And second, it can help you bring the saving message of Jesus

Christ to a toiling and weary soul attempting to reach heaven through Mormonism.

Elyse Fitzpatrick
Biblical counselor, national speaker and
Author of *Women Helping Women*

At last! A book that not only exposes the misleading doctrines of Mormonism, but shows Christians how to share the *real* Jesus with their Mormon friends. I highly recommend it to any Christian who struggles with questions about Mormonism, or just wants to reach a friend who desperately needs the truth.

Cindi McMenamin
Women's Bible teacher, national speaker, and
Author of *When Women Walk Alone*

I started recommending this book before I finished reading it! I really like the style. It feels like 'light' reading, yet is as thoroughly documented as a research paper. It is a wonderful balance of suggestions for asking 'gentle' questions of my Mormon friends and visitors, as well as the theological essentials with Bible references. I am cutting out the 'Mormonism Fact Sheet' so I can put it in my Bible near the front door!

Claire Blackwell, Professor
The Master's College

Donna has a good formula; this book is fascinating, clear, and well outlined for easy referencing. I even caught my pastor-husband reading it twice! I will be able to approach my next encounter with a Mormon with more confidence. I look forward to her future books!

Meg Glass
Missionary and Pastor's Wife
France

Dear Donna, ...*I wish every Christian pastor would read your book.* They need to know about Mormonism, in order to warn their congregation; in order to keep one of their flock from straying into the unknown. Mormonism, as it pertained to its doctrines, was certainly unknown to me. I blindly got baptized into the church (a requirement for marrying a Mormon), and simply thought Mormonism was just another Christian religion. My parents thought this way, and so too did my Christian pastor. He had known me all my life, and knew I was marrying a Mormon. Rather than warn me, he gave me his blessing.

How I wish I had known what I was stepping into! I should have known something was wrong when the Mormon church wouldn't allow my parents, siblings, and relatives attend my own Temple wedding. [Note: non-Mormons are not allowed to enter the Temple.] Since getting married I have brought into this world eight children. Among them, my 5 boys became missionaries and all my children married Mormons, and have been, for many years now, having *lots* of Mormon babies.

Recently, my last child left home, and got married in the Utah temple. At the same time, I bought your book. Wow! You sure spelled things out as they are, doctrinally, and every other way, in the Mormon church. After reading your book (and being convicted) I knew what I had to do—leave the Mormon church, and get back to following truth—truth found only in Jesus Christ. Sadly, as a result, my husband divorced me, and is now getting remarried. Donna, you know the reason for that—so that he can get into the Celestial Kingdom and experience, in full, his exaltation (*which means everything to him*). Sadly, my children refuse to speak to me. I am now viewed as a son...or rather, a 'daughter of Perdition.' Words can't express how painful this is.

Donna, please get my message out to others, and have Christians give their pastor this book. If only my pastor would have warned me—how different my life would have been! Instead of marrying a Mormon, I would have waited until a godly Christian man came along. Instead of raising children for the Mormon church, I would have raised children for Jesus—and the following generations would have sung His praises, rather than that of the prophet, Joseph Smith. *While I rejoice that I'm now walking in Christ, I'm sure you can imagine the burden I now carry as I realize what I have done.* Please pray for me and my family....Helen

Dear Donna,

My name is Sarah. I wanted you to know that you have helped me, my oldest son, and my family, with your book on Mormonism.

My son became good friends with a young Mormon man last year, his senior year in high school. We live in a town in northern Michigan and had no knowledge of the Mormon religion. My son is very shy and so when a new, good friend, came into his life we were happy for him. I thought that Mormons were exactly what they claim to be but, a little bit more than Christians, they believed in present day prophets. My son started to go to church with the Mormon family while still attending the Christian church.

Last fall I was overcome with panic inside about my son and the Mormon church. I felt as though I had this sucking hole in me. I believe now that God was telling me to wake up and do something. So, I started to have frank discussions and fights with my son about Mormonism (admittedly, the fights weren't good). I told him what I believed and what I saw as huge differences, and how I thought they were wrong. My son has been a student of the Bible, so I was shocked that he could fall for this. Of course, he was swayed by the Mormon's kindness, telling him he was part of their family. He even applied to BYU!

I prayed, I cried, we threatened, we limited his access to the Mormons. But, still he believed. Then, I got your book and you are so right—the things you said in your book are exactly what my son started saying to me. I not only read your book, but my son was willing to read it *under one condition*. That is, if after reading the book, that my husband and I would leave him alone if he desired to stay in the Mormon church. We agreed.

I just wanted to let you know that you helped bring my son out of Mormonism and into a true faith in Jesus Christ. He's now considering being a missionary to Mormons in Salt Lake City! Please know, that there is a mom in Michigan who knows that God has brought you into her life through your book. Again, thank you! Sarah

What Do I Say

to

Mormon Friends

and

Missionaries?

DONNA M. MORLEY

FAITH & REASON PRESS
SANTA CLARITA, CALIFORNIA
FAITHANDREASONPRESS.COM

WHAT DO I SAY TO MORMON FRIENDS AND MISSIONARIES?
Expanded Edition
Formerly titled, *A Christian Woman's Guide to Understanding Mormonism.*

Copyright © 2003, 2011, 2015 by Donna Morley
Published by Faith & Reason Press
Santa Clarita, California 93222

Cover design: *Faith & Reason Press*

Front cover picture: *John Morley of JK Morley Photography.*

Library of Congress Cataloging-in-Publication Data

Morley, Donna
What Do I Say To Mormon Friends and Missionaries?
p. cm. Includes bibliographical references.
ISBN 978-0-9841501-2-0 (pbk.)
1. Mormon Church—Controversial literature. 2. Evangelistic work. I. Title.
1-8APGY5   1-501713748
289.3—dc21

To Brian,
the epitome of
the Christlike life.

I wish for every wife
a husband like him,
for every child
a father like him,
for every student
a professor like him,
and
for every Mormon
a friend like him.

Acknowledgments

This book was made possible because of the efforts of many people, nameless and known, who have labored to make valuable sources available. This includes archivists, historians, and editors like Dan Vogel, whose multivolume *Early Mormon Documents* provides convenient access to a wealth of documents, and Scott Faulring's *An American Prophet's Record* provides in their entirety Joseph Smith's personal diaries and journals. Some, like D. Michael Quinn, have published their research and views at great personal cost. Once on the staff of the LDS church historical department, he was excommunicated from the church in 1993 for publishing on Mormon women and the priesthood. I would especially like to thank Jerald and Sandra Tanner, who have worked tirelessly for decades to bring to light the sometimes unflattering truth about Mormon origins. Their perseverance has benefited anyone interested in the history and teachings of Mormonism.

I have appreciated and benefited from access to the many writings treasured by Mormons—*Journals of Discourses, History of the Church, Doctrines of Salvation, Gospel Principles, Gospel Doctrine, The Articles of Faith, Principles and Practices of the Restored Gospel*, and more. They have all been helpful. They have provided great insight into the minds and hearts of those I care so much about and for whom I and many other Christians desire to reach—the Mormon people. It is our hope that they will find the truth that can set them free (John 14:6).

Thanks must also go to the many people who are mentioned in this book. Most names, and in some places even the gender and location, have been changed to protect identities. In order to give the presentation an even flow, in some places, a few conversations have been combined into one. I also want to thank Sandra Tanner of Utah Lighthouse Ministry and Lane Thuet of Mormonism Research Ministry for reading the manuscript and providing feedback; and to Steve Miller for his editorial skills. If there are any shortcomings that exist in this work, I take sole responsibility for them.   I also want to thank the following: First, the *Utah State Historical Society* and Douglas G. Misner for graciously waiving the use-charge of their pictures. As well, to Lorraine Crouse and Kristin Giacoletto at the *J. Willard Marriott Library*, Utah State University, for their helpfulness and cheerful spirit. Also, I'm grateful to the *Library of Congress* for the many pictures they have made available. I would also like to express my appreciation to my husband Brian for his support, encouragement, advice; to my children for their loving prayers over this project. Last, but by no means least, words can't express my gratitude to my Lord and Savior Jesus Christ for giving me His divine enablement to write this book. *To God be the glory!*

CONTENTS

And the Lord's servant
must not be quarrelsome
but kind to everyone,
able to teach,
patiently enduring evil,
correcting his opponents
with gentleness.
God may perhaps grant
them repentance
leading to a knowledge
of the truth....

2 Timothy 2:24-25

THEY SOUND JUST LIKE US!

One day after my husband's Sunday school class ended, a woman named Kaitlyn said, "I have decided to start going to the Mormon church."

Surprised at such a remark, I asked, "What led you to this decision?"

Kaitlyn replied, "Well, my husband and I have been getting visits from Mormon missionaries. We've been impressed by their sincerity and the fact that they have the same theology as any other Christian church. So…why not attend their church?"

Becoming more concerned, I asked, "Kaitlyn, how do you know they have the same theology as any other Christian church?"

Kaitlyn simply answered, "Because they sound just like us!"

"What do you mean?" I asked

She said, "When the missionaries came to our house, they talked lot about God. They too believe in Jesus Christ, and often referred to Him as 'the Lord.' They opened up the Bible often to prove their points about doctrine; they say that they too are born again; and their church name is The Church of Jesus Christ of Latter-day Saints. Obviously they're Christians. If there are differences between what they believe and what we believe, I certainly don't see them."

Kaitlyn is not alone in this observation—in fact, many people think Mormons and Christians are the same. Not only do they sound like us, but Mormons hold to many of the same values that we as Christians hold dear to our heart. Like us, they are pro-life. They are strong on law and order, they are responsible citizens, and they put the family high on their priority list. And as a church they take care of the needs of their own. It's been said that during the depression not one Mormon stood in soup lines. In many ways, we can't help but respect Mormons.

Yet because a clear and correct understanding of the Bible and the gospel message can mean the difference between eternal life and eternal separation from God, we need to ask: "Are there truly differences between Mormonism and biblical Christianity? Are Mormons really Christians? Are their doctrines really biblical? While they use the same words as we do, such as born again, are their underlying definitions truly biblical?"

Perhaps you know men and women like Kaitlyn, and you have wished you could help them discern whether Mormonism and Christianity are significantly different. And maybe you have Mormon friends you've wished to share your faith with, but you're not sure how to do so.

It's for these reasons I've written this book. It's not in any way, shape, or form intended to be an attack on Mormons, to belittle Mormons, or to communicate an attitude that is "anti-Mormon." Rather, it's a book about loving the Mormons—loving them as we take the time to understand what they believe and how we can effectively reach out to them.

What Do I Say to Mormon Friends and Missionaries? will…

• Help you understand Mormonism's history, terminology, and doctrines.

• Help you understand the mindset of your Mormon friends and missionaries and why they believe the way they do.

• Help you (and your children) with a comparison of Mormonism and the Bible.

• Help you share about Christ and the Bible at a moment's notice with the use of the Fact Sheet found at the end of this book.

Before we get started, and learn about Mormonism, let's not ever forget one thing. We have something many people are looking for—*Jesus.* Therefore, let's make sure *we are prayerful,* in this process of equipping ourselves, and reaching out to Mormons.

Let's pray that when Mormon missionaries knock on our door, we'll offer them acceptance—not of their theology, but of them as individuals created in the image of God.

Let's pray we'll be ready to make a defense to Mormons who ask us to give an account for the hope that's in us (1 Peter 3:15).

Let's pray that when we converse with a Mormon we'll maintain a gracious spirit, knowing that Christ never "yelled" anyone into His kingdom. While frustrations can surface when we disagree with a Mormon, let's pray for a humble spirit, asking the Lord to keep us mindful of those dark and sinful days when we too were lost.

And let's pray for *patience* in our sharing. It's not often that a Mormon instantly comes to Christ—it's a process. This is the hard part of sharing Christ with others. Sowing seed is not the same as planting a full-grown tree. It could be soon, later, or never that we see the fruit of our labor. But does it really matter *when* the fruit comes? Not from an eternal perspective. We may want instant results, but we need to trust God's timing. If it is His will to do so, He will bring about the people and circumstances that will lead a person to Christ—on His perfect timetable.

Be encouraged. *As you involve yourself in the harvest, others will follow you to heaven.* And it may be that one day in heaven, you will be singing a "new song" (Revelation 14:2-3) side by side with a former Mormon in whose soul you planted the seed of the gospel. Can you imagine what a wonderful moment that will be?

Until that day, Jesus reminds us, "The harvest is plentiful, but the laborers are few; therefore beseech the Lord of the harvest to send out laborers into His harvest" (Luke 10:2).

May you and I be those laborers...and serve as men and women of the harvest. Let's get started!

The Spirit of the Lord God

is upon me;

because the Lord

hath anointed me

to preach good tidings

to the meek;

He hath sent me to

bind up the brokenhearted,

to proclaim liberty

to the captives,

and

the opening of the prison

to them that are bound.

Isaiah 61:1

PART ONE

WHAT

IS

MORMONISM

ALL

ABOUT?

Mormonism, as it is called, must stand or fall on the story of Joseph Smith. He was either a prophet of God, divinely called, properly appointed and commissioned, or he was one of the biggest frauds this world has ever seen. There is no middle ground.

If Joseph Smith was a deceiver, who willfully attempted to mislead the people, then he should be exposed; his claims should be refuted, and his doctrines shown to be false, for the doctrines of an imposter cannot be made to harmonize in all the particulars with divine truth.

If his claims and declarations were built upon fraud and deceit there would appear many errors and contradictions, which would be easy to detect.[1]

—Joseph Fielding Smith
Tenth President and Prophet
of the Mormon Church

WHO WAS JOSEPH SMITH?

I have more to boast of than ever any man had. I am the only man that has ever been able to keep a whole church together since the days of Adam. Neither Paul, Peter, nor Jesus ever did it. I boast that no man ever did such a work as I. The followers of Jesus ran away from Him; but the Latter-day-Saints never ran away from me yet.

Joseph Smith
LDS History of the Church 6:408-409

We're all familiar with stories that have sad beginnings but happy endings. The one I am about to share has a happy beginning but ends in complete tragedy. As you will soon see, the drama unfolds and the plot thickens like a Shakespearean play, except the story isn't make-believe. It's real. It happened. And the saga still continues as millions of people carry on the belief that Joseph Smith was a prophet of God. Fortunately, we can give this story a new ending—a happy ending—as we involve ourselves in reaching Mormons for Christ. But before we learn how to do that, it's important to understand what the Mormon story is really all about—its history, its people, its doctrine. And because Joseph Smith is the founder of Mormonism, let's begin by learning about who he was and what he did.

A Prophet Is Born

Joseph Smith, Jr. was born on a cold winter night in Sharon, Vermont, December 23, 1805. His parents, Joseph Smith, Sr., and Lucy Mack Smith, welcomed their newborn as the fourth of nine surviving children. While there was great reason for celebration this winter evening, life wasn't always so joyous for the Smiths. The family came close to tragedy sometime between 1811 and 1813 (Lucy Smith could not recall the exact year), when misfortune struck all of the children. They became ill with typoid fever. At one point Joseph's sister, Sophronia, came close to death. The doctor had given up all hope for her survival.[1] After months of severe illness, all the children managed to survive. Sadly, Joseph (between 5-7 years old at the time) developed a severe typhoid infection in his leg, a condition that usually required amputation. Through several painful surgeries, which involved opening his leg and taking "away large pieces of the bone"[2] Joseph's leg was spared.

In the years that followed, the Smith family experienced crop failure after crop failure, which impoverished them. Older brothers Alvin and Hyrum hired themselves out as farm laborers, while the sisters made and sold pies, cakes, and root beer at public events, and Lucy painted on oilcloth. [3]

In 1816, when the other side of the world experienced a volcanic explosion (Tambora, Indonesia), causing the globe to have a "year without a summer,"[4] Joseph, Sr. moved his family to the small town of Palmyra in upstate New York. There, older brother Alvin died from bilious colic. [5] The Smith family, of course, mourned over their irretrievable loss. Lucy said that they "could not be comforted."[6]

After Alvin's death, the family continued on with life the best they could, but little did they know during those dark days that Joseph would become known throughout the world as the American prophet. Millions would praise him. But, too, just as many would vilify him. For instance, in the town Joseph was born in, the citizens put up a plaque with the following inscription:

> This is the birthplace of that infamous impostor,
> the Mormon prophet Joseph Smith,
> a dubious honor Sharon would relinquish
> willingly to another town. [7]

"For good or for evil," wrote poet and journalist John Greenleaf Whittier, Joseph Smith "has left his track on the great pathway of life; or, as to use the words of Horne, [Smith] 'knocked out for himself a window in the wall of the nineteenth century,' whence his rude, bold, good humored face will peer out upon the generations to come." [8]

Smith not only had a negative image amongst the people of his time, but also upon the generations that followed. For better or for worse, he changed the course of life for millions of people. And how did this one man accomplish such a feat? Mormons claim it was God, others blame the devil. Still others would add that Joseph was a product of his ancestors, and in particular, his parents. Let's take a look and see what we can learn about him.

Generations of Influence

We could say it was Joseph's misfortune to have been born into the Smith family, which was no ordinary family. His ancestry goes back to the Salem witch trials, during which two of his ancestors accused two women of witchcraft—Mary Easty of committing acts of witchcraft five years before the trials, and Sarah Wilds of witchcraft 15 years before. Both women were hanged. [9]

While Smith had some ancestors who were accusers, others were users of witchcraft. B.H. Roberts, an official Mormon historian, wrote that "it may be admitted that some of them [Smith's ancestors] believed in fortune telling, in warlocks and witches." [10]

These beliefs would be passed down many generations, eventually affecting Joseph Smith, Jr. A man who spoke at length with Joseph's father wrote: "This Joseph Smith, Senior, we soon learned, from his own lips, was a firm believer in witchcraft and other supernatural things; and had brought up his family in the same belief." [11]

Joseph Smith, Sr. was not only known for being a superstitious mystic, but he was also known for being a drinker of alcohol (some claim to an excess[12]), a money digger for 30 years (so he claimed[13]), And a counterfeiter (in 1842 he was accused of being "connected with a band of counterfeiters." [14]

Joseph's mother, Lucy Mack Smith, was raised to read the Bible and pray. Despite this, she struggled over which church to join, "seeing they are all unlike the Church of Christ, as it existed in former days!" [15]

Lucy was not only confused about religion, but like the man she married, she was superstitious. Anna Ruth Eaton, who had known Lucy for over a decade, said she was "superstitious to the last degree. The very air she breathed was inhabited by 'familiar spirits that peeped and wizards that muttered.'" [16]

Both Lucy and Joseph Smith, Sr. looked to dreams—called "visions"—for spiritual guidance. [17] And so too would their son Joseph—visions that would start the Mormon religion (we'll talk about these visions in upcoming chapters).

As you can see, Joseph had eccentric parents, and unfortunately he ended up becoming just like his parents—especially his father, as a sworn affidavit from residents of Palmyra, New York reveals:

> We, the undersigned, have been acquainted with the Smith family, for a number of years, while they resided near this place, and we have no hesitation in saying, that we consider them destitute of that moral character, which ought to entitle them to the confidence of any community. They were particularly famous for visionary projects, spent much of their time in digging for money which they pretended was hid in the earth; and to this day, large excavations may be seen in the earth, not far from their residence, where they used to spend their time in digging for hidden treasures.   Joseph Smith, Senior, and his son Joseph, were in particular, considered entirely destitute of *moral character, and addicted to vicious habits.* [18]

Joseph's own character, apart from his family, would soon be in question.

Joseph in Court

In 1826 Joseph was accused of money digging and was required to appear (March 20, 1826) in the Bainbridge, New York courtroom. As Joseph stood before Judge Albert Neeley, he explained that he came from Palmyra and spent most of his time at the house of Josiah Stowel. He admitted that part of the time he had been looking for mines, but most of his time was spent working for Stowel on his farm, and going to school. Joseph further explained that he had a certain stone that he occasionally looked at to determine where hidden treasures were. He claimed that with the stone he could locate gold mines at a distance underground. Several times he had looked for Mr. Stowel to inform him where he could find those treasures, and Mr. Stowel would then dig for them. Smith said that while at Palmyra he had pretended to tell where coined money was buried and where lost property was through the use of his stone. For three years he had occasionally been in the habit of looking through the stone, but lately he had given up the practice on the account of injuring his health, especially his eyes, which were sore. Joseph ended his defense by saying that he didn't solicit business of this kind, and had always rather declined having anything to do with searching for treasure.[19]

The practice of treasure digging, in Smith's day, was illegal and found horrid in the eyes of many. While Joseph "admitted to his 'glass looking' practices and was accordingly found guilty of breaking the law...no sentence is recorded."[20]

Soon after the 1826 court hearing (and there would be another in 1830 for "pertending [sic] to see underground"),[21] 20-year-old Joseph decided that he wanted to get married. He had his eyes on one particular woman, and he was determined to get her no matter what it took.

Joseph Gets Married

Joseph asked Emma Hale's father, Isaac, permission to marry his daughter. Isaac refused. In fact, both parents were "bitterly opposed" to Joseph.[22]

In denying Joseph, Isaac cast serious doubt on his character:

> ...his occupation was that of seeing, or pretending
> to see by means of a stone placed in his hat, and
> his hat closed over his face. In this way he
> pretended to discover minerals and hidden
> treasure. His appearance at this time, was that of a
> careless young man—not very well educated, and
> very saucy and insolent to his father...[23]

Disregarding Isaac's feelings, on January 18, 1827, Smith arrived at the Hale home when Isaac was away and took Emma. Carrying her off on horseback, he took her to the local parson and got married. Shortly thereafter, the newlyweds moved into the Smith home, where Emma got acquainted with her in-laws. She soon realized her life would never be the same—little did she know that she was going to get *a lot more* than she bargained for (as we'll see, when discussing polygamy).   When Isaac found out what Joseph had done, he confronted him. In a flood of tears he said, "You have stolen my daughter and married her. I had much rather have followed her to her grave. You spend your time in digging for money—pretend to see a stone, and thus try to deceive people."[24]

Joseph consoled Isaac, promising him that "he had given up 'glass looking,' and that he expected to work hard for a living, and was willing to do so."[25] Soon after Joseph's promise to give up his treasure-seeking ways, he and Isaac's son Alva brought over to Isaac's house "a wonderful book of Plates"[26] that Joseph dug up.

Isaac said,

> I was shown a box in which it is said they
> [the plates] were contained...however, I was
> not allowed to look...I became dissatisfied,
> and informed him that if there was any thing
> in my house of that description, which I
> could not be allowed to see, he must take it
> away; if he did not, I was determined to see
> it. After that, the Plates were said to be hid in
> the woods.[27]

We'll talk about these plates soon, and how Joseph "transcribed"
them into what is commonly known as the *Book of Mormon*. But
for now, let me just share that as Joseph "translated" the allegedly
ancient language into English, he came up with the idea that he
"should preach and have revelations."[28]

Establishing the Mormon Church

On April 6, 1830, in the town of Fayette, New York, Joseph
formally organized his church with just a few people. It is said that
on this day a lengthy revelation from the Lord was given to Joseph:

> Behold, there shall be a record kept among you; and in it
> thou shall be called a seer, a translator, a prophet, an
> apostle of Jesus Christ, an elder of the church through the
> will of God the Father, and the grace of your Lord Jesus
> Christ....Wherefore, meaning the church, thou shalt give
> heed unto all his words and commandments which he
> shall give unto you as he receiveth them, walking in all
> holiness before me....For his word ye shall receive, as if
> From mine own mouth, in all patience and faith. . . .For
> thus saith the Lord, him have I inspired to move the cause
> of Zion in mighty power for good, and his diligence I
> know, and his prayers I have heard. . . . [29]

Although the Mormon church was getting converts because of Joseph's revelations, it is very likely that there were people staying away because of them. Contemporary Charles Dickens said, "What Mormons do seems to be excellent; what they say is mostly nonsense [because] it exhibits fanaticism in its newest garb," namely "seeing visions in the age of railways."[30]

While Joseph began giving revelations from the Lord in New York, four of his emissaries went out to Kirtland, Ohio to preach.[31] There, the church began to grow and it wasn't long before Joseph received a commandment from the Lord that he should go to Ohio and there he would be "endowed withpower from on high."[32] But by the time Smith and some followers arrived in the city of Kirtland all wasn't well. "They had some difficulty because of some that did not continue faithful, who denied the truth and turned unto fables."[33]

While some were leaving the church, others became quite loyal followers of Smith. Some of them would eventually (in Far West, Missouri) join his "Danite band" (also referred to as "Destroying Angels" and "a man of war"[34]). By the way, second prophet Brigham Young had a Danite band too (a story for another time).[35]

Joseph's Danite Men

According to apostate Mormon apostle Thomas Marsh, the Danites were "considered true Mormons."[36] They would do anything for Joseph Smith.

Former Danite William Swartzell explained that each Danite was given by the high priest the following charge: That he "must hold himself in readiness, at a moment's warning, by day or by night. Each one of you must be equipped with a gun, or a cow-skin, or a pistol, [and] according to your different stations; each one of you to have on hand (when called upon to go at a moment's warning, asking no questions), one pound of powder, and one hundred bullets."[37]

The Danites had a rule: "all the enemies of Joseph Smith should be killed."[38] Alexander McRae put it this way: "If Joseph should tell me to kill Vanburen [sic] in his presidential chair I would immediately start and do my best to assassinate him let the consequences be as they would."[39]

Smith's enemies weren't just political figures. They were non-Mormons and Mormons alike. Former Mormon bishop John C. Bennett reported that Smith "meditates the total overthrow, not only of our government and of our social fabric, but of all creeds and religions that are not in perfect accordance with his own bloody and stupid imposture."[40]

Two Mormon men, Nathan Marsh and John Sapp, signed affidavits stating that "a growing intolerance among the Mormons made it difficult, even dangerous, for Mormons to criticize Joseph Smith and other Church leaders."[41]

Marsh said, "I have left the Mormons [and] Joseph Smith, Jr. for conscience['s] sake, and that alone, for I have come to the full conclusion that he is a very wicked man; notwithstanding all my efforts to persuade myself to the contra[ry]."[42] In fear of their lives, Marsh and other dissenters had to secretly flee from their homes during the night.[43] Non-Mormons too had to leave their homes when the Danites came to burn down their town. Some of the Danites engaged in these burnings said "it was a revelation from Joseph that every house in the county should be burned excepting those in Diahman."[44]

In the Missouri town Gallatin, for example, the Danites looted the small shops, piled clothes, bedding, and other merchandise in the street, and then loaded the goods on their horses and wagons. Before leaving, they set fire to the town.[45] After burning two towns, Gallatin and Millport,[46] it was said that "there was scarcely a Missourian's house left standing in the county."[47] Along with the burning of the post office in Gallatin,[48] it was estimated that "the Mormons burned about fifty cabins and stores, and drove one hundred non-Mormon families from their homes."[49]

After the burnings, the men brought the confiscated goods to the city of Diahman in response to Joseph's teaching that "the ancient order of things had returned and the time had arrived for the riches of the Gentiles to be consecrated to the house of Israel (Mormons)."[50] Smith called this activity "milking the Gentiles" (non-Mormons).[51]

Joseph Smith's church historian and recorder, John Whitmer, wrote that the Mormons justified the stealing and burning because "we are the people of God, and all things are God's; therefore, they are ours."[52]

Eventually Joseph and other Mormon leaders were arrested on the charge of treason. "Witnesses testified that (1) Mormon leaders publicly declared they would resist state authority; (2) Mormon soldiers attacked state troops, burned two towns, and drove settlers from their homes; (3) Mormon leaders directed the secret Danite organization, which threatened and forcibly expelled from their homes Saints who would not obey the Prophet...."[53]

Because the governor of the state couldn't legally authorize execution "after having found them guilty of many breaches of the law of the land,"[54] Smith and his Danites were handed over to civil officers. Just before they were to go to court they "hired the guard to let them go."[55]

John Whitmer (who later became a Mormon dissident) reported that upon Joseph's release, Joseph informed the brethren that an angel had delivered him and the other Danites from the guard.[56] But Whitmer recorded that rather than it being an angel, "money hired those base and corrupt men [the guards], who let them go [Joseph and the Danites], and...through the wickedness...these men escaped the Justice of the law of the land...and went unpunished."[57]

Although Joseph escaped justice, he did find himself back in jail—in other places. For instance, Joseph was arrested for the attempted murder of Grandison Newell but was later released because the material witness did not appear in court. [58]

Joseph physically assaulted the county tax assessor, for which he pled guilty and paid a fine.[59] He was arrested for assault and battery on his brother-in-law, Calvin W. Stoddard, most likely the result of "Stoddard charging Joseph with being a false prophet."[60] He was also arrested for instigating an attempt to assassinate ex-governor Boggs of Missouri.[61] As well, Smith was arrested because of his illegal banking practices.

Smith's Banking Practices

It was while in Kirtland, Ohio that Smith's critics accused him of making counterfeit money, creating fraudulent transfers of property, and creating an illegal church "bank"[62] that went into bankruptcy. Joseph (treasurer of the bank) and Sidney Rigdon (secretary) were arrested in March 1837 on charges of violating the banking laws of Ohio.[63] A suit by Samuel D. Rounds and the state of Ohio demanded that Smith and Rigdon each pay a penalty of $1000 (an enormous sum in 1837). Both men were found guilty, so they appealed the decision. However, the case never went to court because both men fled the state before it could be heard.[64]

During this same time, from June 1837 to April 1839, 17 lawsuits were brought against Joseph in the Geauga County court for debt involving original claims of $30,206.44.[65] Unfortunately, these people never recovered their losses.

Now, let's take a look at Joseph's final days on earth.

Joseph's Final Days

On May 10, 1844, Joseph Smith's former counselor William Law (who was excommunicated from the church) and several other former Mormons (who were known for criticizing Joseph) had distributed throughout the town an announcement about a new newspaper, *The Nauvoo Expositor*. It advertised that the first issue, forthcoming June 7, would promote the repeal of Nauvoo's charter and expose the "gross moral imperfections" occurring in Nauvoo. The prospectus also gave reference about Nauvoo's "SELF-CONSTITUTED MONARCH."[66]

When the paper hit the streets, it included the following proclamation: "We will not acknowledge any man as king or lawgiver to the church: for Christ is our only king and lawgiver."[67] This first issue promised that details of all the allegations against Smith and the church (and especially the polygamy issue) would appear in the next edition.[68]

Joseph was seething with anger and in three days, *The Nauvoo Expositor* was destroyed. Immediately the owners of the press went to the justice of the peace in Carthage and obtained "a warrant against the authors" of the destruction.[69] They firmly believed that Joseph and 17 others had not only started a riot but, with the use of force and violence, broke into the *Nauvoo Expositor* printing office and "unlawfully burned and destroyed the printing type and other "property of the same."[70]

After the destruction, William Law wrote, "I could not even suspect men of being such fools."[71] Newspapers all over were also reacting to the destruction. One newspaper, *The Quincy Whig*, called the attack on the *Expositor* "an example of the Mormon attitude toward law and rights."[72]

In a letter, Governor Thomas Ford of Illinois told Joseph that his "conduct in the destruction of the press was a very gross outrage upon the laws and liberties of the people."[73] Ford explained to Joseph that "there are many newspapers in this state which have been wrongfully abusing me for more than a year, and yet....I would shed the last drop of my blood to protect those presses from any illegal violence."[74]

The governor demanded that Joseph and his accomplices submit to arrest and stand trial in Carthage, Illinois. Smith refused to surrender unless the governor could guarantee his safety. The governor not only guaranteed Smith's safety but the safety of all persons brought to Carthage from Nauvoo either for trial or as witnesses.[75]

Smith wasn't too keen on the idea of turning himself in. So he and his brother Hyrum, Williard Richards, and bodyguard Porter Rockwell (known as an outlaw and protected by Smith[76]) fled Nauvoo at midnight on June 22.[77] They crossed the Mississippi River around 2 A.M., arriving at daybreak on the Iowa side of the river.[78] They then sent Rockwell back to Nauvoo with instructions to return secretly the next night with horses for Joseph and Hyrum so that they could escape to the Great Basin in the Rocky Mountains.[79]

When Rockwell returned to Joseph, it wasn't done in secret. With him was a letter to Joseph from Emma, along with a party of Mormon men, including Reynolds Cahoon, whom Emma had asked to persuade Joseph to come back and give himself up. As these men surrounded Joseph, several of them accused him of cowardice,[80] including Cahoon, who said, "You always said if the church would stick with you, you would stick with the church; now trouble comes and you are the first to run!"[81]

Smith responded, "If my life is no value to my friends it is none to myself."[82]

The following day, June 24, 1844, at 6:30 A.M., Joseph, Hyrum, and the group of men (several of whom were involved in the destruction of the press, and some who were not) set out for Carthage. The men entered the town at five minutes to midnight.

The following morning Smith and his men voluntarily surrendered themselves to the constable.[83] Later in the day Smith's companions were released on bail while Joseph and his brother Hyrum were kept in custody with an added charge against them—treason against the state of Illinois. The treason charge came as a result of Joseph's June 18 speech of unlawfully declaring martial law in Nauvoo.[84]

While they were in the two-story Carthage jail, some friends smuggled in a six-shooter for Joseph and a single-barrel pistol for Hyrum.[85] It turned out the prisoners would need their guns because on Thursday, June 27, 1844, at around 5:00 P.M. an angry mob of 100 to 200 men[86] broke into the jail and began to randomly shoot their pistols. Joseph and his brother naturally got in on the act and started shooting as well. Bullets were flying everywhere, and while Hyrum was shot dead,[87] Joseph continued to fight. He eventually made an attempt to escape by jumping out of the second-story window. Smith's secretary, William Clayton, reported what happened next: "Joseph jumped through the window and was immediately surrounded by the mob. They raised him up and set him against the well-curb; but as yet it appears he had not been hit with a ball. However, four of the mob immediately drew up their guns and shot him dead. This was all the work of about two minutes. The mob then fled as fast as possible."[88]

This was a horrible event, no doubt. The Mormon paper *Times and Seasons* reported that Joseph and his brother Hyrum were "shot by a Mob [sic] for their religion!"[89] And the Mormon scripture known as *Doctrine and Covenants* tells us that Joseph died a martyr's death. The scripture quotes Joseph saying, "I am going like a lamb to the slaughter; but I am calm as a summer's morning; I have a conscience void of offense towards God, and towards all men..." (D&C 135:4). Yet contrary to *Doctrine and Covenants*, and contrary to what most Mormons believe, Joseph was no passive victim. Rather than die like a lamb without putting up a fight (a prophecy Christ fulfilled, Acts 8:32), Joseph "died like a raging lion."[90] Pulling out from his pocket the gun that Mormon Cyrus Wheelock snuck into prison, Smith killed two men and wounded a third.

Even though the local newspaper, the *Bloomington Herald*, opposed the way Joseph Smith and his brother were killed, it added, "Smith was an evil disposed man, dangerous in community, we cannot dispute...."[91]

Although Smith's followers were angry, one observer noted that, "there is but one feeling throughout the country in regard to this last tragedy, [and] that is, that merited venge[a]nce has fallen on the right men; at the same time all regret that it happened while he [Joseph Smith] was prisoner [and] had a right to expect protection. It is regretted because his followers will now claim that he died a martyr when, if he could have been tried on the charges and convicted, he would have died a felon."[92]

While Smith's life ended in tragedy, Mormonism didn't die with him. It had really only just begun. Puzzling, isn't it? After reading about Smith's life, we may wonder how the Mormon church could have grown to what it is today. Anna Ruth Eaton (who, as we learned earlier, knew Joseph's mother) gave us her insights on this. On July 28, 1881 she spoke at a Union Home missionary meeting and said:

> Mormonism may have risen from neglect on the part of Christian workers. We have no knowledge of the religious influences thrown around the Smith family when living in Vermont...in a community distinguished for the godliness of its early settlers...ladies of piety and culture never visited Mrs. Smith in her home...never sat down by her side, and in a unpatronizing manner, sympathized with her in her many cares and labors...and by all possible methods made them feel that they loved their souls....

Why was not more done to win them to a better life[?], I received this reply, — 'Oh, they were such an awful family....Why, they were the torment and the terror of the neig[h]borhood.'

Our beloved Master 'came to seek and to save that which was lost.['] They said of Him, 'He was gone to be guest with a man that is a sinner.' He was not ashamed or afraid to touch with His hand-mark, with His hand—the demoniac and the leper.

Had His dear children in early day reached out theirs to this poor, outcast household, possibly this terrible ulcer of Mormonism might not now be corroding into the very vitals of the nation's purity and life.[93]

Wow, Eaton's words are quite sobering! May it *never* be said of us that we were neglectful in reaching Mormons for Christ.

Let's continue to follow the Mormon story, looking next at Joseph's first vision.

CHAPTER 2

WHY IS JOSEPH'S FIRST VISION SO IMPORTANT?

One of them spake unto me, calling me by name and said, pointing to the other—*This is My Beloved Son. Hear Him!* My object in going to inquire of the Lord was to know which of all the sects was right, that I might know which to join....I was answered that I must join none of them, for they were all wrong; and the Personage who addressed me said that all their creeds were an abomination in his sight...

Joseph Smith (italics in the original)
Pearl of Great Price, Joseph Smith 2:17-19

Excuse me, but who are you?" asked my mother sharply. The two men, sitting in our living room, were startled by my mother's entrance and harsh tone of voice. So was I. She wasn't expected home for another few hours. Dressed in bleached white shirts and black ties, they introduced themselves as Elder Johnson and Elder Stone (all young "worthy male members" of the Mormon church become elders at age 18 or older).[1] They explained to my mother that some of my high school friends thought I might enjoy a visit.

My mother asked, "A visit? What for?"

Recognizing them to be Mormons, my mother added, "We're Catholic. If my daughter needs religious instruction, we can get it from our priest."

As my mother continued with her words, Elders Johnson and Stone's easy going personalities changed. They became uptight, as if they were expecting something unpleasant to occur. Looking at each other, they decided to make a run for the front door. My mother helped them, and to put things mildly, she kicked them out of the house, telling them, "We aren't interested in becoming

Mormons. Don't come back."

Oh, how sorry I felt for these missionaries! Let me tell you what they shared with me before my mother came home.

Elders Johnson and Stone began their talk by giving me a full account of Joseph Smith's First Vision (and later, the Second Vision). With much zeal, Johnson said, "We firmly believe that Joseph Smith, our prophet, stood before the Father [in the flesh] and the Son, telling him all churches were corrupt. Joseph was called to restore the church. And, he did. It's called, the Church of Jesus Christ of Latter-day Saints. It's the true church. We're known as Mormons."

As Johnson continued his talk about the Father, the Son, and the Prophet, I couldn't help but think that those three figures comprised some sort of new Trinity. It was as if Joseph had replaced the Holy Spirit. Anyway, Johnson obviously believed with all his heart in Joseph's First Vision and, although I had been raised to believe that I was already in the true church, I wanted to believe Johnson. I wanted to believe not because I thought that the Father, Jesus, and Joseph had truly congregated together, but because these missionaries were so kind and sincere. *Certainly they wouldn't intentionally mislead me*, I thought. And, I admit, there was another reason why I wanted to believe. I had been in a "puppy love" relationship since fifth grade with one of Joseph Smith's descendants. Although I was only in the ninth grade, I was already thinking of my future. *Hmm...if I am going to be Mike's wife one day, certainly I would have to become a Mormon. Of course, Mom and Dad would say Mike has to become a Catholic.* As the missionaries saw me in deep thought, they pressed the issue with me, saying, "What 14-year-old boy could make up such a story?"

Not having the ability to challenge such a statement, I simply thought, *Yes, they're right. Certainly there had to be a greater power!* It was at this point, when I was believing that I must become a Mormon, that my mother entered the scene.

Hindsight shows me that the Lord was truly protecting me even before I knew Him! Many times since that encounter I have thought that if my mother hadn't entered the room when she did, I could have easily slipped into Mormonism—not because of concrete facts, but because I came to like the missionaries and I was in a platonic relationship with a Mormon.

There are many people every day who embrace the First Vision and thus Mormonism for similar reasons. I have had several conversations with Mormon men and women who have admitted to marrying into the church without taking the time to get to know any of the church's theology. With this in mind, let's take a closer look at the First Vision. It's possible the Lord may use your knowledge of this vision to help those who desperately need His truth. As well, you may possibly spare someone from entering the Mormon world.

The Details of the Vision

Joseph Smith, in his First Vision story, which he said took place in the spring of 1820 when he was 14 years old (he would turn 15 in December), said that during those days there was a great revival in the land. People were becoming converted in large numbers—some to the Methodist faith, some to the Presbyterian, others to the Baptist. Joseph was confused. He asked himself, "Who of all these parties are right; or, are they all wrong together? If any one of them be right, which is it, and how shall I know it?" (*Pearl of Great Price,* Joseph Smith 2:10).

While Joseph was struggling over this question he read James 1:5, which reads, "If any of you lack wisdom, let him ask of God, that giveth to all men liberally, and upbraideth not; and it shall be given him."

Joseph said he went into the woods and asked of God which religion was right. Suddenly, Joseph experienced something rather amazing. He tells us,

I was seized upon by some power which entirely overcame me, and had such an astonishing influence over me as to bind my tongue so that I could not speak. Thick darkness gathered around me, and it seemed to me for a time as if I were doomed to sudden destruction. But exerting all my powers to call upon God to deliver me out of the power of this enemy which had seized upon me....when I was ready to sink into despair and abandon myself to destruction....[2]

Just as the enemy was starting to overpower Joseph, a pillar of light came over his head and descended upon him (*Pearl of Great Price*, J.S. 2:15-16). And then standing before Joseph were two personages. Joseph said, "One of them spake unto me, calling me by name and said, pointing to the other—'This is My Beloved Son. Hear Him!" (*Pearl of Great Price*, J.S. 2:17).

The personages, the Father and Son, whom Joseph claimed were both in physical form, told Joseph that he wasn't to join any of the religions. One of the personages told Joseph that all "their creeds were an abomination in his sight" (*Pearl of Great Price*, J.S.2:19).

Shortly after he experienced this vision, Joseph told a Methodist minister about it. The preacher wasn't impressed. Rather, he was quite alarmed and said, "It was all of the devil; that there were no such things as visions or revelations in these days"(*Pearl of Great Price*, J.S. 2:21).

After his talk with the preacher, Joseph claimed he was persecuted in the community. He explained, "I soon found, however, that my telling the story had excited a great deal of prejudice against me among professors of religion, and was the cause of great persecution, which continued to increase...men of high standing would take notice sufficient to excite the public mind against me, and create a bitter persecution; and this was common among all the sects—all united to persecute me" (POGP, JS 2:22). While a longer version of this First Vision is found in *Pearl of Great Price* (JS 2:1-27), the account provided here gives you much of what you need to know. And, know it we must, because the Mormon church considers the First Vision so important that acceptance of it is "necessary before baptism."[3]

This is a crucial point to recognize because in Mormon theology, Christ doesn't cleanse one's sins—rather, baptism does. And, cleansing is made possible only through the Mormon church. Therefore if a person rejects Joseph's vision, he can't be baptized, can't be cleansed of his sins, and can't have "eternal life," at least in the Celestial Kingdom (more on that later).

To the Mormon missionary who may tell us this vision story, to our Mormon friend who simply doesn't know, and to the person looking into Mormonism...let's challenge them with some facts about this First Vision, starting with the great revival.

Problems with the Vision

The Great Revival

Joseph claimed in his First Vision story that in 1820 there was a great revival of all the religions in the area (Smith lived on the Palmyra/Manchester township line).[4] There was "unusual excitement on the subject of religion...great multitudes united themselves to different religious parties..." (*Pearl of Great Price*, J.S. 2:5). This is an important part of his vision story. Without a revival, Joseph wouldn't have been confused, nor would he have asked God which church to join. And God wouldn't have told him to "join none."

We can ask our friend, "How do you know there really was a revival in 1820?"

If this great revival did take place, it would have been reported in the local newspapers. The newspapers, always hungry for local news would have written about it. Yet nothing is reported. Researcher Wesley P. Walters said that,

...the point at which one might most conclusively test the accuracy of Smith's story has never been adequately explored. A vision, by its inward, personal nature, does not lend itself to historical investigation. A revival is a different matter, especially one such as Joseph Smith describes, in which "great multitudes" were said to have joined the various churches involved. Such a revival does not pass from the scene without leaving some traces in the records and publications of the period.[5]

After his own study on the Palmyra revival and the surrounding areas (which included Manchester), Walters concludes that "Mormons account for the origin of their movement by quoting from a narrative written by their prophet Joseph Smith, Jr., in 1838. In this account he claims that a revival broke out in the Palmyra, New York area in 1820....Information which we have recently uncovered conclusively proves that the revival did not occur until the fall of 1824 and that no revival occurred between 1819 and 1823 in the Palmyra vicinity."[6]

The 1824 revival mentioned by Walters *did* appear in newspapers between 1824 and 1825. Joseph Smith's brother, William, may have been thinking about this revival (though off a year) in his book *William Smith on Mormonism*. He said, "About the year 1823, there was a revival of religion...and Joseph was one of several hopeful converts....the people in his neighborhood were stirred up over the   preaching of Mr. Lane, an elder of the Methodist church. He was known as a great revival preacher."[7]

Mr. Lane preached a sermon entitled, "What church shall I join?" (The same question Joseph asks in his vision.) The burden of Lane's discourse "was to ask God, using as a text, 'If any man lack wisdom let him ask of God who giveth to all men liberally [James 1:5]'"[8] (the same verse Joseph uses in his vision).

In an interview with E.C. Briggs, William said that Joseph heard Lane's message and afterwards, "Joseph went home and...looking over the text he was impressed to do just what the preacher had said…"[9]

The Mormon paper *Messenger and Advocate* verified in 1834 that Joseph heard Lane's speech and afterwards his "mind became awakened."[10]

We must ask: Could Joseph have simply made an innocent mistake and gotten the year wrong? Could the revival mentioned in his First Vision account have really occurred in 1824 instead of 1820? Possibly. But if so, then this means the personages visited Joseph at age 19 rather than when he was "between fourteen and fifteen years of age," as he claimed (*Pearl of Great Price*, J.S. 2:22).

Too, it creates a timeline problem in regard to Joseph's Second Vision, which Joseph said occurred in 1823 when he was 17.

The Mormon church and its members affirm that the First Vision (and thus the great revival) took place in 1820 because their scripture confirms it (*Pearl of Great Price*, J.S. 2:5,14). Yet history doesn't confirm this. Researchers like Wesley Walters do not confirm this. Even Joseph's mother doesn't confirm this. She wrote, "From this time until the twenty-first of September, 1823, Joseph continued, as usual, to labour with his father, and nothing during this interval occurred of great importance."[11] In 1831 Lucy wrote to her brother "the full details of the *Book of Mormon* and the founding of the new church, [but] said nothing about the 'first vision.'"[12]

One of the witnesses to the *Book of Mormon*, Oliver Cowdery, doesn't confirm it. In 1834 (14 years after the vision supposedly took place), Joseph collaborated with Oliver Cowdery to put together the first published Mormon history. And in this first official book of the church, the First Vision is completely ignored. [13] Nor does Joseph himself even confirm the First Vision (and thus the great revival)—at least, not immediately. The First Vision wouldn't be mentioned by Joseph either through writing or in print until 18 and 22 years later.

Dr. Hugh Nibley of Brigham Young University, admitted that "Joseph Smith's 'official' account of his first vision…was written in 1838 and first published in the *Times and Seasons* in 1842."[14] Those are some serious facts our Mormon friends need to think about.

Now, what about God's command that Joseph should not join any of the churches of his day?

The Command from God

Joseph's statement that God told him not to go to any of the churches around him raises several more questions we can ask our Mormon friend: If the Smith family believed Joseph's 1820 vision, why were they (except for Joseph and his father) members of the Presbyterian church four years *after* the First Vision took place?[15] And why were brothers Hyrum and Samuel active members of the Presbyterian church for eight years *after* the First Vision?[16]   And finally, if the First Vision really took place, why was Joseph attending a Methodist church with Emma? Marvin S. Hill, professor of history at BYU, admits that "Joseph tried to become a Methodist in 1828."[17] This was *eight years* after he was supposedly commanded by the Lord to join no other church.

Joseph would have continued attending the Methodist church if it had not been for Emma's cousin, Joseph Lewis. He, along with the pastor, Rev. McKune, pulled Smith aside and candidly asked him not to visit anymore because "it would be a 'disgrace to the church to have a practicing necromancer, a dealer in enchantments and bleeding ghosts, in it.' Furthermore, his 'habits, and moral character were at variance with the [church] discipline.'"[18]

Smith was told that if he wanted to stay in the church, there would have to be "recantation, confession, and at least promised reformation."[19]

Smith refused, so he left the church. Now, what about the great persecution?

The Great Persecution

Joseph said that after he had his vision, there was a great persecution against him from religious leaders as well as the general public. "...I was hated and persecuted for saying that I had seen a vision, yet it was true..." (*Pearl of Great Price*, J.S. 2:22,25). We can share with our friend that if there had been a public protest and "great persecution" against Joseph because of the vision, it would have also caught the attention of the local papers, always eager for local gossip. And, the local religious leaders certainly would have written articles regarding Joseph's visions. Yet we find nothing of the sort. Now, this is not to say Joseph and his family didn't endure persecution. They did—especially Joseph. But the backlash was in no way directed at the First Vision story. Rather, it resulted because of Joseph's digging for hidden treasures.[20]

While Joseph's claims of a revival, of the exhortation not to join any religion, and of the persecution against him are unsupported outside his own testimonies, these problems fade in comparison to the next discrepancy.

Who Approached Joseph in the Woods?

This is an important question to ask because Mormon leaders have publicly maintained that Smith told only *one story* concerning the First Vision. Preston Nibley declared, "Joseph Smith lived a little more than twenty-four years after this first vision. During this time he told but one story...."[21]

Contrary to what Mr. Nibley said, Joseph Smith gave three different accounts of the First Vision. In fact, the account of the Father and Jesus coming to 14-year-old Joseph (found in the *Pearl of Great Price*, J.S. 2:17-20) is Smith's third account. Most church members do not know this. The apostle John A. Widtsoe and other Mormon writers have taught that from the beginning Joseph Smith openly proclaimed that he had seen the Father and the Son. Why do these church leaders teach that the Father and the Son were with Joseph if perhaps they know there are differing accounts of the First Vision? In our search for an answer, we can gain some insight from James B. Allen of Brigham Young University. He says the present-day Mormons use the account of the Father and the Son to demonstrate "the concept of God and Christ as distinct and separate physical beings."[22]

In *Doctrines and Salvation* we find this: "The vision of Joseph Smith made it clear that the Father and the Son are separate personages, having bodies as tangible as the body of man."[23]

If you were to show your Mormon friend Joseph Smith's very *first* account of the First Vision, she would discover that the Father isn't even present—only Jesus. We know this personage is Jesus because He tells Joseph, "I was crucified for the world."[24] In this first account, Joseph said he was 16 years old at the time of the vision. There is no mention of the enemy trying to overcome him, and most importantly, no mention of a revival. Your friend would be even a bit more surprised to discover that Joseph's second version of the First Vision doesn't have either the Father or the Son present. Instead, there are angels. Joseph said, "...I received *the first visitation of angels*, which was when I was about fourteen years old...."[25] Again, there is no mention of the enemy trying to overcome him or a revival.

Second president Brigham Young affirmed in 1855 Joseph's angel version of the First Vision and actually denied that the Lord appeared to Joseph. He said, "The Lord did not come...but he did send his angel to this same   person, Joseph Smith junior, who afterwards became a Prophet...."[26]

Third president John Taylor also said on March 2, 1879 that it was an angel who spoke to Joseph in that First Vision. [27]   Many others, including Joseph's own brother William spoke of the personage in the First Vision as "an angel."[28]

The Mormon church didn't pay attention to the words of their former prophets, leaders, or Smith's brother. Instead, the church changed this second account in their recent editions of their *History of the Church.* Taking out Smith's words about *the first visitation of angels,* the account now reads, "...I received *my first vision,* which was when I was about fourteen years old...."[29]

The Differences in the Visions

As we can see, there are a few differing accounts of the First Vision. Interestingly, researcher Wesley Walters said, "Mormon leaders have repeatedly asserted that the foundation of their church rests on the truthfulness of Joseph Smith Jr.'s First Vision Story. If that story is false, they have declared, the whole of Mormonism is a fraud."[30] We must ask our Mormon friend: Which vision account is correct, and why? Let's take a look.

FIRST ACCOUNT ACCOUNT	SECOND ACCOUNT	THIRD
Jesus appears to Joseph.	**Angels** appear to Joseph.	**The Father and the Son** appear to Joseph.
Joseph is **16** years old.	Joseph is **14** years old	Joseph is **14** years old.
No enemy overpowering Joseph is mentioned.	**No enemy** is mentioned.	**Enemy** overpowering Joseph **IS** mentioned.
No revival mentioned.	**No revival** mentioned.	**Revival is** mentioned.

As we can see from the chart, Mr. Nibley was horribly wrong when he said that Joseph Smith gave one story. And what a deceptive story Joseph told! It's a story that provides false security for those searching for "something" —a story that keeps people away from the true message of Jesus Christ. Thankfully, we have a different story—a true story—to tell Mormons and non-Mormons alike .

> *Tell them the story of Jesus*
> *Write on their heart every word*
> *Tell them the story most precious*
> *Sweetest that ever was heard.*[31]

But, before we share our story with our Mormon friends and the missionaries at our door, it would help us to know what Joseph's Second Vision is about (discussed in the next chapter). The Mormon is thankful for this vision because it resulted in Joseph receiving golden plates which, when translated, became their *Book of Mormon*.

Let's move along and learn how the *Book of Mormon* came about, and see how this information can help us as we attempt to reach out to our Mormon friends.

Thinking It Over

1. Explain Joseph Smith's First Vision. Who are the main characters? What message was Joseph given?

2. What are some of Joseph's claims, and those of the Mormon church, regarding the First Vision? What are some discrepancies

CHAPTER 3

WHAT IS THE
BOOK OF MORMON ABOUT?

By the power of God I translated the Book of Mormon from hieroglyphics, the knowledge of which was lost to the world, in which wonderful event I stood alone, an unlearned youth, to combat the worldly wisdom and multiplied ignorance of eighteen centuries, with a new revelation.

Joseph Smith
History of the Church, 6:74.

One day, Brian, the kids, and I decided to have a family picnic at a city park. As Brian was driving around the playground searching for the perfect spot to park, I shouted, "Stop here!

Brian asked, "Why here?"

I replied, "Look across the street. You won't believe it."

Brian observed what I was seeing. Two clean-cut male Mormon missionaries were going house to house on one side of the street, moving their bicycles along with one hand and holding their *Book of Mormon* in the other. On the other side of the street were two nicely dressed female Jehovah's Witnesses, with their *Watchtower* magazines, also going door to door.

Brian parked the car and the kids hopped out. I remained in the car for a moment, thinking, *Oh how I wish I could go across the street and share Christ with those four lost souls!* Since we were having a promised "family time," I resisted approaching them, knowing that talking with them would probably last an hour or more. Wanting to observe this peculiar sight a few more minutes, I asked my anxious cherubs, "Would you like to play on the swings for awhile?" Excitedly they shouted, "Sure!" And off they went.

As the kids played and Brian unpacked the car, I got out and watched the four across the street.

The Mormons were being rejected by every person on the right side of the street, and the Witnesses were getting the same treatment on the left side. At one point, the Witnesses and Mormons passed each other. Interestingly, the Mormons didn't try to share with the Witnesses, and vice versa. Daydreaming a bit, I said to Brian (who by this time had his arms filled with picnic items), "Wouldn't it be wonderful to get those Witnesses and Mormons in a room together? Could you even imagine what a time of sharing we would have?

I then followed Brian to a table, rambling on, "While the Mormons would talk about Joseph Smith and their *Book of Mormon,* the Jehovah's Witnesses would talk about their founder, Charles Taze Russell, and their scripture. Then you and I could share the false prophecies, false scriptures, and false doctrines of both belief systems and introduce them to Jesus Christ and His Word."

Leaving the picnic goods on the ground for me to set up, Brian replied, "Well, that's a nice thought, but you could never get the two groups in a room together."

I knew Brian was right, but I couldn't help but wish it were possible. For a few more minutes, I watched the Mormons and Jehovah's Witnesses at a distance. The rejection they were receiving reminded me of the day when, in the early 1970's, the missionaries Elders Johnson and Stone (whom we met in the previous chapter) were abruptly escorted out of my parents' house. I wonder about them to this day. Do they still believe the message they gave to me? Or might they have come to a saving knowledge of Jesus Christ? While I hope for the latter, let me share with you what they said about Joseph Smith's Second Vision.

Examining the Second Vision

On the evening of September 21, 1823, 17-year-old Joseph Smith was in his room praying to God. Suddenly an angel, sent from God, appeared at Joseph's bedside. The angel's name was Moroni (originally recorded as Nephi[1]). Moroni, as Joseph tells us, was once a man here on earth. He was the son of a "prophet" named Mormon and one of the last Nephites. And, he too was "an ancient prophet who lived upon this continent."[2] And, in honor of Moroni, the top of several LDS temples are graced with him in the form of a 12-foot bronze statue blowing a horn.[3]

Now Moroni told Joseph that God had a work for him to do, and that Joseph's name "should be had for good and evil among all nations, kindreds, and tongues...it should be both good and evil spoken of among all people" (*Pearl of Great Price,* J.S. 2:33).

Moroni went on to tell Joseph that there was a book deposited, written upon gold plates, giving an account of the former inhabitants of this continent, and the source from whence they sprang. He also said that the fullness of the everlasting Gospel was contained in it, as delivered by the Savior to the ancient inhabitants.[4]

Moroni told Joseph he would have to dig up the gold plates in the hill called Cumorah (near where Joseph lived). God would provide for him two stones, called the Urim and Thummim, which he was to use for the purpose of translating the book. Having "removed the earth," Joseph saw the plates. But he was not to dig for the plates "until four years from that time" (*Pearl of Great Price,* J.S. 2:52-53). Smith was to meet with Moroni each year until he was given the plates on the fourth year (*Pearl of Great Price,* J.S. 2:53). Elders Johnson and Stone then explained that once the plates were in Smith's possession, young Joseph translated them from an ancient language into English. That's how the *Book of Mormon* came about. This was a bit difficult for me to swallow, for the missionaries said that Joseph was only 17 years old at the time. So I asked them, "How could Joseph Smith have translated the plates into English if he was still young and would obviously have had no knowledge of ancient languages?"

Elder Johnson answered my question by pointing to his *Book of Mormon,* saying, "Donna, if this book were written in Chinese, you would be able to read it and even write the language. All you need is faith. Joseph Smith had great faith; that's why he had no problem in the translation process. It's really a miracle as to how this book came about."

Was it really a miracle, as Elder Johnson said? Let's take a closer look at this Second Vision account and see.

Elements Related to Joseph's Second Vision
The Ancient Inhabitants
Who Are the Ancient Inhabitants?

Who are the ancient inhabitants mentioned in the *Book of Mormon* and first introduced to Joseph in his Second Vision? They are said to be descendants of Jews belonging to the House of Israel. This is how the story goes:

Lehi, a prophet and leader, brought his family and other Israelites from Jerusalem by the command of God and came to America in 600 B.C. Before departing from the land of their nativity, the travelers secured certain records, which were engraved on plates of brass.[5] After arriving in their new country, the families grew apart, each multiplying to become separate peoples—the Nephites (who followed Lehi's son Nephi) and the Lamanites (who followed another son—Laman). While the *Book of Mormon* mentions some smaller groups such as the Jaredites (Ether 1:5), the two main groups are the Nephites and Lamanites. The Nephites were the ones that Christ (soon after His resurrection) visited personally to minister to. He gave them their doctrines and outlined for them the plan of salvation. The Lamanites (whom Mormons believe to be the American Indians, who supposedly descended from Israel) were at one time "white," but God cursed them with a "skin of blackness" because of their sin (2 Nephi 5:21). The *Book of Mormon* says that they will again be a "white and delightsome people" (2 Nephi 30:6).[6] This promise will be fulfilled only for the righteous Lamanites who will become "white like unto the Nephites" (3 Nephi 2:15).

Now that we've been introduced to the inhabitants in the *Book of Mormon*, we must ask our Mormon friends how they know whether the Nephites and Lamanites were real people groups.

Are the Inhabitants for Real?

A few years ago a survey showed that most Mormons believe the *Book of Mormon* is "an actual historical record of ancient inhabitants."[7] Your Mormon friend might tell you (and a Mormon missionary will, too) that there are many archaeological proofs and artifacts. In a letter, some LDS members were told that The Smithsonian Institution has officially recognized the *Book of Mormon* and that "the Institute has made remarkable study of its investigations of the Mexican Indians and *it is true that the Book of Mormon has been the guide to almost all of the major discoveries.*"[8]

Have There Been Archaeological Findings?

However, The Smithsonian Institution, contrary to what the Mormon church says, does *not* back up the archaeological or historical data in the *Book of Mormon:* "The Smithsonian Institution has never used the Book of Mormon in any way as a scientific guide. Smithsonian archeologists see no connection between the archeology of the New World and the subject matter of the Book." [9]

The National Geographic Society has also denied that their Society has used the *Book of Mormon* to locate historic ruins in America or elsewhere. [10]

The ancient inhabitants described in the *Book of Mormon* are said to have numbered into the millions, yet they left no linguistic or archaeological trace. Archaeologists have never found chariots, coins, metal, or armor to indicate any battles took place as described in the *Book of Mormon*. In one of the battles, 6,562 Nephites were said to be slain along with 12,532 Amlicites (Alma 2:19). In another battle "thousands and by tens of thousands" of Gadianton robbers were killed (3 Nephi 4:21). In still another battle there are "men, women and children [Jaredites] being armed with weapons of war, having shields, and breastplates, and head-plates, and being clothed after the manner of war—they did march forth one against another to battle; and they fought all that day, and conquered not…" (Ether 15:15). In regards to this battle, the *Book of Mormon* makes a commentary that says "millions go down to death."[11]

It would seem that after so many millions of people have been slaughtered, we would find remnants that confirm the battle actually took place. Yet not one artifact (such as shield, breastplate, or head plate) has ever been recovered. We can share with our Mormon friend that while there isn't one bit of evidence to affirm the existence of the ancient inhabitants in the *Book of Mormon*, the opposite is true about the people and places described in the Bible. Archaeologists have uncovered entire Bible cities, found ancient documents bearing the names of those cities, and unearthed significant artifacts that clearly were made or owned by the inhabitants of those places. What's more, not only does archaeology disprove the ancient inhabitants in the *Book of Mormon*, so also does DNA testing.

What About Scientific Findings?

Let's recap for a moment just so you'll understand what the DNA studies are all about. According to the *Book of Mormon*, some Israelite groups, which include the Lamanites, left Israel and came to ancient America. Later, some of Lehi's descendants (Lehi was a Hebrew Lamanite prophet in the *Book of Mormon*) set sail from the Americas and "eventually peopled the lands of Polynesia."[12]

While most of us were never taught this "history" in school or college, most Mormon children will have been taught this at an early age. In a "Special Lamanite Section" in a 1971 edition of the *Ensign,* an official publication of the LDS church, we read,

> For [Mormons] one of the keys to this great pattern of existence is the group of people known as Lamanites. Those not of the church call these people Indians, although the term actually refers to a broader group than that. Most members of the church know that the Lamanites, who consist of the Indians of all the Americas as well as the islanders of the Pacific, are a people with a special heritage.[13] Once again, the heritage is that the Native Americans and Polynesians are descendants of Israel. Such a teaching, according to Navajo Mormon Art Allison "really opens a lot of Native Americans to the teachings of Mormonism."[14] It "singles them out as special."[15]

Former Mormon president Gordon B. Hinkley (now deceased) considered the Native Americans as special, too. He said, "It has been a very interesting thing to see the descendants of Father Lehi in the congregations....So very many of these people have the blood of Lehi in their veins...."[16]

What we must ask is, does DNA research back up this claim that the Native Americans are descendants of Israelites? This question and more is what Brigham Young University (BYU) would like to answer scientifically. They are currently doing a DNA study to verify the true migration patterns of Native Americans and Polynesians. Simon Southerton, a former Mormon bishop and molecular biologist who has extensive background in DNA research, says that past DNA studies at other universities have *already* shown no evidence of a connection between American Indians and Israel.[17]

Southerton left the Mormon church when he started realizing that "the [existing] DNA research shows overwhelmingly that Native Americans and Polynesians are descended from Asian ancesters."[18] He predicts, as BYU continues their research, that they will come up with the same data. Southerton asks, "Is it honest to keep church members in the dark about the mountains of evidence for these facts while discussing the power of this technology to reveal genealogical relationships?"[19]

Along with Southerton, there are others who believe the DNA evidence is crystal clear. Scientist Author Crawford said that all the evidence gathered so far "powerfully demonstrates the Asian American Indian connection that it is as close to a 'truth' as science can get."[20]

While the current DNA evidence is quite damaging to the credibility of the *Book of Mormon* in regard to the origin of the ancient inhabitants of North America, there's additional damaging evidence, including the words of Joseph's mother.

What Lucy Said About the Inhabitants

Lucy Smith shared in her biography these endearing words about Joseph when he was a young child:

During our evening conversations, Joseph would occasionally give us some of the most amusing recitals that could be imagined. He would describe the ancient inhabitants of this continent, their dress, mode of travelling, and the animals upon which they rode; their cities, their buildings, with every particular; their mode of warfare; and also their religious worship. This he would do with as much ease, seemingly, as if he had spent this whole life with them."[21]

You might be wondering why modern-day Mormons don't seem to be concerned with Lucy's description of Joseph giving "amusing recitals" about the ancient inhabitants. The reason is that few know about this information. When Lucy's book came out, President Brigham Young suppressed it the best he could. In an article published on August 24, 1868, Mormon elder Thomas Job stated, "Brigham Young lately traversed every settlement in the Territory, collecting up all the copies of the Biographical Sketches of Joseph Smith the Prophet and his Progenitors, by Mother Lucy Smith. He said that they are nothing but falsehoods, that were 'more lies in them than Lucifer ever told.'"[22]

Young explained, "We could go through the book and point out many false statements which it contains, but we do not feel to do so. It is sufficient to say that it is utterly unreliable as a history...."[23] Young also condemned Lucy's mental competence: "Mother Smith was seventy years old, and very forgetful...."[24]

Young told church members that if they didn't destroy the book there would be consequences for disobedience.[25] After ordering the destruction of Lucy's book, Young "instructed church historians to begin working on a corrected version."[26]

In summary then, there is a complete absence of evidence that North America was populated by the civilizations named in the *Book of Mormon*. No trace of their languages, battles, or artifacts have ever been found. If you are a bit shy about pointing this out to your Mormon friend, simply ask, "Can you get some information for me showing that these people really existed? There's a lot of evidence supporting the civilizations mentioned in the Bible, but I have never heard of documented historical or archaeological evidence on these groups."

Next, let's take a look at the Urim and Thummim, the stones that are said to have been provided by God for Joseph to translate the *Book of Mormon.*

The Urim and Thummim

According to early Mormon leader Orson Pratt, there are certain spiritual gifts that have been "imparted to the Church."One of those gifts is "seeing by the Urim and Thummim."[27] Pratt tells us that Joseph described the Urim and Thummim as a "white stone."[28]

In the *Pearl of Great Price,* Joseph described them as "two stones in silver bows" (J.S. 2:35). According to Pratt, it is "by this sacred instrument he [Joseph Smith] translated that divine and holy record, the *Book of Mormon,* or the sacred history of ancient America."[29]

While Joseph credits the Urim and Thummim for assisting him in his translation of the *Book of Mormon* (*Pearl of Great Price,* J.S. 2:62), in another account he doesn't credit the Urim and Thummim. Why? The reason may have to do with the following facts: in 1833, Willard Chase filed an affidavit in Manchester, Ontario County, New York, testifying that Joseph *stole* from him a unique stone. It so happened years earlier that when Chase showed Joseph his stone, Joseph grabbed it out of Chase's hand. Smith asked Chase if he could keep the stone. Chase said no, simply because he was so curious about the stone himself, but that he would lend it.[30]

Chase said that after Joseph received the stone he, "began to publish abroad what wonders he could discover by looking in it, and made so much disturbance among the credulous part of [the] community, that I ordered the stone to be returned to me again. He had it in his possession about two years."[31]

Hyrum Smith approached Chase and said that he wished to borrow the same stone because "they wanted to accomplish some business of importance, which could not very well be done without the aid of the stone." [32]

Chase agreed under the condition that Hyrum "pledge me his word and honor, that I should have it when called for."[33] Hyrum agreed.

When Chase later tried to get the stone back from the Smith brothers, he reminded Joseph that the stone didn't belong to him. Joseph said, "I don't care who in the Devil it belongs to, you shall not have it."[34] In April of 1830 Chase tried once again to get the stone from Joseph and Hyrum. But Hyrum told Chase he couldn't have it, "for Joseph made use of it in translating his Bible."[35] And even Joseph Smith acknowledged that "if it had not been for that stone...he would not have obtained the book"[36] referring to the *Book of Mormon.*

While there is quite a discrepancy as to which stones were actually used to translate the *Book of Mormon*—the stones God gave, or the stone Smith stole—there is an even larger problem the Mormons must face: the credibility of the *Book of Mormon* witnesses. Remember, these witnesses claim they saw the golden plates. The Mormon church considers these witnesses fully trustworthy, and Mormon apostle John A. Widtsoe said that the witnesses all had "spotless reputations....They remained true to their testimonies without deviation or variation."[37]

Do the facts bear them out?

The Witnesses
Who Were They?

The three main witnesses to the golden plates (which bore the text for the *Book of Mormon*) are Oliver Cowdery, David Whitmer, and Martin Harris. These men signed a testimony stating that "an angel of God came down from heaven, and he brought and laid before our eyes, that we beheld and saw the plates...."[38]

Eight other witnesses, Christian Whitmer, Jacob Whitmer, Peter Whitmer, Jr., John Whitmer, Hiram Page, Joseph Smith, Sr., Hyrum Smith, and Samuel H. Smith, testified Joseph was indeed the translator of the *Book of Mormon* and that Joseph had showed them the plates.[39]

While it's possible to question the credibility of all 11 witnesses, it's sufficient for us to examine the trustworthiness of just the three main witnesses.

Oliver Cowdery

In 1838 Oliver Cowdery was arrested for stealing, but this isn't what got him excommunicated from the Mormon church on April 11, 1838. The charges were numerous, but to name a few, Cowdery was excommunicated for "persecuting the brethren by urging on vexatious law suits against them...seeking to destroy the character of President Joseph Smith, Jun., by falsely insinuating that he was guilty of adultery...treating the Church with contempt by not attending meetings ...disgracing the Church by being connected in the bogus business [making counterfeit money], as common report says...."[40]

But Cowdery had a different story to tell. He met with a Methodist church committee and, according to G.J. Keen, Cowdrey "expressed a desire to associate himself with a Methodist Protestant Church of this city."[41] At a church meeting he "admitted his error and implored forgiveness, and said he was sorry and ashamed of his connection with Mormonism."[42]

This leaves us with two very contradictory accounts about Cowdery's departure from Mormonism. Should we believe Cowdery, or the Mormon church?

David Whitmer

Along with being accused of not obeying the Word of Wisdom, David Whitmer was accused of deceiving, cheating, counterfeiting, and defrauding the saints out of their property.[43] Whitmer denied these accusations.[44] In a letter to the Mormon church's High

Council, Whitmer said, "I hereby withdraw from your fellowship and communion—choosing to seek a place among the meek and humble, where the revelations of heaven will be observed and the rights of men regarded."[45] And just before his death, Whitmer published *An Address to All Believers in Christ,* in which he said,

> If you believe my testimony to the Book of Mormon; if you believe that God spake to us three witnesses by his own voice, then I tell you that in June, 1838, God spake to me again by his own voice from the heavens, and told me to "separate myself from among the Latter Day Saints...."[46]

Martin Harris

Martin Harris was very enthused about the *Book of Mormon* not just because he was a witness to the golden plates, but because he was making money from it. Joseph Smith and Martin Harris' asking price for the book was 14 shillings. Jonathan Lapham, a justice of the peace, told Smith, "I would not give so much." Smith told Lapham that they "had a revelation that they must be sold at that price. "But then some time later, Harris approached Lapham, saying, "They had a new revelation, that they might be sold at ten shillings a piece."[47]

Abigail Harris (Martin's sister-in-law and the wife of a Quaker minister[48]) seemed quite taken aback over the discussion of the profit that could be made out of Mormonism. In a sworn court affidavit (November 28, 1833) she said that when Martin Harris and his wife were visiting her in her home, they were having a conversation about "Mormonites." Abigail observed that Martin's wife wished her husband would quit Mormonism "as she believed it was all false and a delusion." Martin's reply to his wife shocked Abigail: "What if it is a lie; if you will let me alone I will make money out of it!"

Abigail ended her testimony with the following: "I was both an eye and an ear witness of what has been stated above, which is now fresh in my memory, and I give it to the world for the good of mankind. I speak truth and lie not, God bearing me witness."[49]

As it turned out, Harris didn't spend his life selling the *Book of Mormon* because he was unofficially excommunicated from the church in December 1837 because of conflicts with Sidney Rigdon and refusal to join Joseph Smith' s Kirtland Safety Society, which was issuing paper money.[50]

The Mormon church publication the *Latter-Day Saints' Millennial Star* said Martin Harris "yielded to the spirit and temptation of the devil…. He was filled with the rage and madness of a demon…. He soon became partially deranged…a 'wicked man' is no other than Martin Harris…the wrath of God is upon him."[51]

What's especially interesting is Joseph Smith's own assessment of his three main witnesses to the golden plates: "Such characters as…D[avid] Whitmer, O[liver] Cowdery and Martin Harris…are too mean to mention…."[52]

The question we could ask ourselves, then, is this: Given the seeming lack of credibility among the members of this group, can we still assume they saw the golden plates?

Did Anyone See the Plates?

Did anyone, especially the three witnesses, actually *see* the golden plates?

Martin Harris gave different answers as to whether or not he had ever seen the plates. In 1838 he publicly stated that the three witnesses saw the golden plates in a vision, *but not with their natural eyes.*[53]

On another occasion Harris said "he never saw the plates…except in vision." He went on to say that "any man who says he has seen them in any other way is a liar, Joseph [Smith] not excepted."[54]

In an 1859 interview in the Mormon magazine *Tiffany's Monthly,* Harris was talking about the golden plates when the interviewer asked, "How did the Lord show you these things?" Harris replied, "I am forbidden to say anything how the Lord showed them to me, except that *by the power of God I have seen them.*"[55]

The most telling conversation of all was the one between Martin Harris and Professor Charles Anthon of Columbia College. Anthon, a professor of classical studies and literature,[56] said, "[I]...asked him what had become of the gold plates. He informed me that they were in a trunk with the spectacles"[57] (Harris told Anthon the spectacles were used to translate the plates). Anthon told Harris to go to a magistrate to have the trunk examined. He replied, "'The curse of God' would come upon him [Harris] if he did."[58]

Anthon said, "On my pressing him, however, to go to a magistrate, he told me he would open the trunk if I would take the curse of God upon myself. I replied that I would do so with the greatest willingness, and would incur every risk of that nature...."[59]

But Harris never showed the professor the golden plates. Instead, Anthon said, "He then left me."[60]

Oliver Cowdery may have never seen the plates either, as the following portions of a Mormon poem written in 1841 indicates:

> Or prove that Christ was not the Lord
> because that Peter cursed and swore?
> Or Book of Mormon not his word
> Because denied, by Oliver? [61]

Not only did certain key people never see the golden plates, but others who were close to Joseph never saw them either. For instance, Joseph had told justice of the peace, Jonathan Lapham, that "no one must see the plates but himself and [his] wife." [62] Yet Emma admitted to having never seen the plates, although she "once felt the plates."

Emma had said that while serving as Joseph's scribe, Joseph was able to translate the *Book of Mormon* without "either seeing the manuscript...."[63] Joseph's brother William and sister Katharine said they never saw the plates "uncovered."[64]

Lucy came the closest to seeing something, but it wasn't the golden plates she "saw". She said, "It [the breastplate] was wrapped in a thin muslin handkerchief, so thin that I could see the glistening metal, and ascertain its proportions without any difficulty.... Joseph placed it in the chest with the Urim and Thummim."[65]

Certainly there was something hidden under a cloth. But were they golden plates? Brigham Young University professor of Asian and Near Eastern languages Daniel C. Peterson says that those "who wish to dismiss the *Book of Mormon* as merely a piece of nineteenth century frontier fiction must explain where the gold plates came from...."[66]

Where Did the Plates Come From?

Mr. Peterson has a point. Where *did* the plates come from? Before answering this question, we must ask another. Since no one has ever *physically* seen the plates Joseph claimed to have found, are we so sure there were plates? And, if there were actual plates, were they authentic? For instance, General George Harris testified that "Joe proposed to me to go to New York, and get some plates engraved, and bring them to him, so that he could exhibit them as the genuine plates of the *Book of Mormon*, which he pretended had been taken from him, and 'hid up' by an angel, and which he would profess to have recovered. He calculated upon making considerable money by this trick, as there would of course be a great anxiety to see the plates, which he intended to exhibit at twenty-five cents a sight"[67] (emphasis in original).

William Smith threatened his brother Joseph, saying that "if he did not give him some money he would tell where the *Book of Mormon* came from; and Joseph accordingly gave him what he wanted."[68]

It does seem that there was something suspicious going on regarding the golden plates. Yet even if we could come up with a satisfactory explanation, we're left with yet another question: Who really wrote the *Book of Mormon?*

The Book of Mormon

Mormon scholar Hugh Nibley said, "There is no point at all to the question: Who wrote the *Book of Mormon?* It would have been quite as impossible for the most learned man alive in 1830 to have written the book as it was for Joseph Smith."[69]

When Brigham Young picked up the *Book of Mormon* for the first time, before reading "half a page, [he] declared 'God or the Devil has had a hand in that book, for man never wrote it.'"[70] Yet some wonder if Joseph had to have written the book because of what Lucy Smith said about Joseph's imagination regarding the tales he frequently told of ancient peoples.

John Gilbert, the typesetter of the *Book of Mormon,* might have wondered if God really wrote the book because he found the manuscripts so "...imperfect...especially in regard to grammar...." When Gilbert explained this to Smith and his party, "he was given a limited discretion in correction... Many errors...nevertheless, escaped correction, as appeared in the first edition of the printed book."[71]

Some say that at least portions of the *Book of Mormon* actually came from Joseph's grandfather's book. Solomon Mack had published his own autobiography, writing about his participation in the French and Indian wars and the American Revolution, his long history of poverty and physical accidents, and his religious conversion.[72]

Others say that Joseph had to have written the Mormon scripture because in the *Book of Mormon* (1 Nephi 8:8-33; 11:21-22,36) are passages that are very similar to what Joseph Smith, Sr. wrote about his 1811 vision (found in Lucy's book, *Joseph Smith's History by His Mother*, p. 58). Both Lehi (of the *Book of Mormon*) and Joseph Smith, Sr., have the same dream. Both men are traveling in this dream. Both dreams compare the field to the world. Both men have a guide. Both men mention broad roads, a narrow path, a stream of water, something extending along the bank of the stream.

Both mention the beauty of a tree, both trees bore fruit. Both compare the whiteness of the fruit to snow. And, there are plenty more comparisons as well.[73]

Some say that the King James Version of the Bible probably had more "influence" on the *Book of Mormon* than any other book. Mormon experts Jerald and Sandra Tanner point out that there are well over 100 quotations from the King James New Testament in the first two books of Nephi *alone*. These New Testament verses in the *Book of Mormon* match the King James Version of the Bible word for word—right down to the old-style English found in the King James Version! But if the *Book of Mormon* was written in ancient languages around 600 B.C., how could it have included word forms that didn't exist until the 1600s?[74]

Others believe Smith got his story from Ethan Smith's (no relation) book *View of the Hebrews*. Mormon historian B.H. Roberts, who was a "key figure in the intellectual history of the Church,"[75] wrote in 1922 (only released by his family after his death) that there was a possibility that *View of the Hebrews* (the first edition was published seven years before the *Book of Mormon*[76]) may have helped Smith write the *Book of Mormon*. Roberts realized that the *Book of Mormon* may not be of "divine origin" at all.[77]

Roberts said, "...if the *Book of Mormon* is of merely human origin, and Joseph Smith is its author, then all these facts here considered would be reflected in the *Book of Mormon*. Are they?"[78]

Roberts allows the reader to answer his question by comparing parallel passages from the *Book of Mormon* and the *View of the Hebrews*. Both books mention the origin of the American Indians, a hidden book (the *Book of Mormon*) and a lost book (*View of the Hebrews*), writing on gold tablets (*Book of Mormon*), and writing on dark yellow leaves (*View of the Hebrews*). Both books also include inspired prophets, Egyptian hieroglyphics, Urim and Thummim, a breastplate, polygamy, barbarous and civilized people, the gathering of Israel, similarities of civilization in America, incidents of antichrists, and a Messiah on the Western continent.[79]

Both books deal with the "Israelitish origin of the American Indians...the destruction of Jerusalem and the scattering of Israel, the future gathering of Israel, and the restoration of the Ten Tribes."[80] Both also emphasize and use much "of the material from the prophecies of Isaiah, including whole chapters."[81] Roberts said that "many passages quoted by Ethan Smith are identical with passages from Isaiah quoted in the *Book of Mormon*."[82] As well, "Isaiah eighteenth chapter is quoted in full by Ethan Smith in his final chapter. He regards it as an address to the Christian people of the United States."[83] Roberts made the observation that "*this is the very mission assigned by the Book of Mormon prophets to the Christian people of the United States...*"[84] (emphasis in original).

Roberts also pointed out strikingly parallel texts that refer to incidents of antichrists in Ethan Smith's book and the *Book of Mormon*.

Referring to the antichrists in the *Book of Mormon*, Roberts says "they are all of one breed and brand; so nearly alike that one mind is the author of them. . . .The evidence I sorrowfully submit, points to Joseph Smith as their creator." [85]

There is much more that Roberts brought out, but let me end with this profound statement he made:

> ...is it much to be wondered at if intelligent people to
> whom the Book of Mormon is presented for
> consideration, should ask: 'Do we have here a great
> historical document, or only a wonder tale, told by an
> undeveloped mind, living in a period and in an
> environment where the miraculous in 'history' is accepted
> without limitations and is supposed to account for all
> inconsistencies and lapses that challenge human credulity
> in the thought and in the easy philosophy *that all things
> are possible with God?*' [86] (emphasis in original).

This statement may give us some insight as to why, during the
last days of his life, Roberts *may* have denied his faith in the *Book of
Mormon.* There are many Mormons who will say he couldn't have
denied the *Book of Mormon* because in his last conference address
to Mormons in April 1933, Roberts "referred to the Book of
Mormon as one of the most valuable books that has ever been
preserved, even as holy scripture."[87] Even a year before his death he
wrote an article for the *Atlantic Monthly* on "What College Did to
My Religion." In this article, he defended the *Book of Mormon.*[88] But
we can share with our Mormon friends that "not quite two months
before his death," Roberts discussed with Wesley P. Lloyd (former
dean of the graduate school at Brigham Young University and a
missionary under Roberts) his thoughts on the *Book of Mormon.* He
told Lloyd that

> ...the plates were not objective but subjective with Joseph
> Smith, that his exceptional imagination qualified him
> psychologically for the experience which he had in presenting
> to the world the Book of Mormon and that the plates with the
> Urim and Thummim were not objective. He explained
> certain literary difficulties in the Book of Mormon such as
> the miraculous incident of the entire nation of the
> Jaredites...the New England flat hill surroundings of a great

civilization of another part of the country. We see none of the cliffs of the Mayas or the high mountain peaks or other geographical environment of early American civilization that the entire story laid in a New England flat hill surrounding. These are some of the things which has made Bro. Roberts shift his base on the Book of Mormon.[89]

While Mormons may believe that Roberts' apparent denial of the *Book of Mormon* doesn't constitute evidence against the *Book of Mormon*, it does, according to Brigham Young University professor Daniel Peterson, have "a certain shock value when used against faithful Latter-day Saints."[90]

While our goal isn't to try to shock, traumatize, or embarrass anyone, I believe the above questions are legitimate ones for us to ask as we help our Mormon friend think a bit deeper about the validity of the *Book of Mormon* and to consider the Bible as God's only authoritative word.

Responding to the Second Vision

We'll never know the full story about how the *Book of Mormon* came about, but evidently Smith took an assortment of ideas from his own life, his family's life, and his father's visions, and blended them with information from books he read on ancient peoples, the Bible, and newspaper articles—taking a bit of this and a bit of that—to develop the *Book of Mormon*.

Does all this make you want to pray more than ever for your Mormon friends? They are putting all their hope in golden plates that most likely never existed or were fabricated, in ancient inhabitants who never lived, and in visions that could not have come from the Lord. All this and more only deceives our friends into thinking they are being offered fulfillment, whereas all they've been given is emptiness—emptiness from a book that offers them a religion, but not the Savior.

> Oh, what emptiness—without the Saviour'
> Mid the sins and sorrows here below!
> And eternity, how dark without Him!
> —Only night and tears and endless woe!
> What, though I might live without the Saviour,
> When I come to die, how would it be?
> Oh, to face the valley's gloom without Him!
> And without Him all eternity!
> —V. RAYMOND EDMAN [91]

Thinking It Over

1. Describe the Second Vision. Who is Moroni? What message did he give to Joseph? Where did the alleged golden plates come from, and what book is a result of the plates?

2. Who are the ancient inhabitants mentioned in the *Book of Mormon?* Which ancient group was Christ said to be reaching? What vision prompted Lehi and his people to come to America? How do we know these ancient inhabitants aren't for real?

3. Who were the three primary witnesses to the *Book of Mormon?* What evidence can easily lead us to doubt they ever saw the golden plates?

4. What are some differing views on how the *Book of Mormon* was written?

DOCTRINE AND COVENANTS—
REVELATIONS FROM THE LORD?

You are about to begin a study of the Doctrine and Covenants. Think for a moment about that title and its significance to you. These revelations contain the truths necessary to save you. They reveal the doctrines of salvation, the principles that will bring men to a fulness (sic) of joy. In the earliest dispensations of the world the Lord made covenants with His children through which they could bind themselves to Him. Now in the last dispensation those covenants have been revealed again. Within the 138 sections of this work you can find the doctrine and the covenants that are more important than all the treasures of the earth. As the Twelve Apostles testified in the introduction to the Doctrine and Covenants, it is a book that is truly "profitable for all men."

Doctrine and Covenants Student Manual
Religion 324, 325, *(2001 edition) Preface.*

We were just getting to our car after church when our first-grader, Johnathan,   said, "Mom, I forgot my Bible in my Sunday school room."

I gave Brian a pleading little smile, to which he responded, "I'll get it."

When he went into Johnathan's classroom a woman was standing there, talking to the Sunday school teacher. She noticed Brian and stopped him, saying, "I need to talk to you. I *really* need to talk to you. Don't leave."

She ended her conversation with the teacher, then went up to Brian, saying, "I saw you a few months ago at a Mormon conference."

"Oh, so you were there as a non-Mormon too?" Brian asked.

Marjorie replied, "Actually, I was there as a Mormon."

Brian inquired, "Are you still a Mormon?"

Marjorie took a deep breath and began to explain: "When I was at the conference I saw quite a number of young people together, and I assumed they were from a very active singles ward [Mormon congregations are called "wards"], so I asked which ward they belonged to. To my surprise they said they were students at a Christian college taking a class on Mormonism and that being at the conference was part of the class. They pointed to their teacher—who was you."

Brian nodded, recalling that day very well. Marjorie continued, "Not long after that I began to study the roots of Mormonism and the background of some of Joseph's revelations [found in *Doctrine and Covenants*]. The more I learned, the more disturbed I became. About a month ago I finally concluded that I was in a false church."

Brian replied, "I'm glad to see you've discovered that."

Marjorie said, "I also have come to realize that traditional Christianity is true. I knew that I had to find someone who knew a lot about both beliefs and I remembered you from the conference; but I had no idea who you were or how to reach you."

Marjorie paused a moment and then said, "I've been praying that God would somehow help me find you."

So amazed at finding Brian in the most unexpected way, Marjorie chuckled a bit and said, "I can't believe this! Just today I decided to pick a Christian church and check it out. I thought I might as well try this church, but I'm not even sure why I came to this Sunday school room just now. Obviously, God led me, and answered my prayer—here you are!"

God used a woman's "chance" glance at Brian, at a distant conference, and a young boy who forgot his Bible to reach out to a woman who was desperately seeking the truth. And in her journey in search of the truth, she ended up becoming disturbed by what she read in the Mormon scripture known as *Doctrine and Covenants*.

What was it that concerned Marjorie? If her discoveries led her to question Mormonism, and you and I want to help our Mormon friends come to see the truth, then it's well worth our time to become aware of what is taught in *Doctrine and Covenants*. As we read, let's think about all the "Marjories" out there who may benefit from the information we are about to learn. Let's start with an introduction to *Doctrine and Covenants*, and then we'll focus on a few key subjects mentioned in the book.

An Introduction to *Doctrine and Covenants*

Your Mormon friend no doubt calls *Doctrine and Covenants* "the word of God."[1] That's what she's been taught. Her Mormon theologians have told her that "the Doctrine and Covenants is the Lord's book and serves as a means to help us become a pure people before the Lord" (D&C 100:16).[2] And her own prophet, Joseph Smith, said that *Doctrine and Covenants* comprises the very words "of the Lord Jesus Christ Himself."[3]

What are some of the things the Lord allegedly says in this book? Well, in some verses He gives straightforward commands, such as the necessity of children being baptized at the age of eight (D&C 68:27). Mormons are also told their tithes should be "one-tenth" of their earnings (D&C 119:3-4), and if anyone sins against God *the fourth time*, they shall not be forgiven (D&C 98:44).

Other verses inform Mormons about the three heavens (D&C 76:70-112), and that the celestial kingdom will include celestial marriages and that will produce "a continuation of the seeds forever and ever" (D&C 132:19-20). By the way, so important is this celestial marriage revelation that Second Prophet Brigham Young said that if a woman was to reject it she "will go to hell just as sure as you are a living woman." [4]

Doctrine and Covenants also gives information on how to be gods (D&C 132:19-20; also see 132:37), baptizing for the dead (D&C 127:5-10; 128:1-18), the Father having flesh and bones (D&C 130:22), salvation coming through baptism (D&C 84:74) and by keeping God's commandments (D&C 30:8; 56:2). The text reveals how to distinguish between good or bad angels and spirits (D&C 129:5-6,8), and declares that *without the priesthood* "no man can see the face of God, even the Father, and live" (D&C 84:22). Hmm, that verse is quite interesting in light of the fact that Joseph supposedly saw the Father in 1820 and lived to tell about it, even though he didn't receive the priesthood until 1829. In regards to "angels" Joseph tells us in his journal that "there are no angels who administer to this earth but who belonged or have belonged to this earth." [5]

Jesus tells Joseph Smith about a "civil war" (D&C 87:1; Joseph later prophecies about it—D&C 130:12). The Lord also says that there will be a "cursing" upon all who are against the Lord's "anointed" (D&C 121:16). He warns that there is judgment for men who marry "not by the Lord." Their punishment? These men will remain for all eternity as angels, serving those who were found to be more worthy (D&C 132:15-16). The Lord also commanded Joseph to rewrite the scriptures (D&C 94:10; 124:89). There is also the command for Joseph Smith to have a house built for him "in which to live and translate" (D&C 41:7); and that the saints should buy up land in Jackson County, which would be the land of Zion "for the beginning of the gathering of my saints" (D7C 101:69-71).

Now, *Doctrine and Covenants* isn't all harsh. We find "good news" as well. The Lord tells Joseph that his father, Joseph Smith, Sr., is sitting "with Abraham at his right hand" (D&C 124:19); that the New Jerusalem will be in Missouri (D&C 84:1-5); and all who marry "by the Lord's word" will become gods and the angels will be subject to them (D&C 132:19-20).

While *Doctrine and Covenants* is primarily about revelations from the Lord Jesus Christ to Joseph Smith, there is some information in this Mormon scripture from Joseph himself. For instance, Joseph reports that John the Baptist came to earth "acting under the direction of Peter, James, and John" to ordain him and Oliver Cowdery to the Aaronic Priesthood (D&C 13). These are just some of the topics found in *Doctrine & Covenants.*

Because we're most interested in helping our Mormon friends determine whether or not these verses are revelations from Jesus

Christ Himself, let's take a closer look at some specific teachings.

The Teachings of *Doctrine and Covenants*

The Word of Wisdom
The Prohibitions

On February 27, 1833, Joseph received a revelation from the Lord commanding the Mormons *to abstain from wine, strong drink, tobacco, hot drinks, and to eat beef and fowl "sparingly"* (D&C, section 89). This "command" is called *The Word of Wisdom*, considered by Mormons as one of their most important revelations. Perhaps, if you didn't understand earlier, you can now understand why Mormons don't drink coffee or tea.

You will notice, in the above paragraph, that I put quotes around the word, "command." This is because some Mormons will tell you that, unlike today, the Word of Wisdom wasn't a command when Joseph first gave his followers the God-given revelation. Therefore, Joseph Smith and the other leaders didn't have to obey it. They will point you to D&C 89:2 which states that the *Word of Wisdom was not to be observed by "commandment or constraint...."* They will also mention that during Smith's day it was just "a word of wisdom for good health."

No one can argue against "good health," but there are some holes in the Mormon's argument that the Word of Wisdom wasn't originally a command. Most of you won't even have this as a discussion with a Mormon friend or missionary. But, if you want a detailed and documented analysis of exactly why the *Word of Wisdom was a command, from the beginning,* I recommend the forthcoming book, *From Cumorah to the Celestial Kingdom.*

Let me just say that most Mormons believe this "revelation" from God proves Joseph is a prophet. Why? Because, as one Mormon woman told me, "Joseph didn't know these things were bad for you back when this command was written. Now, over a hundred years later, we know of their harmfulness."

Today, Mormons believe there are four promises to those who abide by the Word of Wisdom. They are health, wisdom, lack of weariness, and that the "destroying angel shall pass by them, as the children of Israel, and not slay them" (D&C 89:18-21). Some Mormons have called this last promise a special type of "spiritual life insurance."[6]

LDS church doctrine states that "accordingly the negative side of the 'Word of Wisdom' is a command to abstain from tea, coffee, tobacco and liquor. Abstinence of these four things has been accepted by the [Mormon] church as a measuring rod to determine in part the *personal worthiness of Church members*"[7] (emphasis added).

While we can agree with Mormons that some of these prohibited substances are harmful for the body, history shows us that this command was not from God, and certainly not from Him to be used as a measuring rod to determine one's personal worthiness. The truth of the matter is, according to Brigham Young (and others), this command really came from Joseph's wife Emma. Let's take a look.

The Historical Background

One day Emma asked Joseph to come up with a revelation that would make the use of tobacco a sin. Emma's reason for making this request was that she was sick and tired of having "so filthy a floor" because of the church leaders smoking their pipes in her home and spitting "all over the room, and as soon as the pipe was out of their mouths a large chew of tobacco would then be taken."[8]

Wanting to be spared Emma's wrath, Joseph took up the matter at a church meeting. One of the leaders at this meeting suggested that the "revelation should also provide for a total abstinence from tea and coffee drinking."[9]

The Mormon leaders had a good laugh, believing this was a counter-dig at the sisters who drank these beverages. The matter was then taken up for a vote, and with a majority in favor, the Word of Wisdom was the result. [10]

Knowing the origin of the Word of Wisdom, it seems Emma may not have taken the Lord's "command" very seriously. One day after a long journey "sister Emma asked [an] old lady if she would have a cup of tea to refresh her after the fatigues of the journey, or a cup of coffee." Appalled at such a request, the old woman's entire family "apostatized because they were invited to take a cup of tea or coffee, after the Word of Wisdom was given."[11]

Sadly, Mormons are taught that they must not only keep the Word of Wisdom in order to have entrance into the Temple, but in order to get to the "celestial kingdom" (the highest of the three Mormon heavens). They are told,

"SALVATION AND A CUP OF TEA. You cannot neglect little things. 'Oh, a cup of tea is such a little thing. It is so little; surely it doesn't amount to much; surely the Lord will forgive me if I drink a cup of tea." Yes, he will forgive you, because he is going to forgive every man who repents; but, my brethren, if you drink coffee or tea, or take tobacco, are you letting a cup of tea or a little tobacco stand in the road and bar you from the celestial kingdom of God, where you might otherwise have received a fulness (sic) of glory....There is not anything that is little in this world in the aggregate. One cup of tea, then it is another cup of tea and another cup of tea, and when you get them all together, they are not so little." [uppercase in original] [12]

Now, let's look at some other topics in *Doctrine and Covenants*.

The Dead Come Back to Earth

Doctrine and Covenants teaches that the dead can reappear on earth, coming back as angels (D&C 129:1-9). Joseph F. Smith said,

> There are no angels who minister to this earth but those who do belong or have belonged to it."[13] These angels bring "from the divine Presence messages of love, of warning, or reproof and instruction."[14] They "are not strangers, but...our fathers, mothers, brothers, sisters and friends who have passed away from this earth." [15]

Past Mormon president Wilford Woodruff professed to have been visited by the dead. He had "many interviews" with Joseph Smith, Brigham Young, and "many others who are dead." Woodruff told the Mormons that these dead "attended our conferences, they attended our meetings."[16] He also said, "After the death of Joseph Smith, I saw and conversed with him many times in my dreams...."[17]

Receiving visitations from the dead was not some odd occurrence with the early Mormon leaders. It was an accepted fact, and they taught it to their church members. For instance, Brigham Young taught:

> There is evil in the world, and there is also good. Was there ever a counterfeit without a true coin? No. Is there communication from God? Yes. From holy angels? Yes; and we have been proclaiming these facts during nearly thirty years. Are there any communications from evil spirits? Yes; and the Devil is making the people believe very strongly in revelations from the spirit world. *This is called spiritualism, and it is said that thousands of spirits declare that 'Mormonism' is true; but what do that class of spirits know*

more than mortals? Perhaps a little more... [18] (emphasis added).

We can show our Mormon friend there are two issues at stake here: The first is that the Mormon church is confusing angels with humans. Second, their current scripture confirms that we get visitations from the dead (D&C 129:1-9). Both of these beliefs originate from a pagan worldview. Let's address them.

Do the dead come back as angels? We can share with our friend that Mormon teaching conflicts with the Bible. Angels are distinct from human beings (Psalm 8:4-5). They cannot reproduce after their kind (Mark 12:25), they are designated by masculine gender in Scripture (Genesis 19:1-5; cf. Zechariah 5:9 for possible exception— although the "two women" aren't referred to as angels. Earlier, in Zechariah 5:1-2, an angel is present who is referred to as "he."). Angels are spirit beings (Hebrews 1:14), and they cannot die (Luke 20:36).[19] Human beings die and after that are judged (Hebrews 9:27). They are then sent to their eternal destination. There is one exception we can find in Scripture that does show a human being coming up from the dead with a warning (see 1 Samuel 28:3-25). However, he is not said to be an angel.

Can we receive consultation from the dead? Communicating with the dead is sorcery or necromancy (which Joseph Smith was accused of practicing[20]). This is forbidden in the Bible (Exodus 22:18; Leviticus 19:31). The apostle Paul said those who practice sorcery "will not inherit the kingdom of God" (Galatians 5:20-21).While few Mormons will say they've received visitations from the dead, their current scripture (D&C 129:1-9), their theology book *Gospel Doctrine* (pp. 435-36), and even an LDS book titled *Temple Manifestations,* which lists numerous encounters with the dead at LDS temples (Joseph Heinerman [Salt Lake City, UT: 1986]), confirm their belief that the dead come back to earth. Nowhere in the Bible (except for the unusual circumstance in 1 Samuel 28:3-25) do we find the dead coming back to earth, or coming back as angels to deliver messages to us.

The Command to Translate the Bible

In *Doctrine and Covenants* the Lord commanded Joseph to "publish the new translation of my holy word unto the inhabitants of the earth. And if he will do this I will bless him, with a multiplicity of blessings" (D&C 124:89-90). In other words, Joseph was told to write a new translation of the Bible itself—one that apparently would be more correct than any other Bible available.

Joseph was also told by the Lord that "it is expedient to translate…it is expedient to continue the work of translation until it be finished" (D&C 73:3-4). That this project was "urgent" is affirmed by the fact that *Doctrine and Covenants* includes 16 more sections of text related to the translation work. This new translation was also said to be needed because they believed that many plain and precious truths had been taken out of the Bible (*Book of Mormon*, 1 Nephi 13:28).[21]

The Reorganized Church of Jesus Christ of Latter Day Saints (RLDS, which now calls themselves the Community of Christ) says that Joseph began his work in June of 1830 and finished it July 2, 1833.[22] But Joseph didn't publish this Bible right after he completed it. This is odd, considering that the Lord told him to be expedient about it. In fact, this Bible wasn't published until 1867 (25 years after Smith's death)—and at that, by the RLDS church, which is a Mormon splinter group.

Why didn't the Mormon church itself publish Smith's Bible? After Smith's death, Brigham Young sent Williard Richards to pick up the Bible manuscript from Emma. Emma told Richards that "she did not feel disposed to give it up at present."[23] Instead, she gave it to the RLDS church in 1866, and it was published and distributed the following year.[24] Joseph's Bible was called the *Inspired Translation of the Bible* (also known as the *Inspired Revision*).

Young didn't like the fact that the RLDS church had Smith's Bible. He considered the church and everyone in it to be apostates. So, rather than promote the translation that was supposedly commanded of God, Young downplayed Joseph's Bible, saying,

> That made us very anxious, in the days of Joseph, to get the new translation; but the Bible is good enough just as it is, it will answer my purpose, and it used to answer it very well when I was preaching in the world…. The Bible is good enough as it is, to point out the way we should walk and to teach us how to come to the Lord….[25]

To this day the Mormon church continues to downplay Joseph's revision. While the church sells it in their bookstores (still published by the RLDS church), the church "uses the King James Version of the Bible because it is *the best version translated by the power of man*"[26] (emphasis in original).

To further downplay Smith's translation, the Mormon church publicly stated that "the revision of the Bible which was done by Joseph Smith at the command of the Lord was not a complete revision of the Bible. There are many parts of the Bible in which the Prophet did not change the meaning where it is incorrect….However, all that he did is very helpful for the major errors have been corrected." [27]

We might want to ask our Mormon friend, "If major errors of the Bible have been corrected by Smith (and most likely 'plain and precious truths' put back in), then why isn't the church using his Bible? Your church includes selections from Smith's translation in the back of the KJV Bible, but why not make the entire translation available? Isn't it still much better to use Smith's Bible than the King James Version of the Bible, which hasn't been corrected at all?"

Permission to Marry Multiple Wives

During the early 1830s, Emma was beginning to have some strong suspicions that Joseph might be involved in infidelity. While these were only suspicions, Oliver Cowdery (one of the three witnesses to the *Book of Mormon*) had proof of Smith's adultery and confronted him about it. Smith denied to Cowdery that he was involved in any such activity. (And, as we read earlier, Cowdery was excommunicated from the church on several counts including, "by falsely insinuating that he [Smith] was guilty of adultery."[28])

Emma's suspicions were confirmed when she caught Joseph and 19-year-old Eliza Partridge locked in a room upstairs together. Emma had hired Eliza to take care of their newborn.[29]

Joseph admitted to his personal secretary, William Clayton, that if he took Eliza and Emily Partridge (twin sisters) as wives, he knew that Emma "would pitch on him and obtain a divorce and leave him."[30] But, Joseph added that "he should not relinquish anything."[31] And he didn't. He would eventually marry the sisters in March, 1843 (without Emma's knowledge).

In the meantime, Smith shared to his friend John Bennett his dilemma and the trouble he was having with Emma. He wondered what he should do, and Bennett replied, "This is very simple. Get a revelation that polygamy is right, and all your troubles will be at the end."[32]

The Revelation

Joseph didn't waste any time. On July 12, 1843 he sat down and wrote a command from the Lord that Emma would be destroyed if she didn't "receive all those that have been given unto my servant Joseph." If she didn't obey this command, not only would the Lord destroy her, but the Lord will bless Joseph and multiply him with "wives and children and crowns of eternal lives in the eternal worlds" (see D&C 132:52, 54, 56, 61-62).

In this same command, Emma was told to forgive Joseph's trespasses if she wanted to be forgiven (D&C 132:56). She was then told that the Lord would justify Joseph: "If he have ten virgins given unto him by this law [the law of priesthood], he cannot commit adultery, for they belong to him, and they are given unto him; therefore is he justified" (D&C 132:61-62).

Interestingly, Martin Harris affirmed Joseph had practiced polygamy as early as 1838—five years before Joseph received his revelation.[33] But after receiving the supposed revelation in 1843, Joseph no longer had to keep his affairs from his wife or the public. And, he made this plural-wife doctrine available to all Mormon men under the condition that they get permission from their first wife. *Doctrine and Covenants* says that the first wife must give consent before her husband can take another wife, yet if she didn't offer her consent "she shall be destroyed saith the Lord your God; for I will destroy her" (D&C 132:64). The second wife also had to be a virgin and not married to any other man. If the first wife consented then the man would not be committing adultery (D&C 132:61). It isn't known if Joseph sought permission from Emma for each of his many wives, but it is known that Joseph didn't just marry virgins. He married other men's wives,[34] and he even asked for the wives of the twelve Mormon disciples (see endnote for documentation of at least some of Smith's documented wives— there may have been more [35] *and* Brigham Young's documented wives[36]). Eighteen of Joseph's wives were single when he married them and had never been married previously.   Another four were widows. But the remaining 11 women were already married to other men, cohabiting with their legal husbands when Smith married them.[37]

In addition, 11 of Smith's wives were 14 to 20 years old when they married him. Nine wives were 21 to 30 years old. Eight of his wives were between the ages of 31 to 40. Two wives were between 41-50, and three wives were between 51 to 60 years of age. [38]

After Smith's death, many more women married him by "proxy," sealed to him for eternity. And for the record, Smith had at least one acknowledged polygamous child named Josephine. The child's mother was Sylvia Sessions Lyon. (See endnote regarding the question of other potential children.)[39]

The Extent

Many Mormons today have no idea how widespread polygamy was. For instance, Mormon singer Donny Osmond believes that "only a relatively small number of church members did so [practiced polygamy] prior to the late 1800s when the Church decreed the practice unacceptable."[40] However, polygamy was an accepted practice and it *wasn't* restricted to a mere few. Let's take a look at what some of the church prophets and leaders said.

First Prophet and President Joseph Smith (1843): "...God...gave me this revelation and commandment on celestial and plural marriage and the same God commanded me to obey it. He said to me that unless I accepted it and introduced it, and practiced it, I, together with my people, would be damned and cut off from this time hence forth.... But we have got to observe it. It is an eternal principle and was given by way of commandment and not by way of instruction."[41]

Second Prophet and President Brigham Young (1865): "...the whole question, therefore, narrows itself to this in the 'Mormon' mind. Polygamy was revealed by God, or the entire fabric of their faith is false. To ask them to give up such an item of belief is to ask them to relinquish the whole, to acknowledge their Priesthood a lie, their ordinances a deception, and all they have toiled for, lived for, bled for, prayed for, or hoped for, a miserable failure and a waste of life."[42]

Third Prophet and President John Taylor (1880): "The United States says we cannot marry more than one wife. God says different...when adulterers and libertines pass a law forbidding polygamy, the Saints cannot obey it....["43]

John Taylor said in 1886: "Thus saith the Lord...I have not revoked this law [plural wives doctrine] nor will I for it is everlasting & (sic) those who will enter into my glory must obey the conditions thereof, even so Amen."[44]

These statements raise some important questions. Did God really use these men, especially Joseph Smith? God's Word says that "*holy* men of God spoke as they were moved by the Holy Ghost" (2 Peter 1:21, emphasis added). Only *holy* men (although not sinless) would be used of God to write His Word. Because of this fact alone, Mormons must question whether *Doctrine and Covenants* is truly the revelations of Jesus Christ.

According to the Bible (especially since the New Testament was written) men are to have only one living wife (1 Corinthians 7:2; Titus 1:6). Because the Bible contradicts *Doctrine and Covenants,* Mormons must question the validity of one or the other. They can't both be right.

If our Mormon friend still believes the Lord gave Joseph Smith and other Mormon prophets a revelation on plural marriage, we can ask this: Why would the prophets (such as Taylor in 1886) say the plural wives doctrine was everlasting, and then some short years later (1890), deny having anything to do with such a doctrine?

In 1869, fourth prophet and president Wilford Woodruff said, "If we were to do away with polygamy...we must do away with prophets and Apostles, with revelation and the gifts and graces of the Gospel, and finally give up our religion altogether."[45] He changed his tune when he wrote an "Official Declaration," also referred to as The Manifesto. He wrote:

Press dispatches having been sent for political purposes...allege that plural marriages are still being solemnized ...that...the leaders of the Church have taught, encouraged and urged the continuance of the practice of polygamy—I, therefore, as President of the Church of Jesus of Latter-day Saints, do hereby, in the most solemn manner, *declare that these charges are false. We are not teaching polygamy or plural marriage, nor permitting any person to enter into its practice....* I now publicly declare that my advice to the Latter-day Saints is to refrain from contracting any marriage forbidden by the law of the land. (emphasis added) [46]

Despite the above statement, the U.S. Senate's Committee on Privileges and Elections submitted a report in which it stated,

"A sufficient number of specific instances of the taking of plural wives since the manifesto of 1890, so called, have been shown by the testimony as having taken among officials of the Mormon church to demonstrate the fact that the leaders in this church, the first presidency and the twelve apostles, connive at the practice of taking plural wives and have done so ever since the manifesto was issued." [47]

The Response

Remember our friend Marjorie, whom we met at the beginning of this chapter? One reason she sought to find Brian was to seek answers to her many questions she began to have. She discovered that the Mormon church first defended polygamy, then said they would stop it. Yet while the church leaders condemned followers who were still in polygamous relationships, some of these same church leaders continued marrying more women—in secret. [48] Marjorie may not have known that the Mormon leadership even considered the idea of secret concubines, wherein men and women could live together in secret. [49] After discovering this apparent hypocrisy, Marjorie became concerned about other revelations that Joseph Smith proclaimed in *Doctrine and Covenants*. But not all Mormons will respond as Marjorie did. There are some who still defend this past church doctrine.

Dialogue: Journal of Mormon Thought tells us one of the reasons Mormons defend the plural-wives doctrine:

> Many Latter-day Saints—especially those that have polygamous ancestors—take pride in the faithful men and women who practiced plural marriage long ago. Even though LDS men take just one legal wife today, many devout Mormons still believe in the "principle" and may be sealed to more than one woman for eternity. The Mormon church's promise of plural marriage in the afterlife, and the current practice of plural marriage among Fundamentalist Mormons, are the legacies of Joseph Smith's revelation sanctioning Nauvoo polygamy as "new and everlasting covenant.[50]

Other Mormons defend Smith's revelation for another reason. For instance, a while ago I asked Pat, a Mormon friend, "Why is it that the Mormon church accepts Joseph's polygamy and that of other church leaders, but condemns it for everyone else?"

After thinking about the question for a moment, Pat replied, "Well, it was a command from God during a very special time only. It was the same command that God gave the prophets in the Old Testament. Also, Joseph was concerned about the widows and the older single women who didn't have a man to protect them. These were the type of women he married. He really had a good heart for doing this."

Surprised at the answer, I said, "But God was against plural marriage in the Old Testament. Only because of the hardness of man's heart He did allow it [see Genesis 16:4-7]. There were also consequences because of polygamy, such as jealousy."

I later shared with Pat (after doing some homework) what Leviticus had to say (since Pat was excusing Joseph's polygamy by pointing to the OT prophets). Let's take a look.

Mormon Friend, Please Consider:

Go to the book of Leviticus. Read Leviticus 18:18, 20; 20:14. Leviticus forbids a man, which included the prophets of the Old Testament, to marry *"a woman in addition to her sister...while she is alive"*(18:18).

Neither was he to marry *"a woman and her mother"*(20:14).

Neither was he to *"have intercourse with your neighbor's wife, to be defiled with her"* (18:20).

After sharing from Leviticus, I told Pat, "You can't defend Joseph Smith's polygamy. He and other Mormon men went completely against the laws of Leviticus. Joseph Smith, for instance, married five pairs of sisters; he married a mother and her daughter; and he took other men's wives (which included Joseph requesting the wives of all 12 Mormon apostles)."

I then gently added, "I know you want to think the best of Joseph Smith. I wish I could, too. But if the Mormon church is about truth, as you say it is, we must look at the truth regarding Smith's life. He didn't just marry widows and older single women, as you've been told. He married pubescent girls, others in their late teens; women in their twenties and thirties, and only a few in their fifties and sixties. Most of these women had never been married or were already married. Few were widows."

Pat was at a loss for words and simply said, "Interesting."

Since speaking to Pat, I also came to realize that according to Mormon Scripture, *Doctrine and Covenants,* Joseph *wasn't* allowed to marry widows, nor currently married women. It states that Joseph was only allowed to marry "virgins," who were *not* vowed to any other man..."then he is justified" (D&C 132:61).

The Turn from *Doctrine and Covenants*

At first Marjorie knew very little about her church's history. It was her careful examination of *Doctrine and Covenants* that opened her eyes to the issues that made her concerned. Eventually Marjorie held the teachings of *Doctrine and Covenants* up to the Bible. And as a result, she decided to trust God and His Word rather than Joseph and his *Doctrine and Covenants*. Marjorie repented of her sins, asked Christ to be her Savior, and committed her life to the Lord, Jesus Christ. Isn't this wonderful news?! You can hope the same for your Mormon friend as you stress that the Bible—God's holy Word—is the *only* Word we can trust.

For feelings come and feelings go,
and feelings are deceiving;
My warrant is the Word of God,
naught else is worth believing.
Though all my heart should feel condemned
for want of some sweet token,

There is One greater than my heart
whose Word cannot be broken.
I'll trust in God's unchanging Word
til soul and body sever;
For, though all things shall pass away,
His Word shall stand forever.

— MARTIN LUTHER[51]

Thinking It Over

1. What is the *Doctrine and Covenants*?

2. What do Mormons believe about the "Word of Wisdom"? How did it come about?

3. If a Mormon excuses Joseph Smith's polygamy, what Old Testament verses can we point to? How do these verses show that Joseph's polygamy was inexcusable.

CHAPTER 5

WHAT DO I NEED TO KNOW
ABOUT OTHER
MORMON SCRIPTURES?

...the translation [of Joseph Smith] was correct, more so than any he [Professor Anthon] had before seen translated from the Egyptian...he said that they were Egyptian, Chaldaic, Assyric, and Arabic; and he said they were true characters.

History of the Church, 1:20

On July 3, 1835 a man by the name of Michael H. Chandler came strolling into Kirtland, Ohio to share something quite extraordinary with the townspeople—four Egyptian mummies. But, that's not all. He also displayed rolls of papyrus covered with hieroglyphic figures. Chandler told the curious observers that the papyrus scrolls were from a catacomb in Egypt. Joseph Smith, one of the observers in the crowd, was fascinated. He asked Chandler if he could examine the scrolls. After receiving permission, Smith looked them over very closely. He then stated that one of the rolls contained the writings of Abraham and another the writings of Jacob's son Joseph, who was sold into slavery in Egypt.

Excited over this find, Smith encouraged the Mormon church to pitch in and buy Chandler's entire collection—and so they did. Joseph then got to work translating the writings of Abraham, which are now known to be part of the *Pearl of Great Price*.[1]

According to the Mormon church, the *Pearl of Great Price* is "one of the standard works of scripture."[2] Because of this volume's important place in the Mormon church, it's good for us to know about its contents.

The Mormon Scriptures
The *Pearl of Great Price*

The *Pearl of Great Price* provides Mormons with access to Joseph Smith's revelations, translations, narrations, and personal history, which includes, of course, his two visions. Along with the last few pages providing the *Articles of Faith*, we can also find a section by the sixth Prophet of the Church, Joseph F. Smith (the nephew of prophet Joseph Smith, Jr.) titled, "Vision of the Redemption of the Dead." That's not all. This volume includes two special books, the Book of Moses and the Book of Abraham. The Book of Moses is comprised of revelations Prophet Joseph Smith, Jr. allegedly received from the Lord on the visions and writings of Moses. And the Book of Abraham is comprised of Joseph's translation of the writings of Abraham while in Egypt…well, sort of.

The Book of Abraham
An Initial Review

Joseph Smith was thrilled to have in his possession "authentic" ancient scrolls. He was also proud of the translation work he did on the scrolls. He wrote, "The remainder of this month, I was continually engaged in translating an alphabet to the Book of Abraham, and arranging a grammar of the Egyptian language as practiced by the ancients."[3]

During the time Joseph was hard at work transcribing his ancient finds, he invited a group of young people to his house to observe his "Egyptian records." One of the young ladies in the group who had been examining them was asked "if they had the appearance of antiquity."[4] She honestly answered that the records didn't look authentic whatsoever. Smith wrote about this incident and what he told that young lady:

On hearing this I was surprised at the ignorance she displayed, and I observed to her, that she was an anomaly in creation, for all the wise and learned that had examined them, without hesitation pronounced them ancient. I further remarked that it was downright wickedness, ignorance, bigotry and superstition had caused her to make the remark; and that I would put it on record. And I have done so....[5]

Yet the young lady wasn't the only one who thought the "ancient records" looked suspicious. While the mummies and scrolls were authentic, dating after the time of Christ, they were not authentic to Abraham's day, as Joseph believed. For this reason, professional scholars known as Egyptologists have clearly stated their own doubts.

A Scholarly Examination

Some of the world's top Egyptologists have carefully reviewed Joseph Smith's "Egyptian Alphabet and Grammar," which he said was used to translate the Book of Abraham. Each and every one of them declared Joseph's work "fraudulent."[6] When Egyptologist Henry Lutz of the University of California took a look at Smith's Egyptian "glyphs" without knowing where they came from or that they had any significance to the Mormon church, he stated that they "are from the Book of the Dead."[7]

When modern-day Egyptologist Samuel A.B. Mercer met with other scholars about Joseph's Egyptian text, he said "all the scholars came to the same conclusion ...Smith could not possibly correctly translate any Egyptian text, as his interpretation of the facsimile shows."[8] (A picture of the facsimiles and Joseph's interpretation of each can be found in the Book of Abraham.) Mercer also said that any pupil of mine who would show such absolute ignorance of Egyptian as Smith does, could not possibly expect to get more "than zero in an examination in Egyptology....I speak as a linguist when I say that if Smith knew Egyptian and correctly interpreted the facsimiles which you submitted to me, then I don't know a word of Egyptian, and Erman's Grammar is a fake, and all modern Egyptologists are deceived."[9]

Despite what Egyptologists have said, Mormons will never know about their findings unless we show them. In fact, they have no reason to question the authenticity of the Book of Abraham, since Smith "proved" he could translate the *Book of Mormon*. In their book *History of the Church*, Mormons can read Columbia College professor Charles Anthon's "endorsement" of Smith's translation of the *Book of Mormon:*

> ...the translation was correct, more so than any he had before seen translated from the Egyptian...he said that they were Egyptian, Chaldaic, Assyric, and Arabic; and he said they were true characters.[10]

Does Anthon's endorsement authenticate Joseph Smith's translation work? Not according to Anthon. Professor Anthon wasn't by any means endorsing Smith's ability to translate Egyptian hieroglyphics. In a letter to E.D. Howe on February 17, 1831, Professor Anthon (again, a professor of classical studies and literature[11]) wrote, "The whole story about my having pronounced the Mormonite inscription to be 'reformed Egyptian hieroglyphics' is *perfectly false*"[12] (emphasis in original).

Anthon explained that Martin Harris, "a plain, and apparently simple hearted farmer,"[13] came to him with a piece of paper. Of the paper Anthon remarked, "This paper was in fact a singular scrawl. It consisted of all kinds of crooked characters disposed in columns, and had evidently been prepared by some person who had before him at the time a book containing various alphabets...the paper contained anything else but *Egyptian Hieroglyphics.*"[14]

Despite the fact that important portions of Anthon's letter to

E.D. Howe are in the Mormon's *Comprehensive History of the Church,* many church members still believe that great scholars such as Anthon have endorsed Smith's work.

While we can encourage our Mormon friends to read B.H. Roberts's *Comprehensive History of the Church* (pages 102-04), we can also share with them that Mormon thinkers are questioning Smith's translation work of the Book of Abraham. In *Dialogue: A Journal of Mormon Thought* we find these statements:

> An obvious question is whether or not Smith's identifications and interpretations are unique to him; i.e., whether or not they can be corroborated egyptologically. Unfortunately, they cannot.[15]

> It is therefore no wonder that apologists for Joseph Smith as a translator are so anxious to divorce him from 1) the "Egyptian Alphabet" manuscripts—a futile attempt, since one was in his own handwriting and the remainder followed his lead; and 2) Book of Abraham manuscripts 1a, 1b, and 2, which were simply scribal copies of his dictated "translation."[16]

So, what *did* Smith "transcribe" from those papyrus scrolls that became the *Book of Abraham?*

Some Apparent Discrepancies

Parts of the *Book of Abraham* include familiar biblical stories, such as the account of Abraham being confronted by the Egyptians in regard to his wife Sarai. Yet there is one big difference in this account as opposed to the biblical account. While the Bible shows that Abraham, of his *own* volition, had wrongly lied about his wife (Genesis 12:11-13), the *Book of Abraham* has God telling Abraham to instruct Sarai to lie to the Egyptians—telling them she's

Abraham's sister (*Pearl of Great Price*, Abraham 2:22-25). Not only can we point out this discrepancy to our Mormon friend, but we can also show them what their *Book of Mormon* says: liars will be thrust down to hell (2 Nephi 9:34), and that God cannot lie (Enos 1:6; Ether 3:12). If God cannot lie, He certainly wouldn't instruct someone else to lie, would He?

An Awkward Controversy

It's important to be aware there are many Mormons who do not want to talk about the Book of Abraham. You see, there's a sensitive portion of text they really would like to forget. I don't blame them—I would want to forget it, too. It involves the Mormon priesthood. Specifically, it says that those who belong to the lineage of Cain cannot enter the priesthood. Even Pharaoh, "a righteous man" in the Book of Abraham, was "of that lineage by which he could not have the right of Priesthood" (*Pearl of Great Price*, Book of Abraham 1:26-27).

Who belongs to the lineage of Cain? According to Joseph Smith, it's the black person. He wrote, "In the evening debated with John C. Bennett and others to show that the Indians have greater cause to complain of the treatment of the whites, than the negroes, *or sons of Cain*"[17] (emphasis added).

David O.McKay, ninth president and prophet of the Mormon church, said, "I know of no scriptural basis for denying the Priesthood to Negroes other than one verse in the Book of Abraham (1:26); however, I believe...that the real reason dates back to our pre-existent life."[18]

Also defending the Book of Abraham doctrine was tenth Mormon president and prophet Joseph Fielding Smith, who said, "The only souls coming into this world who are under restriction are the Negroes, and they cannot hold the priesthood; but Negroes may be baptized...." [19]

Apostle and theologian Bruce McConkie supported his father-in-law, Joseph Fielding Smith, by saying, "Negroes in this life are denied the priesthood; under no circumstances can they hold this delegation of authority from the Almighty...."[20]

Those of us who are familiar with the 1960s will remember the strong messages of Martin Luther King and others who said a man shouldn't be judged by the color of his skin. It was during this era that the Mormon church began being criticized for its "black policy."

Students in Tuscon, Arizona, asked the Western Athletic Conference to "break ties with Brigham Young University" because of the school's connection with Mormonism's racial policies.[21] The NAACP threatened to picket Temple Square if the church didn't "present an 'acceptable' statement on civil rights."[22] And the Boy Scouts of America pressed charges against the church because a 12-year-old black boy was not permitted to become a senior patrol leader. Apparently one of the requirements for becoming such was to be a deacon's quorum president [23] within the church, a position he could not hold without entering the priesthood.[24]

Bruce McConkie tried to defend the church's position, saying, "Am I valiant if I am deeply concerned about the Church's stand on who can or who cannot receive the priesthood and think it is time for a new revelation on this doctrine?"[25] Church president Spencer W. Kimball spoke to the Brigham Young University (BYU) faculty and student body in 1977, stating that "the gospel is made up of absolute truths that do not change regardless of contrary opinions or beliefs of men."[25]

Despite Kimball's words about "absolute truths" that never change, just a year later, in 1978, he "received a revelation from the Lord directing that the gospel and the priesthood should now go to all men without reference to race or color."[26] Perhaps embarrassed over this change, Bruce McConkie said to the seminarians and institute teachers at BYU, "Forget everything that I have said, or what President Brigham Young or whomsoever has said in days past that is contrary to present revelation...they don't matter any more...."[27]

If only the Mormon church had known from the beginning what God says about the subject. He says, "God is not one to show partiality, but *in every nation* the man who fears Him and does what is right is welcome to Him" (Acts 10:34-35, emphasis added). You might be wondering about the Mormons themselves. Have any left the church upon discovering the church's former "black policy"? It's uncertain to know. But one thing is certain: According to Jerald and Sandra Tanner, "there are a growing number of Mormons who are rejecting the Book of Abraham."[28] Many members, however, have stayed within the church while rejecting the book. Marvin S. Hill, a professor of history at Brigham Young University, explains the reason: "While Mormons venerate their sacred books...the final word comes not from any scriptural passage but from the living oracles...."[29]

So a Mormon can reject certain written scriptures as long as they are obeying the Living Oracles—the unwritten scripture.

The Living Oracles

The Living Oracles are "words from the Lord" given to the Mormon prophets, presidents, and those in the leadership of the LDS priesthood. The oracles are considered scripture[30] and are passed on to the members of the church with the expectation that they be obeyed.

In the Mormon study guide *Gospel Principles*, Mormons are told to "believe in and follow the living prophet.... sustain the President of the Church as prophet, seer and revelator.... Study his words...follow his inspired teachings completely. We should not choose to follow part of his inspired counsel and discard that which is unpleasant or difficult. . . . The Lord will never allow the President of the Church to lead us astray." [31]

President Brigham Young wanted his people to understand very clearly the importance of following his words. So, with an air of drama, he took the Bible and laid it down; he took the *Book of Mormon* and laid it down: and he took the *Book of Doctrine and Covenants,* and laid it down before him, saying,

> ...when compared with the living oracles, those books are nothing to me; those books do not convey the word of God direct to us now, as do the words of a Prophet, or a man bearing the Holy Priesthood in our day and generation. I would rather have the living oracles than all the writing in these books.[32]

President Ezra Taft Benson wanted Mormons to have an unfailing allegiance to the Living Oracles, so he said, "Always keep your eye on the President of the Church, and if he ever tells you to do anything, and it is wrong, and you do it, the Lord will bless you for it."[33]

The Living Oracles are of such importance that, according to Bruce McConkie in *Mormon Doctrine,* a Mormon "may accept or reject" the Oracles but they must keep in mind that "acceptance brings salvation; rejection leads to damnation."[34] Apostle Heber Kimball stressed very clearly, "When a servant of God counsels you, it is your duty to hear and obey his words.... You have no salvation only what you get through that source, and every true hearted Latter-day Saint believes so."[35]

Imagine—no salvation except through the president of the church! Debra, who is currently spiritually confused, just left the Mormon church because of the Living Oracles. She sums up the Oracles this way: "Once a church leader has spoken, the thinking has been done."

Does it make sense that human leaders of a church can contradict what a perfect, all-wise God says in the Bible and still be correct? Or that you will be blessed for following a church president even if what he says is wrong? And if he's wrong when giving an oracle—a prophetic message—wouldn't that make him a false prophet? If so, then the following Bible verse would apply to him: "as for the prophet or the priest or the people who say, 'The oracle of the LORD,' I will bring punishment upon that man and his household" (Jeremiah 23:34).

If only the church leaders could be aware of God's warning! But, until they are made aware, they will continue to warn church members, telling them, "Your safety and ours depends upon whether or not we follow the ones whom the Lord has placed to preside over his church."[36]

The True Scriptures

Wouldn't it be wonderful if we could introduce our Mormon friends to the Bereans? Remember them? They were a group of people to whom the apostle Paul preached in Berea. Although they "received the word with great eagerness," they didn't accept even an apostle's sermon at face value. Instead, they checked the Scriptures to see if what Paul was saying to them was true. The Bible commends the Bereans not for being simpleminded, but rather for being noble minded (Acts 17:11).

Just as you and I strive towards noble mindedness, we can help our Mormon friends in this area, too. It begins by encouraging them to take the time to discern whether or not something is true. And that's what we've been learning about in the first portion of this book by looking at the historical background and early teachings of Mormonism. The facts we've examine not only challenge Joseph Smith's credentials as a prophet, but they have opened the eyes of many Mormons, prompting them to seek the truth. Thus one of the best ways to help our Mormon friends is to help them compare God's truth with Mormon doctrines and see the discrepancies—and so it's the truths of His Word that we will focus upon in the rest of the book. Are you ready for the challenge? So am I! But, before we begin, let's keep in mind that Mormons are proud of their church doctrine. Such pride has a legacy going back to Brigham Young, who said,

> "if you can find a truth in heaven, earth, or hell,
> it belongs to our doctrine.
> We believe it; it is ours; we claim it"
> (*Journal of Discourses*, April 24, 1870).

Thinking It Over

1. What do Egyptologists say about the Book of Abraham?

2. What is the book's most controversial teaching? How have some Mormons responded to this teaching?

3. Although the church has now changed its "revelation" in regard to blacks and the priesthood, why do you think they haven't changed the teaching in the Book of Abraham?

4. What are the Living Oracles? What authority do they have in comparison to the scriptures? Explain.

Do not be ashamed to
testify about our Lord....

I am not ashamed, because
I know whom I have believed,
and am convinced that He is
able to guard what I have
entrusted to Him for that day.

What you have heard from me,
keep as the pattern of sound teaching,
with faith and love in Christ Jesus.

2 Timothy 1:8,12,13

PART TWO

QUESTIONS
TO
ASK
OUR
MORMON
FRIENDS

The doctrine the prophet Joseph teaches is all I care about. Bring anything against that if you can. As for anything else, I don't care if the prophet Joseph acted like the Devil. He brought forth a doctrine that will save us if we will abide by it. He may have got drunk every day of his life, slept with his neighbor's wife every night, run horses and gambled every day; I care nothing about that, for I never embrace any man in my faith.

The doctrine the prophet produced will save you and me and the whole world. If you can find fault with his doctrine, find it.[1]

—President Brigham Young

WHY DON'T YOU BELIEVE THE
BIBLE *ALONE* IS SUFFICIENT?

Thou fool, that shall say:
A Bible, we have got a Bible, and we need no more Bible.

Book of Mormon: 2 Nephi 29:6

D o you know that we who are Christians are confusing to our Mormon friends? Yes, we are confusing to them. You see, while Mormons respect the fact that we believe in the Bible, they are puzzled over our stubbornness to believe the Bible alone is sufficient to find God's truth.

In *Doctrines of Salvation*, Mormon prophet Joseph Fielding Smith tells his followers that you and I lack understanding, that we believe there is no more revelation, that Scripture is full, and that "the Lord has no more doctrine to reveal through prophets...."[1] (Smith is correct on the last three points—Christians believe the Bible is complete.)

Smith then continues by quoting from the *Book of Mormon*, saying, "Truly do they cry, 'A Bible! A Bible! We have got a Bible, and there cannot be any more Bible' " (2 Nephi 29:3). Continuing his contention, Smith tells his listeners that because you and I are trusting only in the Bible we are "helplessly groping in the dark."[2]

So, as you can see, your Mormon friend pities you. You are groping in the dark because you won't go beyond the Bible and seek the "light" that the *Book of Mormon* offers. Because of that *you are lost*. Knowing this is what Mormons believe, it's easy to understand why they are so zealous for us to embrace their book.

With that said, we—not them, but we—will need to offer sensitivity.

Offering Sensitivity to Mormon Individuals

Many faithful Mormons read the *Book of Mormon* daily because they firmly believe it's the Word of God. One Mormon woman I know prides herself in the fact that she reads the entire *Book of Mormon* once a month. She covets every word on those printed pages.

Knowing that Mormons cherish their Mormon scripture, we need to be very sensitive when we talk to them about the Bible.

Keep in mind that our goal is to talk with them about the *Bible's authority*—to show them it's the only Word of God given to mankind. But, in striving toward that goal, and hopefully reaching it, we'll be stripping away something very precious to them—their scripture.

Back in chapter 3, we discovered why the *Book of Mormon* is not valid when it comes to history. In this chapter, we'll be looking at how the *Book of Mormon* compares to the Bible—and see why the *Book of Mormon* cannot be called God's Word. Imagine what this means to a person who not only treasures her Mormon scripture, but includes it as part of his (or her) testimony—a testimony that gives him acceptance into the Mormon church and from other Mormons.   What is his testimony? It's the same for all Mormons:

I know this Church is true,
I know Joseph Smith was a true prophet,
I know the modern Prophets are true
I know the *Book of Mormon* is true.

Your Mormon friend would not only receive rejection if he denied his testimony, but in his mind, he would lose something even greater. Joseph Smith, Jr., explains what that greater thing is:

"Take away the *Book of Mormon* and the Revelations and where is our religion? We have none." [3]

Quite a sobering and truthful statement, isn't it? Thankfully, we have Jesus to offer our friend. If he embraces Him, he doesn't lose a thing—he only gains!

So as we begin to question our friends about their Mormon doctrines and showing the truths from the Bible, I highly recommend you use the King James Version of the Bible. That's because Mormons, who believe the Bible has been corrupted, will trust only the King James Version. They say it's "the best version translated by the power of man." [4]

Responding Biblically to Mormon Arguments

When you ask, "Why don't you believe the Bible alone is sufficient?" be ready for the following memorized response:

> We believe the Bible to be the word of God
> as far as it is translated correctly;
> we also believe the *Book of Mormon*
> to be the word of God. [5]

As you may have noticed, the response to your question can become a nice transition for your Mormon friend to begin talking about the *Book of Mormon*. And, the subject will indeed change to the *Book of Mormon*. This is just fine; we'll still be able to talk about the Bible. As your friend (or a Mormon missionary) talks about the *Book of Mormon,* he will begin sharing with you either its history (meaning, Joseph's vision), telling you of its importance to mankind (God's Word to the world), or he may instead just share with you on a more personal level, telling you about his "burning in the bosom."

The Burning in the Bosom

Several years ago, I had the opportunity to meet with a former high school friend who had become a Mormon. We'll call her Maureen. It was such a delight to see her after 25 years of changes. We had a lot of catching up to do. Along with the usual talk of marriage and children, I shared with her how I had become a born-again Christian. She, in turn, shared with me how she became a Mormon (prior to marrying the man who helped her join the church).

As she shared, Maureen said, "Donna I know the *Book of Mormon* is true. I prayed to Heavenly Father, asking Him if it was true."

Maureen and all other Mormons believe that the angel Moroni bids everyone to pray about the *Book of Mormon*. With a sincere heart we are to ask "the Eternal Father in the name of Christ, if these things are not true." Only then will the Holy Ghost "manifest the truth of it unto you" (Moroni 10:4).

Maureen went on to explain that after she prayed she got a "burning in the bosom" that confirmed to her the *Book of Mormon*'s truthfulness. She then told me that if I were to sincerely pray, I too would feel the same burning. What my former high school pal and other Mormons are communicating is that the "burning" experience qualifies the *Book of Mormon* to be true.

Because Maureen and I used to joke around a lot, I replied, "What if the burning in the bosom is really heartburn or a terrible case of indigestion? Wouldn't this mean that the *Book of Mormon* isn't true?"

Maureen didn't seem to appreciate the humor. So I said in all seriousness, "Maureen, I remember a very zealous Muslim telling me the same thing about the Quar'an. That is, that I can pray about it, and if it's true, I'll get a burning in the bosom. Obviously, we can't go by this; otherwise, we'll be saying the Qur'an is true too."

I continued, "We must look to the Bible. It's the only book that has stood the test of time and has been affirmed ever since Moses as the divine Word of God. There have been no changes, no contradictions, no opportunities for a person to slip in his own opinion and doctrines. The Bible is authoritatively God's Word."

As a side-note, Mormons have no problem dismissing the Bible, as they put their trust in the *Book of Mormon*—which is completely unverifiable (other than the truth of it being confirmed by their own subjective feelings). The prophet Jeremiah tells us, "The heart is deceitful above all things, and desperately wicked; who can know it? (Jeremiah 17:9).

With concern I continued, "Maureen, you know I would never want to hurt you. So please accept it when I say, with a sincere heart, that the Bible shows us the *Book of Mormon* can't be true. Can I show you?" Maureen nodded. Taking my pocket Bible out of my purse, I read Galatians 1:6-8 to her.

Mormon Friend, Please Consider:

The Bible shows that the Mormon scriptures can't be true.

Read Galatians 1:6-8. Paul said,

I marvel that ye are so soon removed from him
that called you into the grace of Christ unto another gospel:
which is not another; but there be some that trouble you,
and would pervert the gospel of Christ.
But though we, *or an angel from heaven*,
preach any other gospel unto you
than that which we have preached unto you,
let him be accursed. (emphasis added.)

The *Book of Mormon*—Another Gospel

After sharing Galatians 1:6-8 with Maureen, I could tell she was quite bothered. Desiring to avoid the issue, she simply said, "Donna, you've got to be sincere in seeking the truth about the *Book of Mormon.*"

Not wanting to let Paul's admonition be swept under the carpet, I said, "Maureen, what do you think about Paul's warning? He is saying, 'Though we, or an angel from heaven, preach any other gospel unto you...let him be accursed.' Didn't an angel approach Joseph Smith with a different gospel?"

Nervous, Maureen said, "I don't want us to talk anymore about this, but let me just encourage you to pray the prayer. You'll come to see that the *Book of Mormon* is true."

On another occasion, I shared Paul's words in Galatians 1:6-8 with a pair of Mormon missionaries, Elders Reeser and Brown. They, too, showed apparent displeasure with the passage.

After Elder Reeser heard me quote Paul's words "we, or an angel from heaven," he said in a bothered tone, "I can see you are not open to truth. We had better leave."

I replied, "I *am* open to truth; that is why I am bringing up these verses. It tells us we are to ignore an angel if it comes to us with a different gospel."

Elder Brown quickly jumped in, saying, "Well, the angel Moroni didn't come to Joseph with a different gospel."

With that answer, I decided to begin asking a few *why* and *what* questions in response to what the missionaries were saying to me. Try to do the same. It challenges your Mormon friends to think carefully about what they really believe. And it will help you to verify the authority of Scripture.

Why Do We Need the Book of Mormon?

Responding to Elder Brown's statement, I asked, "If Moroni didn't come to Joseph with a different gospel, why then must we even have the *Book of Mormon?*

Elder Brown answered, "The *Book of Mormon* is the Bible's 'second witness.'"

"But," I questioned further, "*why* would the Bible need a 'second witness' when it already has many witnesses, such as the 40 authors who wrote the 66 books of the Bible? You can't say they weren't witnesses."

Elder Reeser answered this time, saying, "Donna, the Bible needs a second witness, a special kind of witness, because scripture says, 'There are many plain and precious things taken away from the book'" (1 Nephi 13:28).

What Was Taken Out of the Bible?

Reeser's comment "scripture says" caused me to ask (let it also cause you to ask), "What scripture are you referring to? And, what plain and precious things have been taken away from *what* book?"

Knowing I wouldn't like his answer, Elder Reeser sheepishly replied, "The *Book of Mormon* is the scripture I'm referring to."

Quickly regaining his confidence, Elder Reeser answered my second question: "And in regard to the 'plain and precious things,' they were eliminated from the Bible. That's why we need the *Book of Mormon*. It's the 'restored gospel.'"

I then asked, "Can you tell me one 'plain and precious thing' that was taken out of the Bible?"

Elder Reeser answered my question indirectly by saying, "Many of the things in the *Book of Mormon* were supposed to be in the Bible, but aren't.

I answered, "That's not really an answer, because you're not giving any examples of what has been taken out. How do you really know if something has been taken out, especially in light of God's promise that He would preserve His Word, the Bible?"

You can also ask the Mormon missionaries, "if *plain and precious things* were taken out of the Bible (thus the reason for the *Book of Mormon* as the "Restored Gospel"), why, then, are there Bible verses in the Book of Mormon?" Actually, why are there 21 *entire chapters* taken directly from the Book of Isaiah, **inserted** into the *Book of Mormon—some verses into the very book of Nephi that claims plain and precious things were taken out?*

Mormon Friend, Please Consider:

• *The Bible is incorruptible.* Read 1 Peter 1:23-25. Note what the passage says about the Word of God. This means that there is no way "plain and precious things" could have been taken out.

• *The Bible says it will endure.* God tells us His truth shall never vanish but will reveal itself to *all* generations (read Psalm 100:5; also Isaiah 40:8; Matthew 24:35; 1 Peter 1:24-25;).

• *Jesus defends the Bible.* Jesus said, "Thy word is truth" (John 17:17 KJV). Therefore the Bible is sufficient to give us truth.

• *We were given the truth once and for all.* The Bible, God's truth, was delivered to the saints once and for all (Jude 3). This indicates that no other truth was going to be given.

• Yes! *Plain and precious things WERE taken out of the Bible and inserted into the Book of Mormon, such as 21 chapters (entire chapters) from the Book of Isaiah and inserted into the Book of Mormon (compare the verses below). Also, compare Genesis 1:2-31 with Moses 2:2-31. Doesn't this appear to be plagiarism? Compare:* 1 Ne.20/Isa.48;
1 Ne. 21/Isa 49; 2 Ne. 7/Isa. 50;   2 Ne. 8/Isa. 51; 2 Ne 12/Isa. 2;   2 Ne. 13/Isa. 3; 2 Ne. 14/Isa 4;   2 Ne. 15/Isa. 5;   2 Ne. 16/Isa. 6; 2 Ne 17/Isa 7; 2 Ne. 18/ Isa. 8;   2 Ne. 19/Isa. 9;   2 Ne. 20/Isa. 10;   2 Ne. 21/Isa. 11; 2 Ne. 22/Isa. 12;   2 Ne. 23/Isa. 13;   2 Ne 24/Isa. 14;   2 Ne. 27/Isa. 29; Mosiah 14/Isa 53; Mosiah 15/parts of Isa. 52; 3 Ne. 22/Isa. 54....and much, much more.

After I mentioned the above Scriptures, I told the missionaries that one of the marks of a false religion is that they hold to extrabiblical revelation. Their *Book of Mormon* and other Mormon scriptures are indeed extrabiblical in that they go beyond the Bible. God's Word forbids this, saying,

> I testify unto every man that heareth the words of the prophecy of this book, If any man shall add unto these things, God shall add unto him the plagues that are written in this book (Revelation 22:18-19 KJV).

While I thought the above warning would cause the missionaries to show at least a bit of discomfort, it didn't. In fact, they had a ready response. Elder Reeser said, "Donna, the apostle John was only warning against adding to or taking from the revelations *he had received and written* while banished upon the Isle of Patmos. And, I agree we shouldn't add to the revelations John was given at that time. But, these verses don't in any way prevent the Lord from adding to what He has already revealed."

Who Really Wrote the Mormon Scriptures?

I simply replied, "While I disagree with your commentary, let's take this one step further: Are the additions, the Mormon scriptures, really of the Lord, or of Joseph Smith and others? Just the *Book of Mormon* alone contradicts the Bible in many areas. Therefore, the additions have to be from Joseph Smith. And, let's not forget Paul's words—the one who gives a different gospel than the gospel of Christ is giving us a distorted gospel. Paul says, 'Let him be accursed' (Galatians 1:8)."

With that I thought I hit the final nail on the coffin, but the missionaries didn't want to give up the fight for the *Book of*

Mormon. You, too, will meet missionaries who are persistent in the battle. Let's just keep on being patient with them.

Remember, they've been instructed that the *Book of Mormon is true.* It's the "keystone" to their religion.[6] And, as we now know, if a Mormon rejects the *Book of Mormon,* he has nothing left to believe in. So, it's not easy for a Mormon to come to terms with the truth regarding their scripture.   Elder Brown continued to defend the *Book of Mormon,* saying, "Donna, the Bible prophesies the coming of the *Book of Mormon.* Therefore, it has to be from God."

Bible "Prophecies" Regarding the *Book of Mormon*

Opening his Bible, Elder Brown read from Isaiah 29:4 (KJV):

> Thou shalt be brought down, and shalt speak out
> of the ground, and thy speech shall be low out of
> the dust, and thy voice shall be, as of one that hath
> a familiar spirit, out of the ground, and thy speech
> shall whisper out of the dust.

With tremendous confidence, Brown declared, "This clearly speaks of the plates that were in the ground before the prophet dug them up and translated them into the *Book of Mormon.*"

Reeser then read me the other "prophecy," found in Ezekiel 37:16-17:

> Moreover, thou son of man, take thee one stick,
> and write upon it, For Judah, and for the
> children of Israel his companions: then take
> another stick, and write upon it, for Joseph, the
> stick of Ephraim, and for all the house of Israel
> his companions: and join them one to another
> into one stick; and they shall become one in
> thine hand.

Reeser explained, "Judah in this verse is referring to the Bible and Joseph is referring to the *Book of Mormon.*"

Unfortunately, because I wasn't prepared for these "prophetic" verses, my only response to the two men was to say, "I don't want to sound disrespectful, but I am not convinced these verses are prophecies for the *Book of Mormon.* As I see it, nowhere does the Bible sanction the *Book of Mormon,* nor does it refer to it by its name."

It's fine if you want to share this same answer with a Mormon. But, if you desire to refute the Mormon interpretations of Isaiah 29:4 and Ezekiel 37:16-17, let's go back to the Word, and take a look at these verses in their scriptural context.

Mormon Friend, Please Consider:

• *Isaiah 29:4 is not about the* Book of Mormon.

—Isaiah 29 is a warning of judgment upon "Ariel" (another name for Jerusalem) because of her hypocrisy (warning starts in verse 1).

—The passage speaks of nations that will be against Jerusalem (Isaiah 29:5-7).

—Isaiah 29 is a foreshadowing of what will happen at the second coming of Christ (Zechariah 14:2-3). [7]

• *Ezekiel 37:16-17 is not about the Bible or the* Book of Mormon. Theologians confirm these verses indicate that God will not only re-gather the Israelites to their land, but will, for the first time since 931 B.C., restore union between Israel and Judah (Ezekiel 37:19,21-22) in the Messianic reign (cf. Isaiah 11:12-13; Jeremiah 3:18; Hosiah 1:11). [8] **The bottom line:** Ezekiel 37:22 shows that the two sticks in verse 16 refer to the *two nations* that God shall bring together, making them into one nation during His Messianic reign.

Elders Reeser and Brown had one more bit of ammunition to give me simply because they wanted me to believe that the *Book of Mormon* was truly from God (while I wanted them to see that it wasn't). So they said, "The *Book of Mormon* was 'translated by the power of God'" (D&C 1:29; 135:3).

Translated by the Power of God

To get our Mormon friends or missionaries to wonder whether their *Book of Mormon* was really "translated by the power of God," we can ask a few questions (although there are *many* more we could ask).

1. If the *Book of Mormon* was translated "by the power of God," can you explain why it includes an incorrect prophecy? As we know, Christ was born in Bethlehem. Micah 5:2 predicted His birth would be in Bethlehem, and Matthew 2:1 confirms this location. But in Alma 7:10 in the *Book of Mormon*, the birthplace is said to be *Jerusalem*.

2. If the *Book of Mormon* was translated "by the power of God," can you explain why there have been close to 4000 changes through the years?[9] For instance, if you were to look at the 1830 edition of the *Book of Mormon*, Mosiah 21:8 refers to "King Benjamin," while modern editions read "King Mosiah."[10]

If your Mormon friend doesn't believe this one point, you can refer him or her to the comments of Dr. Sidney Sperry of Brigham Young University, who confirmed the change had to be made. Why? Because, as Sperry puts it, "the reading 'king Benjamin' would have made a contradiction in the *Book of Mormon* because king Benjamin had been dead for some time."[11] With these words, Dr. Sperry is admitting to the fact that the "Mormon Church leaders deliberately falsified this verse to eliminate contradiction."[12]

Why would church leaders deliberately alter t[
Mormon? I cannot read their minds or hearts, but I can read Joseph's Smith's words. He said that not only had the *Book of Mormon* been translated by the power of God, but that it was "the most *correct book on* earth."[13] Maybe this is our answer for why the Mormon church has had to make thousands of changes to the book.

Along with what we've just read, we can of course share with our friends some of the information in chapter 3 that challenges the *Book of Mormon*. And, be encouraged, for although there are millions of Mormons who stand by the *Book of Mormon*, there are many others who have questioned or are questioning whether it really is God's Word.

Observing Uncertainty in Some Mormons

A few years ago Brian was a guest speaker at a Mormon symposium (he's even been asked back; all things are possible with God!). Brian challenged the audience to think about the lack of objective evidence for their views. He pointed out that the Mormon church used to claim that their beliefs are supported by contemporary evidence, such as archaeological finds. But over the years as researchers have explored North American historical and archaeological data, we've learned that Mormon beliefs simply are not supported by the data. Whereas Mormons used to point more confidently to evidence, they now rely more on the "burning in the bosom," which is a feeling. Furthermore, Mormons used to say they were the only true church and the reason they exist is because God told Joseph Smith that all other churches were corrupt and abominable. But the trend now is to convince everybody that they are just another Christian denomination that has received a bit more revelation beyond the Bible. After Brian's 40-minute talk, he asked if anyone had a question.

One woman stood up and said angrily," You have completely ruined my faith!" She then marched out of the room. (I have since prayed for this woman, hoping her "ruined faith" will lead her to find "true faith.") However, not all were upset with the message. Several Mormons asked Brian some soul-searching questions. After the question-and-answer period was over, one man remained in the room. He eagerly wanted to talk to Brian, alone. His name was Frank. He was a lifelong Mormon and the father of five missionary boys. He said to Brian in a low voice, "You know, everything you said today is absolutely true. I have come to not believe the *Book of Mormon* and other Mormon writings. I believe only in the Bible."

Imagine a Mormon saying that! Frank later called Brian at home about historical evidence for the Bible (then for reasons unknown, abruptly discontinued the discussions).

While we are discouraged that Frank didn't continue to dialogue with Brian, we can also be encouraged by the knowledge that there are more "Franks" out there who are questioning the *Book of Mormon*. All they want is the truth. Let's tell them that they can know the truth, and that . . .

The truth

will make

you free.

John 8:32

Thinking It Over

1. What response will you get from a Mormon when you ask, "Why don't you believe the Bible alone is sufficient?"

2. What is the "burning in the bosom"?

3. Based on what the apostle Paul said in Galatians 1:6-8, what might he say about the *Book of Mormon?*

4. When a Mormon tells you that the *Book of Mormon* is the restored gospel, how can you show the Bible alone is sufficient, and therefore we don't need a restored gospel?

5. When you are told that Isaiah 29:4 and Ezekiel 37:16-17 are Bible "prophecies" regarding the *Book of Mormon*, what can you say?

6. What are some points you can make to the Mormon who says that the *Book of Mormon* was translated "by the power of God"?

Be wise in the way
you act toward outsiders;
make the most of
every opportunity.
Let your conversation be
always full of grace,
seasoned with salt,
so that you may know
how to answer everyone.

Colossians 4:5-6

CHAPTER 7

WHY DO YOU TRUST IN JOSEPH SMITH FOR YOUR SALVATION?

No man or woman of this dispensation
will enter the Celestial Kingdom
without the consent of Joseph Smith.

Brigham Young
Journal of Discourses, 7:289

In 1996 the Mormon church was (and has been, off and on) running national television ads for a video entitled *Family First*. Intrigued, I called the phone number on the screen to ask if they could mail the video to me.

The woman operator taking my request informed me, "It's our custom to have a missionary deliver it to your home."

With an upbeat voice I replied, "I appreciate that, but I have to be honest with you. While your missionaries are welcome to come to my home, you need to know that I'm not searching for truth. I have already found it. It's in the Bible from Genesis to the book of Revelation. I'm just curious about what the Mormon church says in this video."

The operator said, "Well, I'll have to get permission on this one."

A few minutes later she returned and said she would send me the video. When I got it, I put it right in the VCR. It basically portrayed Mormon families as the happiest people in the world.

Anyway, *four years* later, the Mormon church had a glitch in their system (perhaps we can credit divine intervention), and for over a week I was getting at least one phone call (sometimes two or three) a day from young male Mormon missionaries at the Salt Lake City church headquarters. Their first question was always, "Did you receive our video *Family First?*

I responded the same way to each one of them: "Yes, four years ago."

Their embarrassment broke down some barriers and I was able to start informal discussions and ask many questions—which they gladly answered. In turn, I tried to show them answers from God's Word.

I'll never forget one missionary who called. We'll call him Elder Ted (although most missionaries only give their last name). He couldn't speak highly enough about Joseph Smith. Ted had such high esteem for the prophet that I couldn't help but ask, "Are you basing your whole eternal destiny upon this one man, Joseph Smith?"

"Absolutely!" he replied.

Now, let me break from my conversation with Ted for a moment and tell you why Ted and other Mormons base their salvation upon Joseph Smith. Mormon scripture says, "Joseph Smith, the Prophet and Seer of the Lord, has done more, save Jesus only, for the salvation of men in this world, than any other man that ever lived in it..." (D&C 135:3). Joseph Young (senior president of the First Council of Seventy), an elder brother of Brigham Young and brother of one of Joseph Smith's polygamous wives said,

> Believe in God, believe in Jesus, and believe in Joseph his Prophet, and in Brigham his successor. And I add, If you will believe in your heart and confess with your mouth that Jesus is the Christ, and Joseph was a Prophet, and that Brigham was his successor, you shall be saved in the kingdom of God....[1]

The tenth Mormon prophet, Joseph Fielding Smith, said there is NO SALVATION WITHOUT ACCEPTING JOSEPH SMITH....*no man can reject that testimony without incurring the most dreadful consequences, for he cannot enter the kingdom of God. It is, therefore, the duty of every man to investigate* that he may weigh this matter carefully and know the truth[2] (emphasis in original).

carefully and know the truth[2] (emphasis in original).

One of the verses that some Mormon missionaries use to explain their belief in Joseph Smith is found in Acts 3:22, which they believe is a prophecy about him. It reads, "Moses said, 'The Lord God will raise up for you a prophet like me from your brethren; to Him you shall give heed in everything He says to you.'"

We can share with the missionary that it's important to consider a verse's context before deciding how to interpret it. In this case, this verse could refer to a number of prophets. For instance, Muslims believe this verse refers to Muhammad.[3] That's why it's important to look at this verse in its context. Doing so, we see it points to none other than Jesus Christ.

Mormon Friend, Please Consider:

• *Acts 3:22 is not about Joseph Smith, but about Jesus.* This is confirmed in the preceding verses (read Acts 3:14-21).

• *Acts 3:22 can't be about Smith because he was a false prophet.* Smith wrongly prophesied many things (for instance, he said the second coming of Christ would occur between 1890 and 1891). God's Word says we aren't to believe false prophets (Matthew 24:23-24, 26). *More about this later.*

Between the comments of Mormon leaders and the Bible "prophecies" that are interpreted as referring to Smith, it's easy to understand why our Mormon friends are very much focused on their prophet. In fact, they sing about him in their churches and homes: "We Thank Thee, O God, for a Prophet,"[4] "Joseph Smith's First Prayer,"[5] and "Praise to the Man."[6]

By the way, if your Mormon friend doesn't bring up the supposedly biblical prophecy of Joseph Smith, you will want to show her in other ways that it is tragic to rely upon a mere man for one's salvation. This is what I had to convey to Ted.

I said with great concern, "Ted, there are people who consider Smith to have been a fraud. How do you know he wasn't?"

With confidence Ted replied, "Had Smith been a fraud, Mormonism wouldn't have grown the way it has. As well, had he been a fraud, he would have been exposed by now."

I said to Ted as gently as possible, "Joseph Smith *has* been exposed as a fraud."

He answered, "There have been attacks on Smith, but they have failed."

"Are you sure?" I asked him.

I continued by inquiring about a particular command found in *Doctrine and Covenants*. "Ted, do you believe that the Word of Wisdom was a revelation from God passed down to Joseph Smith?"

Ted responded, "Certainly. The Word of Wisdom and all the Mormon scriptures—*Doctrine and Covenants*, the *Book of Mormon*, and the *Pearl of Great Price* came from God, just like the Bible did. These scriptures are the cornerstone to our beliefs."

I continued, "Isn't it true that the Word of Wisdom stresses a Mormon is to abstain from drinking wine, strong drink, and tobacco?" (As you know from Chapter 4, it also says they aren't to drink hot drinks, but I didn't address that issue.)

Ted quickly replied, "That's right. I guess you can say that the Word of Wisdom proves Smith was a prophet of God. Even before these things were known to be bad for the body, Smith gave us the revelation by God not to have them."

I asked Ted, "Do you abide by the Word of Wisdom?"

With conviction in his voice Ted replied, "Yes I do!"

"Well Ted, your prophet didn't."

"What do you mean?

Answering the question, I said, "Joseph drank liquor and smoked.

A bit startled, he said, "That can't be true. If there is record of him doing so, it had to be before he became a Mormon."

"No Ted, it was after. The years in his own diary verify quite clearly it was not only after he started Mormonism, not only after he wrote the Mormon scriptures, but after he wrote the Word of Wisdom command" (D&C 89).

My husband Brian, having heard what I was saying to Ted, quickly brought to me *The Diaries and Journals of Joseph Smith.*

Fortunately, a few years earlier, I had tabbed all the references to Smith's drinking, so I was able to quickly refer to many of those episodes.

I quoted for Ted an entry dated January 20, 1836, which told of Smith and several Mormon elders at a wedding. They were drinking wine and, in Joseph's words, "Our hearts were made cheerful and glad...we had taken our fill."[7]

Ted answered, "Well, that's innocent, it was a wedding."

I asked, "Does the prophet make allowances for Mormons, telling them when drinking is acceptable?"

Ted was silent, so I continued on. I read about Elder Hyde commenting to Joseph about an "excellent white wine he drank in the east [Palestine]." In response to Hyde, Smith "prophesied in the name of the Lord that he would drink wine with him in that country" (January 20, 1843).[8]

The last account I read to Ted was, "Drank a glass of beer at Moissers..." (June 1, 1844, weeks before Smith's death).[9]

I also explained to Ted that Joseph Smith had had "no objection to having a brewery put up" in town.[10] In fact, he obtained a liquor license so that he could "sell or give spirits of any quantity... to...travelers or other persons as shall visit his home from time to time."[11]

Joseph had even put a bar in his home while his wife Emma was out of town (upon Emma's return she told Joseph he had to choose between the bar or her[12]). Also, the formerly Mormon-owned store called Zion's Cooperative Mercantile Institution sold tea, coffee, and tobacco—all forbidden under the Word of Wisdom.[13]

With resolve I said, "Ted, while all this is hypocritical, it's still nothing compared to many other things Smith did in his life, such as having plural wives, and creating an illegal church 'bank' that went into bankruptcy and impoverished many of his followers."

"Ted, I could go on and on. I could tell you about him being a Mason,[14] his conversation with the devil,[15] his instigation of the salt sermon that called for a formation of 'Gideonites' [who were all dedicated followers] who would drive out anyone who disagreed with the church;[16] and his [with the help of others] defrauding non-Mormons out of their property in Missouri.[17]

"But," I said, "the greatest atrocity was Joseph Smith's false prophecies."

I then gave Ted a verbal resume of those prophecies (some of which we'll look at, shortly). Ted then lowered his voice to a whisper (remember, he's calling from the church headquarters).

He said, "If what you are saying is true, I am stunned."

"I can imagine." I then pleaded, "Ted, you've got to get more background on the prophet and the church. Why don't you start by reading Joseph Smith's own diary? You'll find some amazing things, such as his King Follet sermon. In that sermon Smith distorts the true God as found in the Bible. It's a real eye opener."

Ted answered, "I can't read Smith's diary. I'm a missionary for the next two years. I'm only allowed to read the *Book of Mormon*."

It was my turn to be stunned. I asked, "You're not even allowed to read your prophet's *own diary?*"

Ted replied, "No. We've never been encouraged to read it anyway." (Ted's statement later prompted me to go to a local Mormon bookstore to see if they even sell Joseph Smith's journal or anything comparable. To my surprise, they didn't—at least they didn't in that store. When I asked the two Mormon employees why the prophet's own writings weren't sold, one of them answered, "I didn't know Joseph Smith wrote a diary.")

Anyway, I began to wind down my conversation with Ted by

asking him to search for truth not in the *Book of Mormon* but in the Word of God—the Bible. I recommended he start with the book of John.

Ted again reiterated to me that the only book he could have on his person for the next two years was the *Book of Mormon*. Not until after his mission was completed could he read the Bible. I thought Ted's comment was peculiar because I've had some Mormon missionaries come to my door with both a *Book of Mormon* and a Bible in their possession.

I couldn't help but say, "Ted, listen to your own words. You have told me that currently you can't read your own prophet's diary. Now you tell me you can't even read God's own Word. Doesn't this sound cultish?"

Ted gave a hint of a laugh and then said quietly, "Yeah, it does."

With alarm I added, "Ted, cults not only distort who Christ is— which Mormonism does—but they tell their followers everything they can and cannot do."

Then I said, "Ted, when you have the courage to step out and read the Bible, you will probably have questions, especially as you discover Mormon doctrines that conflict with the teachings of the Bible. If you feel okay about this, I want you to write down my name and my husband's, and our phone number. Put it in your wallet; call us anytime."

Ted responded, "One day I just may call you back."

I replied, "I hope you will. In the meantime, I'll pray for you and your journey. I hope you find 'the way, and the truth, and the life'"(John 14:6). I ended the conversation with a few points to think about from God's Word:

Mormon Friend, Please Consider:
- *Salvation is through Jesus Christ* (John 14:6; Acts 16:30-31; Romans 5:10).
- *Salvation is in no one else* (Acts 4:12).
- *We are to confess Jesus only* (Romans 10:9).

In Ted's case, a few facts about Prophet Joseph Smith were enough to make him wonder if he really had the truth and to motivate him to start searching. As you converse with your Mormon friend, you may find that he, too, trusts in Joseph Smith for his salvation.

While you don't want to be rude or denigrating, if the situation is right, you can use some of the preceding information (or information from chapter 1) to ask a few serious questions about Smith. And, if the opportunity seems right, you can also point your friend to a few of Smith's false prophecies.

A Sampling of Joseph Smith's False Prophecies

You Are to Go to Toronto

Early in his prophetic career, Joseph received a revelation from God to send a few Mormon men to Toronto, Canada, and there, they would sell the copyright of the *Book of Mormon*. Wanting to obey God, the faithful men made the long and uncomfortable wagon ride. Once in Toronto, the men soon discovered that no one was interested in the *Book of Mormon*. They couldn't give the copyright away free if they so dared. Defeated, they made the long journey back home, arriving exhausted, disappointed, and deeply puzzled. Faced with the failure of his prophecy, Joseph offered an explanation that would astound anyone used to the biblical standards of prophecy: "Some revelations are of God; some are of man: and some are of the devil."[18]   To their credit, Mormon church officials don't cover up this incident. They explain that Smith received his revelation "through the Seer stone," and admit that it "fails its purpose."[19] Unfortunately, blaming the stone won't absolve their prophet, who relied on it.

The New Jerusalem to Be in Missouri

Joseph prophesied that the New Jerusalem (also referred to as Zion—D&C 84:2) and the temple, "appointed by the finger of the Lord," shall be built "in the western boundaries of the State of Missouri [Jackson County[20]]...*this generation shall not all pass away* until an house shall be built unto the Lord" (D&C 84:2-3, emphasis added; also see D&C 57:1-3; 97:19-20; 101:16-20). Understandably, those who heard the original prophecy were quite excited, and in 1832 they left their jobs and property because they believed Joseph's vision" of the promised land. Mormon Ezra Booth said that when they arrived at their destination, "we discovered that *prophecy and vision* had failed, or rather had proved false"[21] (emphasis in original).

This false prophecy became notorious, the evidence against it being so clear that no one could miss it. Sidney Rigdon (one of the most important Mormon leaders at the time) said that "Joseph's *vision* was a bad thing"[22] (emphasis in original).

Joseph, as we know, was speaking to the 1832 generation. He prophesied that *their* "generation shall not all pass away" until the New Jerusalem and temple were established in Missouri. Even if we take the statement in the *Book of Mormon* that a generation equals 100 years (4 Nephi 1:22) we still have a problem. Over one hundred and eighty years have passed, and still nothing has been built. Now, the Mormon church still defends this prophecy. They say that the New Jerusalem wasn't built in Smith's day because they were "hindered by their enemies,"[23] and that it will indeed be "built before the Second Coming."[24] In the meantime, Salt Lake City is the church's headquarters.[25] But of course, that's not what the prophecy said.

There Will Be a Civil War

The Civil War prophecy is the one Mormons are most proud of. Many are convinced that Joseph Smith is a true prophet because of it.[26] In *Doctrine and Covenants*, Joseph prophesied that there would be a rebellion in South Carolina, that the Southern states would be divided against the Northern, and that many would die (D&C 87:1-3).

Regarding this prophecy, sixth president and prophet Joseph F. Smith said this:

> I will refer the congregation to the revelation given December 25, 1832, in relation to the great war of the Rebellion, with which all are more or less familiar (*Doctrine and Covenants* 87). A portion of that revelation has been literally fulfilled, even to the very place indicated in the prediction where the war should commence; which, as was therein stated, was to terminate in the death and misery of many souls.[27]

Let's consider three facts our Mormon friends are probably unaware of:

• *The Civil War prophecy in Doctrine and Covenants wasn't in the first edition of the book.* The prophecy was made, then suppressed when it looked as though it would not come to pass. It was first published in 1851 in the *Pearl of Great Price* [28] (seven years after Smith's death).

• *Predictions of a civil war appeared in U.S. newspapers six months before Joseph's December 25, 1832 prophecy.* It was a common belief that there would be a civil war.

• *Five months prior to Joseph's prophecy, Congress passed a tariff act (July 14, 1832) that South Carolina refused to accept.* This raised tensions and everyone looked to South Carolina as the likely flashpoint for future conflict.

With a bit of objectivity, our friends can see that forecasting a civil war beginning with South Carolina is not remarkable— others were predicting the same at the time. Even the Frenchman Alexis de Tocqueville predicted America's Civil War. [29]

The Overthrow of the United States

In 1843, Joseph Smith said,

> I prophesy in the name of the Lord God of Israel, unless the United States redress the wrongs committed upon the saints in the state of Missouri and punish the crimes committed by her officers that in a few short years the government will be utterly overthrown and wasted, and there will not be so much as a potsherd left.[30]

Smith also said,

> I prophesied…in the name of the Lord Jesus Christ, that, if Congress will not hear our petition and grant us protection, they shall be broken up as a government….[31]

These prophecies were never fulfilled, for the United States never broke up, nor was it overthrown and wasted despite the fact that Congress did not grant Smith's petition, nor did the government redress any wrongs. Incidently, documents show that the Mormons weren't entirely innocent victims in Missouri.[32]

The Revelation of Apostle David W. Patten:

Doctrine & Covenants 114:1 provides a specific revelation, from the Lord, on April 17, 1838. David Patten was to "settle up all his business as soon as he possibly can, and make a disposition of his merchandise, that he may perform a mission unto me next spring, in company with others, even twelve including himself, to testify of my name and bear glad tidings unto all the world."

With Patten's other companions they were to "next spring let them depart to go over the great waters, and there promulgate my gospel, the fullness thereof, and bear record of my name. Let them take leave of my saints in the city of Far West, on the twenty-sixth day of April next, on the building-spot of my house, saith the Lord" (D&C 118:4-5, July 8, 1838).

There's only one problem with this prophecy. Patten was to leave with the others in the spring of 1839 (April 26, 1839, to be exact). I guess the Lord didn't know that Patten would die in October 1838 defending Mormon Territory in the Mormon Missouri War. In Joseph Smith's own words, he tells us that "Captain Patten, who instantly fell, mortally wounded, having received a large ball in his bowels" (*History of the Church*, 3:171).

This false prophecy has been excused by Mormons saying that the Lord changed his mind, due to Patten being found unworthy. While this argument could be plausible, it won't hold water only because Joseph Smith said, "Brother Patten was a very worthy man, beloved by all good men who knew him" (Ibid.)

The Second Coming of Christ

Joseph wrote in his diary, "There are those of the rising generation who shall not taste death till Christ comes.... I prophecy in the name of the Lord God, and let it be written, that the Son of Man will not come in the heavens till I am 85 years old, 48 years hence or about 1890."[33]

As we know, the "rising generation" is gone; 1890 has come and gone; and Smith never made it to age 85. He died at the age of 38.

We can also lovingly show our friend that Jesus Himself said no one can predict the date of His return (Matthew 24:36).

The Messiah Would Be Born in Jerusalem

During Christmastime it's a certainty that everyone from little children to the elderly in the Mormon church will sing the song "O Little Town of Bethlehem." In their singing, however, they are confirming that their prophet gave a false prophecy. The prophecy, which can be found in the *Book of Mormon* (Alma 7:10), is that the Messiah would be born in Jerusalem. The Mormon defense is that the *Book of Mormon* was just referring to the general area of Christ's birth. This is a weak argument, for the *Book of Mormon* refers to Jerusalem as a distinct city (1 Nephi 1:4). Though Bethlehem is near Jerusalem, it too, is a distinct town. We can share with our Mormon friend that the Holy Ghost (it's best to use the word *Ghost* with our friend rather than *Spirit*—at least until we get to the chapter on the Trinity), who inspires Scripture, wouldn't make such an error. Nor would the Holy Ghost contradict Himself by stating two different birthplaces for Jesus. The Bible said the Messiah would be born in Bethlehem (Micah 5:2), and this prophecy was correctly fulfilled, according to Matthew 2:1.

The Prophet Will Be Protected

"And thus prophesied Joseph, saying
'Behold, that seer[meaning Joseph Smith]
will the Lord bless; and they that seek to destroy him
shall be confounded....Behold, I am sure of
the fulfilling of this promise" (2 Nephi 3:14).

William Clayton, Joseph Smith's personal secretary, wrote that Joseph "prophecied [sic] that 'not all the powers of hell or earth combined can ever overthrow this boy' for he had a promise from the eternal God."[34]

But contrary to his prophecy, Joseph was killed by those who sought to destroy him. The prophecy, in 2 Nephi 3:14, found in the *Book of Mormon*, disillusioned many Mormons of that era.

Sarah Hall Scott wrote to her parents after Smith's murder, saying, "Joseph also prophesied on the stand a year ago last conference that he could not be killed within five years from that time; that they could not kill him till the Temple would be completed, for that he had received an *unconditional promise from the Almighty* concerning his days"[35] (emphasis added).

In August 1843, when Joseph gave his prophecy to the Mormon congregation, he had assumed he still had a long life ahead of him. Now some Mormons may still argue this point. They will insist that Joseph prophesied an early death. We can mention to our Mormon friends that Apostle Erastus Snow and other early Mormons didn't think that Joseph prophesied his death. Instead, according to Snow, they "supposed that our Prophet was going to continue with us, to lead us on until the coming of the Savior."[36]

It's true that the possibility of death crossed Smith's mind during his six-month imprisonment (1838-39) in Missouri for treason (he escaped);[37] and again in 1842–43 when he feared being extradited or kidnapped back to Missouri.[38] Yet thoughts of death are common when a person is nervous about what might happen to him. We shouldn't interpret such thoughts as a sign of prophecy.

Quite to the contrary, *after* Smith's fear of extradition to Missouri was laid to rest, and *after* he felt safe from the law, he gave his prophecy of protection from his enemies.

Believing firmly in the prophecy he gave in 1843, Smith became an enthusiastic candidate for the U.S. presidency in January 1844.[39] This makes it clear Smith expected to live many more years and that he truly did believe his enemies would be confounded, he would live to see the temple completed, and he would live at least another five years. Well, as we know, he didn't. Five months after Smith announced his candidacy, his enemies killed him.

The Bible's Standard for a True Prophet

Joseph Smith once said that "every man has a right to be a false prophet, as well as a true prophet."[40] We must ask our friend, "Which type of prophet was Joseph Smith?" We can help our friend answer this question by reminding him or her of the true biblical standard for a true prophet.

Mormon Friend, Please Consider:

• *All it takes is one false prophecy to mark a man as a false prophet.* Scripture tells us "when a prophet speaks in the name of the LORD, if the thing does not come about or come true, that is the thing which the LORD has not spoken" (Deuteronomy 18:22). The passage also says "the prophet shall die" (verse 20). Smith died an early and tragic death.

• *We are to avoid anyone who gives a false prophecy.* Read the following Bible verse: For thus saith the Lord of hosts, the God of Israel; Let not your prophets and your diviners, that be in the midst of you, deceive you, neither hearken to your dreams which ye cause to be dreamed. For they prophesy falsely unto you in my name: I have not sent them, saith the Lord (Jeremiah 29:8-9).

After sharing with our friend about Joseph Smith and his false prophecies, we can point out that no false prophecies have ever been found in the Bible—and that every biblical prophecy about Jesus Christ's first coming was fulfilled perfectly. That's why we can tell our friend that Jesus alone is all she needs.

> *I've tried in vain a thousand ways,*
> *My fears to quell, my hopes to raise,*
> *But what I need, the Bible says,*
> *Is ever only Jesus!*
> *My soul is night, my heart is steel,*
> *I cannot see, I cannot feel,*
> *For light, for life, I must appeal,*
> *In simple faith to Jesus!* [41]

Thinking It Over

1. Mormons believe that Acts 3:22 is a prophecy about Joseph Smith. How can we show that this verse is speaking about Jesus Christ?

2. Mormon theology teaches there is no salvation without Joseph Smith. What Bible verses can we share that shows salvation is in Christ alone?

3. What are some of Joseph Smith's prophecies?

4. Describe Smith's prophecy regarding the Civil War. How can we explain to a Mormon that this wasn't really a unique prediction on Joseph's part?

5. Read Deuteronomy 13:1-6. Is a false prophet considered false only because he is wrong about a prophecy, or is there more we need to keep in mind? (Notice in verse 2 that the false prophet's sign comes true.)

6. What can we share with our Mormon friend about those who prophesy falsely? What does God say in Deuteronomy 18:20-22 about those who prophesy falsely?

For it is all for your sake,
so that as grace extends
to more and more people
it may increase thanksgiving
to the glory of God.

2 Corinthians 4:15

CHAPTER 8

WHAT DOES GOD'S GRACE
MEAN TO YOU?

Some of our old traditions teach us that a man guilty of atrocious and murderous acts may savingly repent on the scaffold; and upon his execution will hear the expression—'Bless God! He has gone to heaven, to be crowned in glory, through the all-redeeming merits of Christ the Lord!' This is all nonsense. Such a character will never see heaven.

Prophet Brigham Young
Journal of Discourses 8:61

On July 24, 1724, in the town of London, a Christian woman gave birth to a son. She named him John. And as the youngster was growing, this dear woman tried to persuade him to receive Christ as his Savior. Unfortunately, her efforts were short lived because she died when John was just six-and-a-half years old.

Being left motherless, John left school, and by the age of 11, he joined the crew on his father's ship. Out at sea, John would learn every curse word, every vulgarity, every evil way of a godless man. He not only became wild, but became an agnostic and a blasphemer.

As time went on, John was forced into the British navy as a midshipman, and war was expected. He wanted no part in this and deserted the military. He was caught and received the consequences. He was stripped, severely whipped, and ordered back to the navy with a lower rank.

After completing his military duties, John became the captain of his own ship, a slave ship. In this lucrative business, John bought, sold, and transported scared, whipped, and helpless Africans to England.

In 1748, while he was recovering from a severe fever, John loaded his boat with slaves destined for England. During this voyage the ship encountered unusually stormy seas for close to a month. Everyone aboard thought they would never get off that boat alive. In the midst of the fear and the devilish business of slave trading, God was working in John's life.

During all the turmoil, John found aboard a book titled *The Imitation of Christ*. Written in 1441 by Thomas `a Kempis (and still in print), the book is about forsaking the selfish life and embracing selflessness by committing one's life to Jesus Christ. Struck by the book's powerful message, John, in the midst of the stormy weather, repented of his sins and gave his remaining years to Jesus Christ.

Naturally, John's life changed. He gave up slave trading, became an ordained minister, and was a great influence in William Wilberforce's life, the politician primarily responsible for eliminating slave-trading in England. John spent the rest of his life rejoicing in God's wonderful grace, mercy, and love.

Have you guessed yet who I am talking about? Yes, John Newton. You probably know him best for the well-known song he wrote, "Amazing Grace." It's the favorite song of many Christians. It's my favorite, too. And you may be surprised to know that it's the favorite song of many Mormons.

I get teary-eyed every time I sing the words, "I once was lost, but now am found, was blind, but now I see." So too does a dear Mormon friend of mine. But we are getting teary-eyed for two very different reasons.

You see, when you and I sing "Amazing Grace," we are rejoicing over the fact that God's grace is free (Ephesians 2:8-9). His grace forgives (Colossians 2:13), His grace saves (Ephesians 2:8-9), His grace allows us to have a relationship with Him now and forever (John 14:2-3), His grace is completely undeserved. His grace spares us from hell and leads us to heaven. And though we'll be there "ten thousand years, we've no less days to sing God's praise." Yes, for eternity we will be praising the Lord for His marvelous grace!

By contrast, when my Mormon friend sings "Amazing Grace"

at her church, she and other Mormons are rejoicing that grace (Mormon grace) is allowing every person on earth to be resurrected from the dead—and nothing more. These resurrected people will still await their eternal destiny, whether that is hell or one of the three Mormon heavens.

What's just as sad is that the Mormon church can't even leave their grace alone—they add to it. They say that "grace and works unite to bring salvation."[1]

Grace Plus Works Equal Salvation

Most Mormons think it's preposterous and a bit arrogant on our part to claim we can get to heaven without earning it. Let's try to gain a bit of understanding here. You and I have been taught from God's Word that we are saved by grace and not works (Ephesians 2:8-9). Mormons have been taught completely the opposite. Their prophet Brigham Young said, "I am the only person that can possibly save myself,"[2] and that "salvation is an individual work; it is every person for themselves."[3]

Another Mormon prophet, Joseph Fielding Smith, sang this same tune when he taught that "man must do all he can for [his] own salvation."[4] Even the *Book of Mormon* tells Mormon church members that "we know that it is by grace that we are saved, *after all we can do*"[5] (2 Nephi 25:23, emphasis added).

While such statements are disheartening, there's more. Mormons have been taught that "Christ alone cannot save you."[6] They have been told that "it is a most serious error to believe that Jesus did everything for men if they would but confess him with their lips, and there is nothing else for them to do."[7] Isn't this sad? Imagine—your Mormon friends, or the missionaries at your door, are actually being discouraged from trusting in Christ alone! How can you help?

You'll want to explain that true grace is a gift. That's what the Bible says —"it is the gift of God" (Ephesians 2:8). We can ask,

"Since when do we pay for a gift given to us? If we pay, then it's no longer a gift!"

God's Grace Excludes Good Works

While your friends may understand what you are getting at, they might, or a missionary will, point out that the Bible says you are to "work out your salvation with fear and trembling" (Philippians 2:12). Don't be intimidated by this. With the assistance of your Fact Sheet (at the end of this book), you can explain what this verse truly means.

Mormon Friend, Please Consider:

• *"Work out your salvation"* is in the context of Paul telling the Philippians not to rely on him. They needed to learn to stand on their own feet, knowing *God* was working in them (Philippians 2:13).[8]

• *"Fear and trembling"* doesn't mean we need to live life in fear—especially in fear of possible damnation. "Fear and trembling" simply refers to us having a healthy fear of not wanting to offend God.

After you explain the meaning of Philippians 2:12, your friend will probably share with you that it's *impossible* to have salvation without being good. One Mormon woman, named Ruth, shared with me that it's by joining the Mormon Church we can become "good." She explained that "the church ordinances and the *Book of Mormon* help me stay on the right track. They help me live a good life."

I asked Ruth to tell me what she thought about the prophet Isaiah's words, "But we are all as an unclean thing, and all our righteousness are as filthy rags" (Isaiah 64:6 KJV). Ruth didn't have an answer, and I explained to her that what we may think is "good" can be filthy in God's eyes. That's why it's impossible to get to heaven on the basis of goodness—we will always fall short, as Romans 3:23 says. Let's help people like Ruth come to really understand God's grace with the following truths:

Mormon Friend, Please Consider:

• *If salvation is by works, we eliminate God's grace—His undeserved favor* (see Romans 11:5-6). If we depend upon our good works for salvation, there is no need for God's grace.

• *If salvation is by works, Christ died needlessly* (see Galatians 2:21). Why would Christ have needed to die on the cross if we could get to heaven on our own?

• *If salvation is by works, then the Bible is wrong.* The Bible says salvation is *not* by works (Ephesians 2:8-9). God's grace provides for us the gift of salvation. To say otherwise is to say the Bible is wrong.

• *Works are a result of our salvation—not the cause of our salvation.* While it is true that God looks at our works and shall one day judge them (Romans 2:5-6,13), we aren't saved by our works (Ephesians 2:8-9). And, genuine works can't be manifested in one's life unless the person has a genuine relationship with Jesus Christ. Even that relationship comes by grace (John 15:16; Ro. 9:15-16).

• *It's God who works in us.* Philippians 2:13 says God is already at work in us. We can't even do "good works" on our own; we can't save ourselves by our works. They aren't our works, they are God's. *Again, it is by grace we have been saved (Ephesians 2:8).*

• *Jesus' answer to the question of "works."* Some people asked Jesus, "What shall we do, so that we may work the works of God?" Jesus answered, "This is the work of God, that you believe in Him whom He has sent" (John 6:28-29).

It's hard to tell if Ruth is open to these biblical truths. Her husband is a Mormon bishop, so I'm sure much of what I have shared with her has been "explained" away.

The fact that salvation is by grace alone is a hard pill for Mormons to swallow. That's because in Mormon theology, not all people can be offered forgiveness. For instance, "there is no forgiveness for murderers."[9]

Now, at this point in your witnessing, be aware that most Mormon women, especially, may not rely so much on the teachings of the church about grace and works but rather more on their emotions. That's fine. But for their sake, we still must understand the doctrine behind their beliefs. And regardless, whether it's your Mormon friend whose belief is more emotional, or a missionary whose belief is more doctrinal, both will most likely tell you not all people can be forgiven, such as murderers. We can agree with them by saying, "You're right—any murderer who does not receive God's pardon will not be forgiven. Without God's pardon, he can't make it to heaven." Let's illustrate.

God's Grace Offers Full Pardon

In 1829, George Wilson was charged guilty of stealing mail and of murder. President Andrew Jackson, for reasons unknown, pardoned Wilson. But, for stranger reasons unknown, Wilson refused the pardon. He sent word back to Jackson, saying, "It's not a pardon unless he [Wilson] accepts it."

This was a point of law that had never yet been raised, and the president called upon the Supreme Court to decide how this should be handled. Chief Justice John Marshall gave the following decision:

> A pardon is a paper, the value of which depends upon its acceptance by the person implicated. It is hardly to be supposed that one under sentence of death would refuse to accept a pardon, but if it is refused, it is no pardon.

George Wilson must be hanged![10]

George Wilson was hanged simply because he refused the pardon.

We can share with our friend or missionary that provisionally, God's grace offers pardon to all "who believe" (Mark 1:15; John 11:25-26), irrespective of what he may be or what he may have done. And so, even the worst of criminals who trust solely in Jesus Christ for their salvation can say, "Where sin abounded, grace did much more abound."[11]

While the message of God's free grace is wonderful news for Mormons, we have another step to take with them. You see, not only does Mormon doctrine reject "grace alone," it also rejects "faith alone."

Faith Alone, or Faith Plus Obedience?

Joseph Fielding Smith said that the faith-alone doctrine is "false"[12]; that by such a doctrine, "mankind is damned,"[13] and that it "denies justice of God."[14] The Mormon church explains that "this false doctrine would relieve man from the responsibility of his acts other than to confess a belief in God and would teach man that no matter how great the sin, a confession would bring him complete forgiveness and salvation."[15] Rather than believe in salvation purely based upon faith in Jesus Christ, Mormons believe that "salvation comes by faith *plus obedience*."[16]

Let's turn the page and see how we can respond to our Mormon friends.

Mormon Friend, Please Consider:

• *By grace you are saved through faith, and that not of yourselves* (Ephesians 2:8-9). No amount of goodness is going to save you (see also Hebrews 11:6).

• *Faith comes not by our righteousness, but through Christ, and* "the righteousness which comes from God on the basis of faith" (Philippians 3:9).

• *True faith is believing what Jesus says.* He says we're saved only through Him (John 11:25; 14:6).

We can share with our Mormon friend that to be spiritually alive, we must have true saving faith; without it, we are spiritually dead. When I shared that with a Mormon missionary I got this response: "The Bible says, 'faith, if it has no works, is dead'" (James 2:17).

Also Consider:

• *Yes! Faith without works is dead,* but genuine faith cannot be "dead" (read James 2:14, 18, 20.)

True faith is going to *result* in good works—not the other way around.

• *Faith works through love.* Jesus said, "He who does not love Me does not keep My words" (John 14:24).

Born-again Christians do not obey Christ in an effort to gain salvation. *They already have salvation,* and express their gratitude and love by keeping Christ's words (John 14:15).

Christ Alone, No Other Way

One of my favorite conversion stories appears in the book of Acts. It involves the jailer who asked Paul and Silas, "Sirs, what must I do to be saved?" (Acts 16:30).

They answered, "Believe in the Lord Jesus, and you will be saved" (Acts 16:31).

Quite simple isn't it? All we must do is put our faith in Jesus Christ for our salvation. God's undeserved mercy is given freely to all who accept it. Paul and Silas didn't tell the jailer to do good works in order to become saved. Throughout the ages, the message of "grace through faith" has been the truth that has stirred men's souls. It was the message that led John Newton to write about it, Martin Luther to take a dangerous stand upon it, Jonathan Edwards, Charles Spurgeon, and others to preach about it. But most of all, it is what led Jesus Christ to die a torturous death on a cross.

At Calvary, Jesus powerfully summed up this message of grace and faith by proclaiming, "It is finished!" (John 19:30). Christ's sacrifice made His righteousness available to us and makes our salvation complete. And this *free* gift of eternal life became available to all who put their trust solely in the once-crucified, now-glorified Redeemer. What good news this is for our Mormon friends!

From the cross uplifted high,
Where the Savior deigns to die,
What melodious sounds I hear,
Bursting on my ravished ear!
Love's redeeming work is done;
Come and welcome, sinner, come.[17]

Thinking It Over

1. What is the Mormon perspective of grace? What is the biblical definition of grace?

2. What do Mormons believe is necessary for salvation?

3. Mormons use Philippians 2:12 to prove that everyone must "work out their salvation." What can we say to them about this verse and about the place works have in a Christian's life?

4. Mormons reject the concept of salvation by faith alone. How can we respond?

5. What is the Mormon belief regarding James 2:17? How can we respond?

CHAPTER 9

WHY DO YOU RELY ON BAPTISMS FOR THE LIVING AND THE DEAD

> The greatest responsibility in this world
> that God has laid upon us
> is to seek after our dead.
>
> *Joseph Smith*
> Journal of Discourses, 6:7

One day I am going to be baptized in the Mormon church. At that time I will be considered a full-fledged Mormon. And, because of my baptism, I will be saved. Does this shock you?

Well, before you start calling me a heretic, you may be stunned to know that one day someone you know—a close Christian friend, a relative, or perhaps yourself—might be baptized in the church, too. It all depends on whether or not the "candidate" meets the conditions. But, before I mention what those requirements are, let me reiterate some background information.

The Mormon Teaching
Baptism for the Living

Brigham Young said the following to his congregation:

> But, brother Mormon, do you really suppose that water will wash away your sins? I will tell you what I suppose. I suppose THE LORD SAID IT WOULD, and further it is none of my business. Baptism has been instituted *for the remission of sins;* I therefore do it to take away my sins..."[1]
> (uppercase in original, emphasis added).

As you can see from Brigham Young's teaching, Mormons attach the forgiveness of sins to baptism. They also believe that when they are baptized in the church, they are born again. *This is an important point to remember.* When a Mormon says, "I am born again," what she is really saying is, "I have been baptized in the Mormon church." By contrast, the Bible does not teach that baptism leads us to be born again.

Mormon Friend, Please Consider:

Being born again is a spiritual rebirth "through the living and enduring word of God" (1 Peter 1:23); in Christ we are a new creature (2 Corinthians 5:17); we are reconciled to God through Christ (2 Corinthians 5:18), *not through baptism.*

Mormons firmly believe that to receive forgiveness and salvation you must be baptized. A verse they often cite is Acts 2:38, which reads, "Then Peter said unto them, Repent, and be baptized every one of you in the name of Jesus Christ for the remission of sins" (KJV). Although Mormons interpret this verse inaccurately, we can understand just by looking at it why Mormons believe the way they do. To better help our friends, let's take a closer look at the passage. (The explanation I'm about to share is detailed, but don't be intimidated by all the information. It's easy to understand, and remember, you can use your Fact Sheet for help.)

In Acts 2:38, the word "for," in the original Greek text, is *eis*. This Greek word can have several meanings, including "result," "to," "towards," and "in regard to."[2] So, which word do we use for Acts 2:38? Well, there is a debate among scholars about that very matter.[3] Some believe *eis* may simply mean that baptism and forgiveness go together. Others believe that *eis* can also mean "cause" or "purpose," and that is why some people argue that baptism causes salvation or is for the purpose of obtaining salvation. But as New Testament scholar F. F. Bruce points out, even if *eis* means "cause" or "purpose," you cannot separate baptism from repentance because the verse connects them![4] Therefore, we can invite our Mormon friend to look closely at Acts 2:38 and ask: "Is it through *baptism* or *repentance* that we obtain the forgiveness of sins?"

If our friend still insists the answer is baptism, or he says it's a combination of both, we can take him to Acts 3:19. There, we see Peter speaking to the Jews of Jerusalem. He tells them that *repentance* brings forgiveness; he says nothing about baptism. So, based on Acts 3:19, it is not baptism that brings forgiveness.

The reason Acts 2:38 mentions baptism, then, is because the New Testament assumes that everyone who repents and comes to Christ will be baptized. That conclusion fits with what the New Testament says about salvation[5] being by grace through faith, and not through anything we can do (Romans 11:6; Ephesians 2:8-9), including baptism.

If you discuss that with Mormon missionaries, be ready for another verse they will use in an attempt to prove that baptism brings forgiveness and salvation. They will take you to Acts 22:16, where Ananias said to Paul, "And now why tarriest thou? Arise, and be baptized, and wash away thy sins, calling on the name of the Lord" (KJV).

New Testament scholar Bruce Demarest says it's important to note that the tense of the verb "calling" shows that it happens *first*.[6]

So *first* you call on Christ, *then* you arise and are baptized. That fits perfectly with Acts 2:38 as well as the fact that no one's sins are forgiven, cleansed, or wiped away through baptism. Nor is the individual saved, redeemed, or set free by being baptized.

Let's summarize all this for our Mormon friend on the following page.

Mormon Friend, Please Consider:

• *Look at Acts 2:38 carefully.* It speaks of repentance and baptism. You cannot separate the two.

> **Mormon friend:** Which is it—through *baptism* or *repentance*—that a person receives forgiveness?" If you say "baptism," take a look at the next point.

• *Repentance brings forgiveness.* Read Acts 3:19. Peter tells the Jews that *repentance* brings forgiveness—he says nothing about baptism. This verse fits what the New Testament says about salvation being by grace alone (Romans 11:6; Ephesians 2:8-9).

• *Salvation comes first, then baptism.* Mormon friend if you believe that Acts 22:13-16 says that baptism washes away our sins, then take a closer look at the apostle Paul. Paul is being exhorted to *first* "call on His name" (the name of Jesus), then be baptized. Remember:

> —It's through Christ that we are saved (Acts 16:30-31).

> —Look again at Acts 3:19. It's through *repentance that* our sins are wiped away.

• *The Lord cleanses our sins, not baptism* (1 John 1:9).

• *Jesus Himself said belief in Him brings salvation.* Nothing is said about baptism (John 3:15; 5:24).

• *The thief on the cross was not baptized*, yet he immediately went to heaven (Luke 23:39-43).

Now, what about baptism for the dead? Or, as Joseph Fielding Smith, Jr. puts it, "What are we doing for the salvation of our dead?"[7]

Baptism for the Dead

Mormons believe that anyone who didn't hear the gospel of Jesus Christ in this life will be given a second chance to hear it in the next. As well, "they get equal blessings if they accept it."[8] How is this second chance possible? With the help of the living Mormons *and* the dead Mormons who are in the "spirit world." Let me explain.

Faithful Mormons who have died are believed to approach the dead heathens in the afterlife (referred to as "spirits in prison"[9]) to share the Mormon gospel. If the heathens accept this gospel, they are on their way to becoming saved. Having accepted the Mormon gospel, they still need a living person on earth to baptize them. Thus, heathens can only be saved through Mormons who are willing to become their saviors. Yes, their saviors.

Saving the Dead

Joseph Smith told his followers that "baptism for the Dead [was] the only way that men can appear as saviors on mount Zion."[10] They were the ones to "save & redeem their dead."[11] He said," A friend [meaning a dead friend] who has got a friend in the world can save him—unless—he has committed the unpardonable sin. *So, you can see how far you can be Savior...*"[12] (emphasis added).

The Mormons have a great burden for bringing salvation to the dead (If only they realized that no one but Jesus can save!). They are told that "the greatest responsibility that God has laid upon us [is] to seek after our dead...they without us can't be Perfect."[13] This point is emphasized in *Doctrine and Covenants:* "For we without them cannot be made perfect; neither can they without us being made perfect" (D&C 128:18).

While the dead and the living are said to be made perfect through this baptism process, there are conditions that determine which dead people are offered proxy baptism—where a living Mormon is baptized by full immersion on behalf of the dead person. Your Christian friend or family member, when deceased, might be one of those people. The Mormon church's policy for determining which of the billions of dead people will have this ceremony performed by a living person are as follows:

1. It's for those who were direct ancestors of a Mormon.
2. It's for those who were known personally by their descendant, and
3. It's for those believed to have accepted the gospel in the spirit world.[14]

If you have a friend who is related to a Mormon, there's a good chance one of her descendants will be baptized for her when she is dead. Or, if she has a Mormon friend who outlives her, there's a good chance the Mormon will be baptized on behalf of your friend. She will tell the church that she's convinced your friend has now come to see the "light" and has accepted the gospel in the spirit world.

Proxy Baptism

Out of obedience to Joseph Smith, Mormons undergo proxy baptism on behalf of their dead. As mentioned earlier, they themselves get immersed in water for the dead person of their choice. This at least ensures the departed one of getting into what's known as the telestial kingdom. So seriously does the Mormon church take this proxy baptism that the temples are typically busy six days a week. Joseph Fielding Smith commented that "the temple in Salt Lake City is frequently so crowded with anxious, earnest workers, that it is necessary many times to turn large numbers away."[15] In 1954, one Mormon official said that "at the rate we are baptizing for the dead in our temples today, plus the baptism of the living, it is estimated that it would take over four thousand years to baptize the two billion four hundred million who are now living on the earth, without counting the dead."[16]

In order that not one dead soul is left behind, the church's world-famous genealogical library in Salt Lake City has hundreds of millions of microfilmed records to help church members identify non-Mormon ancestors for proxy baptism.[17] But what did the apostle Paul say about genealogies? He said to not "pay attention to...endless genealogies" (1 Timothy 1:4). Although it's not clear what Paul was talking about (most likely Jewish genealogies), this can hardly be taken as an endorsement of Mormon devotion to their genealogies.

You might be wondering how this baptizing-the-dead doctrine got started. Possibly it began at the deathbed of Joseph's father. In Lucy Smith's biography of her son Joseph, she wrote about her dying husband's concerns. He was worried about his son, Alvin, who died without being baptized. Joseph, Jr. comforted his father by saying it was "the privilege of the Saints to be baptized for the dead."[18] This delighted Joseph's father, and he requested that "Joseph should be baptized for Alvin immediately."[19]

Now, how do Mormons defend their belief in baptism for the dead?

The Mormon Defense

Many years ago when I first heard that Mormons carry out baptisms for the dead, I dismissed this as an "anti-Mormon" (using their term) rumor. I thought it was just too bizarre to be true. So, when shortly thereafter two Mormon missionaries came to my door, I told them that I had heard something quite ridiculous and wanted to hear from them that it wasn't true.

I asked," Do Mormons perform proxy baptisms for the dead?"

Elder Phillips replied, "Yes, we do." I was stunned. I could only say one word: "Why?"

He answered, "Because, for one reason or another, the dead didn't have the opportunity to be baptized in the Mormon church when they were alive. We're giving them that chance."

Shocked, I said, "But that's not biblical!"

Elder Phillips answered with great confidence, "It certainly is biblical! Paul the apostle is the one who began the practice."

Phillips had only his *Book of Mormon* with him, so he asked me if he could borrow a Bible. I handed one to him, and he read First Corinthians 15:29 (KJV):

> "Else what shall they do
> which are baptized for the dead,
> if the dead rise not at all?
> Why are they then baptized for the dead?"

Elder Phillips explained, "Right here, Paul is showing that without us baptizing the dead, they will not rise. We are giving them a second chance at getting to glory."

I couldn't believe what I was hearing. Not wanting to show how shaken up I was, I simply said, "Well, I don't believe that is what Paul is communicating."

After my short time with the missionaries, I knew I had to find out the true meaning of 1 Corinthians 15:29. I'll show you what I learned on the following page.

Mormon Friend, Please Consider:

• *First Corinthians 15:29 is not about proxy baptism.*

Throughout chapter 15, Paul has been reinforcing the resurrection. And although there are Christian commentators and theologians with different interpretations of verse 29, *none of them* say that the Bible directs us to perform proxy baptism.

Mormon friend, take a close look. Throughout the entire chapter 15, *except* verse 29, Paul speaks in terms of "I", "we", and "you." But in verse 29 he says **"they."** It seems that Paul was disassociating himself from the doctrine and those who practice it. He doesn't say, "What shall *we* do," but "What shall *they* do"[20] (it may be that Paul's opponents were baptizing their dead[21]).

Again, after verse 29, Paul shifts back to "I", "we," and "you."

What's more, we can't be baptized on behalf of the dead because...

• *After death, there are no second chances.* "It is appointed unto men once to die, but after this the judgment" (Hebrews 9:27 KJV). Also, there is no escaping judgment; it will be everlasting (Matthew 25:41, 46).

• No human can redeem any other human. As God's Word tells us:

> *None of them can by any means redeem his brother,*
> *nor give to God a ransom for him.* (Psalm 49:7)

The Biblical Truth

Throughout this book, we have seen that the Mormon church completely distorts the true message of Jesus Christ. Baptism doesn't save; Jesus saves! Mormons can't be saviors; Jesus is the only Savior. Baptism doesn't make a person born again; only through Jesus are we born again. Baptism can't cleanse a person of sin; only Jesus can cleanse sin. Just as important, it's too late for the dead to gain salvation, for judgment comes immediately after death. How scary it is to consider that the Mormon prophets and other leaders in the church have misled not only your friend, but millions of others! Our hearts should mourn over this deception, and we should hope for opportunities to share the truth that salvation is in Jesus alone.

What can we do while it is still day?
Proclaim that they can be *saved.*
Not from water—it doesn't cleanse sin.
But through Jesus—in your heart—let Him in!

—D.M.

Thinking It Over

1. What do Mormons believe about baptism?

2. What is proxy baptism? Why do Mormons see this as necessary? Which dead people are allowed to receive these baptisms?

3. What Bible verse do Mormons use to defend their practice of baptizing the dead? What does this verse *really* talk about?

CHAPTER 10

IN YOUR VIEW,
WHO IS JESUS CHRIST?

"In bearing testimony of Jesus Christ, President Hinckley
spoke of those outside the Church who say Latter-day
Saints 'do not believe in the traditional Christ.' *'No, I
don't. The traditional Christ of whom they speak is not
the Christ of whom I speak."*

President Gordon B. Hinckley
LDS Church News, June 20, 1998, p.7, italics inserted

Years ago, while working in a hospital, I had the opportunity
to reach out to an elderly Mormon woman named Mrs.
Hendrickson. Her husband, Robert, was a patient in the hospital.

Sadly, he was very ill and in a coma. For nearly two weeks, I made
it a point to see Mrs. Hendrickson, who faithfully sat by her
husband's side. I so much enjoyed her warmth and prayed for the
right moment to talk to her about Jesus.

One day, as I was beginning my lunch hour, I felt a prompting
from the Lord to go see the Hendricksons. As I approached the
room, Mrs. Hendrickson walked out. She looked physically and
emotionally worn out. Extending my hand out to her, I asked, "How
are you holding up?"

Trying to control her emotions, she said, "Robert won't be with
me much longer."

I said, "Mrs. Hendrickson, Jesus can help you during this time.
Can I tell you how?"

Mrs. Hendrickson said with assurance, "Oh, I know all about
Jesus. I belong to His church, the Church of Jesus Christ of Latter-
day Saints."

I remarked, "So I guess you believe in the Mormon Jesus."

Mrs. Hendrickson looked a bit surprised. "I've never heard anyone refer to Him as a Mormon."

"Well, actually, Mrs. Hendrickson, I don't believe Jesus was a Mormon. It's just that the Mormon church has a different Jesus than the one in the Bible. That's why I referred to him as the Mormon Jesus."

Mrs. Hendrickson asked, "What's the difference between the two?"

Before I tell you what I shared with Mrs. Hendrickson (basically the following Mormon views compared to the Bible), we must first ask this: Do our different views of Christ really matter?

Do Our Different Views of Christ Really Matter?

I once had a Christian friend say it doesn't matter so much if Mormons are wrong about the biblical facts regarding Jesus. What matters is that they accept Him.   What do you think? Is it okay if Mormons believe wrongly about Jesus as long as they accept Him? I pondered the question myself and found from God's Word that it *does* matter what they believe about Christ. Jesus said that our worship of Him must be *in truth* (John 4:24).He Himself was concerned that people think accurately of Him. He asked, "What do you think about the Christ?" (Matthew 22:42).

Let's help our Mormon friends think accurately about Christ by asking a few questions that may help lead them to the *real* Jesus.

What Do Mormons Believe About Christ?

The Mormon View of Christ's Conception

Years ago, I saw a movie on Mormonism (not an LDS film). It showed the Father of heaven knocking on Mary's door. As she opens it, the Father enters the home, then closes the door behind Him. The rest of the scene is left to the imagination for you and me, but not for Mormon church leaders. Many of them have taught that the Father entered Mary's home to have physical relations with her. Jesus is the literal son of Mary and the Father in heaven (whom Mormons believe has flesh and bones). Prophet Brigham Young said that Jesus "was begotten of his Father, as we were of our fathers."[1] He also said that Jesus was *not* begotten by the Holy Ghost.[2]

Prophet and tenth president Joseph Fielding Smith affirmed what Young said by saying, "Christ was begotten of God. He was not born without the aid of Man, and that Man was God!"[3] Admittedly, many Mormons today have never heard this teaching, but it is current LDS doctrine. Even though in our minds this means that the Father had a *sexual* relationship with Mary, Mormons today might not think of it that way. In any case, their view of Christ's origin is radically different from that given in Scripture.

It's also good to point out that the *Book of Mormon* says Jesus was conceived by the Holy Ghost as well. Now, Joseph Fielding Smith has openly denied this fact. He wrote in his well-received work, *Doctrines of Salvation*, that those who "claim that he [Jesus] was begotten of the Holy Ghost, and they make the statement that the scriptures so teach....they do err not understanding the scriptures. They tell us the *Book of Mormon* states that Jesus was begotten of the Holy Ghost. I challenge that statement. The *Book of Mormon* teaches no such thing! Neither does the *Bible*"[4] (italics in original).

Mormon Friend, Please Consider:

*The Bible says Jesus was conceived
by the Holy Ghost.*

(Matthew 1:18, 20; Luke 1:34-35).

The challenge Smith gives us isn't really that difficult. Along with the verses from the Bible, we can refer our Mormon friends to their *Book of Mormon*, which specifically says that Mary "shall be overshadowed and conceived by the power of the Holy Ghost" (Alma 7:10—while this verse is correct about the role of the Holy Ghost, it's incorrect about where Christ would be born).

Ask your friend: "Who is correct regarding Christ's conception? Your prophets or your *Book of Mormon?*"

The Mormon View of Jesus and Lucifer

When I first heard that Mormon doctrine says Christ and Lucifer are spirit brothers, I was just as dumbfounded as I was when I heard about proxy baptisms. I just couldn't believe it. I thought, *Surely the average Mormon doesn't know this is part of their doctrine. Surely they, too, would be just as appalled.* Then one day I asked Rodney, a Mormon seminary student, about this. "Rodney, do most Mormons, like you, know that the church teaches that Jesus and Lucifer are spirit brothers?"

He responded, "Sure they do. It's what we are taught."

From Rodney's response, I could tell that he and other Mormons take the Living Oracles seriously, not daring to question church authority. If Joseph Smith, Brigham Young, and the church hierarchy say that Jesus and Lucifer are spirit brothers, then they are spirit brothers (Jesus is thought to be the older brother).[5]

I told Rodney that although it's admirable to be submissive, it's unwise to submit to untruth. I then shared with him the following:

Also Consider:

- *Jesus created all things.* The Bible says that Jesus created all things—both in heaven and on earth (Colossians 1:16).
- *Mormon friend:* How could Jesus and Lucifer be brothers if Jesus created Lucifer?

When I asked this question of Rodney he didn't have an answer, but it did get him thinking.

The Mormon View of Jesus' Death on the Cross

As I continued to share with Rodney, I brought up Christ's death on the cross. To Christians, Christ's willingness to die on the cross is the epitome of self-sacrifice, an incredible display of love. We are astounded when we consider that He loved us even though we were wretched sinners bound for hell. Christ, the sinless one, died for utterly lost sinners like us (2 Corinthians 5:21). He became a "curse" for us (Galatians 3:13) and endured great torture to cleanse us from sin (1 Corinthians 15:3) and kept us from eternal torture. What sacrifice, what humility, what love!

A Diminished Perspective of Christ's Blood

For Mormons, including Rodney, Christ's sacrifice doesn't seem nearly as significant. In fact, Rodney talked more about the fall of mankind and how it was the best thing that could have ever happened (see endnote for the Mormon view on the Fall, [6]). While I didn't understand Rodney back then, I certainly do now because of what I've learned through the years. In the popular LDS book *Mormon Doctrine*, we are told that "all who would believe and obey his [Christ's] laws would be cleansed from sin through his blood.[7] But, "man may commit certain grievous sins...that will place him beyond the atoning blood of Christ."[8] At least all who obey Christ's laws (and thus get cleansed from sin) gain immortality."[9] This immortality doesn't mean eternal life with Christ, as discussed in Chapter 8, it simply means that Christ's death allows everyone to be resurrected. Joseph Fielding Smith explained that Christ's "death upon the cross brought salvation to every living soul, *so far as the resurrection from the dead is concerned*"[10] (emphasis added).

Mr. Smith had put emphasis on the fact that it's "through the blood of Christ" we will be resurrected.[11] How unfortunate that Christ's cleansing blood, according to Mormon theology, is based on works (obeying Christ's laws) and merely resurrects us but does not guarantee eternal life. By contrast, the Bible says "in Him we have redemption through His blood, the forgiveness of our trespasses, according to the riches of His grace" (Ephesians 1:7).

The blood Jesus shed cleanses us from our sins and grants us a total salvation that includes eternal life with Him. From what we've learned in the previous chapters, we can almost understand why Mormons can't accept the idea that Christ's death on the cross cleanses us from sin. We have learned that their idea of salvation is works oriented and that baptism is what cleanses us from sin. They can't envision such *power* as the blood of Christ. One Mormon leader put it this way: *"It is said that the blood of Jesus cleanses from all sins. Then why is it we remain sinners? It is simply because the blood of Jesus has not cleansed us from sin...."*[12]

Since the beginning of the Mormon church, the cleansing power of Jesus' blood has never been rightly understood. Yes, the church did believe at one time in blood atonement, but it's not what you think. Blood atonement, years ago, had to do with the sinner's own blood being shed to cleanse him from sin. Moreover, most present-day Mormons don't know about this doctrine, and when they learn about it, they're usually stunned. For example, when Sandra Tanner (a former Mormon and one of the premier researchers of Mormon history) found out that her famous great, great grandfather taught this doctrine, she said, "I was shocked! I knew what Brigham Young was saying was wrong but I couldn't reconcile these sermons with the things I had always been taught concerning him. I knew these were not the words of a Prophet of God." [13]

Let's take a look at this doctrine.

An Unbiblical Demand for Human Blood

Joseph Smith told the city of Nauvoo council," I was opposed to hanging, even if a man kill another, I will shoot him, or cut off his head, spill his blood on the ground, and let the smoke thereof ascend up to God; and if I ever have the privilege of making a law on that subject, I will have it so."[14]

After Smith was killed a year later, Brigham Young further defined Smith's teaching, referring to it as the act of "blood-atonement." Young preached that blood atonement was necessary for the forgiveness of certain sins that couldn't be forgiven any other way. The person "must die by having his throat cut" [from ear to ear] "so that the *running of his blood* would atone for his sins"[15] (emphasis in original).

Blood-atonement sins included adultery,[16] apostasy,[17] stealing,[18] speaking evil against the Prophet,[19] not obeying the Priesthood,[20] "covenant breaking," counterfeiting, murder, not being "heartily on the Lord's side," profaning "the Lord's name," and sexual intercourse between a "white" person and an African American,[21] and it was for those who were "so foolish as to raise his voice against any act committed by order of the Church authorities."[22]

If a person was caught in these sorts of sins, he was told he would be spared from blood-atonement if he "fully confessed" his sins;[23] if he agreed to "obey any and all orders of the Priesthood," and if he would "refuse all manner of assistance, friendship or communication with those who refused a strict obedience to the authorities of the church."[24]

It's difficult to tell how many people actually went through with blood atonement, but we get an idea that there were quite a few, according to John D. Lee, a Mormon bishop and guard to Smith and Young.[25] Lee said, "The most deadly sin among the people was adultery, and many men were killed in Utah for that crime."[26]

We can't help but be saddened that early Mormon church members didn't understand that Christ's blood shed on the cross atoned for all sins for all time. And for Mormons today, we can't help but feel sadder still. While blood atonement is no longer taught as official Mormon doctrine, the message of the cross, and the total cleansing power of Christ's blood, is still hidden from them.

Mormon Friend, Please Consider:

• *Christ's death brings forgiveness.* Without the shedding of blood there is no forgiveness (Hebrews 9:22). Redemption comes solely and totally through the blood of Jesus (1 Peter 1:18-19).

• *Christ's death relieves us of judgment.* Christ became the substitute of judgment, bearing the sins of many (Hebrews 9:26-28). "Therefore there is now no condemnation for those who are in Christ Jesus" (Romans 8:1).

• *Christ's death allows us to have the very righteousness of God* (2 Corinthians 5:21; Romans 3:22-26). When we trust Christ as our Savior, we don't have to trust in our "righteousness" (Isaiah 64:6) to get us to Heaven. Instead Christ's righteousness is imputed to us, and God no longer sees our sinful state. Because of the blood of Jesus, He sees His Son's righteousness in us.

• *Christ's death brings reconciliation.* Sin severs us from God; Christ's death removes sin and restores our relationship with God (Romans 5:1; Hebrews 2:17).

Christ's death is proof of God's love for us (John 3:16; Romans 5:8). And, it's His love we will want to highlight to our Mormon friends. They have no idea of the extent of His love—a love that forgives, a love that died that we might live. It was this divine love that brought former Mormon Sandra Tanner to Christ.

A Total Redemption Through Christ's Love

On the morning of October 24, 1959, Sandra turned on the radio and a Christian station caught her attention. A minister was preaching on the great love of God and the mercy offered to us through Jesus Christ. The message of God's love struck her with great force. She immediately opened her heart to God and accepted Christ as her personal Savior. The Holy Spirit flooded her soul with such joy that she wept for over an hour.

Sandra began visiting some Christian churches. Listening to various sermons, she came to realize that God was not concerned with people's church affiliations, but with a personal relationship.

Christ taught a way of love, not a religious system.... God reaches out to man, not because he deserves it, but because God loves him...(1 John 4:10)."[27]

If only Mrs. Hendrickson had made the same discovery as Sandra! Unfortunately she was not only stuck on the Mormon Jesus, but she was having a hard time with the simple message the *real* Jesus came to give us.

What Is the Message of the *Real* Jesus?

After sharing with Mrs. Hendrickson some of the differences between the Mormon Jesus and the *real* Jesus, I said as sensitively as possible, "Mrs. Hendrickson, your Jesus leads you to trust in Joseph Smith to save you, baptism to save you, the church ordinances to save you, and good works to save you. Your Jesus puts a great burden upon you. The *real* Jesus has taken away our burdens."

"If I don't believe what my church says about Jesus, then I would be rejecting Mormonism," she said.

Again, with gentleness, I said, "Mrs. Hendrickson, to believe what your church says about Jesus is to reject what the Bible says about Jesus. Therefore, rejecting the Bible's Jesus is rejecting the only Jesus."

I added, "You must come to see yourself as a sinner, rather than righteous. You must see your need for Jesus rather than your need for your church. The Bible tells all of us to repent and receive the Jesus of the Bible. The Bible tells us, "Now is 'the day of salvation' " (2 Corinthians 6:2). Jesus promises eternal life to all who believe in Him (John 11:25). Isn't this good news? Would you like to receive the *real* Jesus?"

Mrs. Hendrickson was quiet for a moment. Then, in a high pitched voice that betrayed her confusion, she uttered, "Repent and believe? It's just too simple. I've been a Mormon all my life. I'll be okay and Robert will be okay. We'll be spending eternity together." Then she smiled and said, "I must see Robert now."   I asked, "Please, Mrs. Hendrickson, will you think about what I've shared about Jesus?"

Mrs. Hendrickson nodded, and then went back into the room. A few hours later, I got word that Mr. Hendrickson had died. I went to his room with the hope that for some reason Mrs. Hendrickson still might be there. Unfortunately, she wasn't. Saddened by the death and that I wouldn't have any more opportunities to talk to Mrs. Hendrickson, I resolved to pray. My one prayer was that she would think about the things I shared, and that other Christians would come into her life and lead her to Jesus. Three weeks after her husband's death,   Mrs. Hendrickson came to the emergency room late at night complaining of chest pains. During those long hours in the hospital, she still had time to give her remaining moments to the *real* Jesus. Whether she decided to or not, I'll never know. All I do know is that she died that night of a massive heart attack.

What If I Forget What to Say?

If you're concerned that you might have a hard time remembering what we've learned in this chapter about Jesus, don't forget about the Fact Sheet at the end of this book. And keep in mind: Even if you didn't have the Fact Sheet—even if you were to forget every thing you just read—there is one thing you will never forget when you share with your Mormon friend: *your testimony.* Like Sandra Tanner, you can share how Christ saved you and what He means to you. And as you share from your heart, you can pray that your Mormon friend will see that you do indeed have a different Jesus—the *real* Jesus—living in you! (Galatians 2:20)

Thinking It Over

1. What does the Mormon church teach about the conception of Christ? What can we show our friend from the Bible, as well as from the *Book of Mormon?*

2. What are some other errors the Mormon church teaches about Jesus?   What does the Bible say or not say regarding these teachings?

3. What does the Mormon church say Christ's death on the cross accomplished for us? What does the Bible say His death accomplished?

I love you, O Lord, my strength.

The Lord is my rock and my fortress

and my deliverer, my God,

my rock, in whom I take refuge,

my shield, and

the horn of my salvation,

my stronghold.

I will call upon the Lord,

Who is worthy to be praised....

For who is God, but the Lord?

and who is a rock, except our God?

Psalm 18:1-3, 31

WHY DO YOU BELIEVE
YOU CAN BECOME A GOD?

Brethren, 225,000 of you are here tonight. I suppose 225,000 of you may become gods. There seems to be plenty of space out there in the universe. And the Lord has proved that he knows how to do it. I think he could make, or probably have us help make, worlds for all of us, for every one of us 225,000.

President Spencer W. Kimball
In a speech to members of the Mormon Church.
Later put in Church publication, *The Ensign*, November, 1975, p. 80

One Sunday after a worship service at a church I formerly attended, I saw my friend Kurt sitting and looking quite depressed. Wanting to find out what was wrong but not wanting to talk with him alone, I grabbed a friend, saying, "Let's go see what's up with Kurt."

Marci and I approached Kurt, and she asked, "Kurt, is something wrong? You looked depressed."

Kurt responded, "Today would have been our sixteenth wedding anniversary." We immediately knew he was referring to his former wife, Patty.

Marci and I sat down. "Do you want to talk about it?"

Kurt burst out, "The Mormon church ruined my marriage!"

"I thought your marriage was ruined because you came to Christ," I inquired.

Kurt nodded. "Certainly my coming to Christ shook my wife up, but at the time we weren't talking about divorce."

Kurt began to tell his story. "It all started when I was questioning the Mormon faith. I had become a Mormon because of my wife. I guess you could say love is blind, because I blindly joined the church without understanding its doctrines."

"Then," continued Kurt, "a buddy of mine started sharing Christ with me. He pointed out some serious doctrinal errors in Mormonism and contrasted them with what the Bible says. This prompted me to take my friend's information and talk to the bishop at the local Mormon ward I was attending. He didn't appreciate me asking what apparently were tough questions for him to answer."

Marci commented, "I would think the church leaders would view you as an earnest seeker and that they would invite questions."

Kurt shook his head, saying, "Oh no...no, not in the Mormon church. In fact, the bishop warned me that I was coming close to disobedience because I wasn't trusting the church prophets and leaders."

He continued, "The bishop told me to relax, assuring me that the prophets of the church have never and would never lead anyone astray doctrinally. Well, I wasn't satisfied with the bishop's response, so I continued to search. And as I searched, I talked to my Mormon friends about my findings."

"I'm sure that didn't please the bishop," I remarked.

Kurt gave a slight chuckle and said, "No, it didn't. In no time, I was ordered to attend the bishop's court. There, I was told that my questioning was stirring up some confusion among the brethren and I needed to just accept Mormonism or leave the church."

Marci said, "Well, since you're sitting here, we can guess what you told them."

Kurt went on: "They weren't happy when I told them I was leaving. They warned me that if I pursued that course, I would be considered a 'son of Perdition.' Being a son of Perdition is not a good thing. Since Satan is called Perdition in the Mormon church, you can guess what they thought about my eternal destiny. But, according to them, it's not hell I would be going to. I would be sent to a place far worse. I would be sent to outer darkness, where Mormons believe is the weeping and gnashing of teeth.

"The most difficult part," sighed Kurt, "is that they told me I could lose my entire family now and for eternity. As you can imagine, I left that bishop's court just steaming. I talked to Patty about it. She tried to be understanding, but it was difficult for her, having been raised in the church. As the months passed by, my non-Mormon friend led me to Christ. I was so zealous after that. I desired more than anything to follow Him with all my heart. Patty noticed the change in me, especially as I began sharing with her God's fabulous truth. She didn't respond as I had hoped. She began freaking out; her parents freaked out; and her friends freaked out. They, along with the church bishop and counselor, were encouraging her to divorce me."

I interrupted Kurt, asking, "Why would anyone in the Mormon church advise divorce when they have such strong family values?"

Kurt replied, "Because I was keeping Patty from being a goddess."

Marci had never heard of the Mormon godhood doctrine before and said, "Come on, is this some sort of a joke?"

Kurt laughed loudly and said, "I wish it was."

Kurt then told Marci, "The Mormons teach that, in the next life, you can be a god. Because I made the decision to leave the church, I was keeping Patty from eternal life in the celestial kingdom, where she could be a goddess. The only way she can attain this state of exaltation is if she's married to a faithful Mormon, and that marriage ceremony must be performed in a Mormon temple and nowhere else.[1] Because I was no longer a faithful Mormon, I was ruining Patty's chance of exaltation, so she had to divorce me."

Kurt added sarcastically, "Well, Patty is now on her way to being that goddess. Shortly after she divorced me she married a Mormon man and quietly moved to Salt Lake City."

I asked Kurt how his teenage boys were doing.

"Since they have been told that Dad is now a 'son of perdition,' they haven't desired to talk to me. Also, Patty and others are afraid that if I spend time with the boys, or even talk to them, I'll convince them to leave the church. But if I ever get that chance, I won't just convince them to leave the church. I'll show them they shouldn't strive to be gods, but rather, that they should turn to the *only* God. Oh, how I hope one day I'll get that chance!"

We, too, hope Kurt gets that chance. Let's take a moment now to look at this godhood theology Kurt was talking about.

Becoming a God

In the early days of the Mormon church, Mormon elder Lorenzo Snow (who later became prophet) gave the church the special revelation that "as man now is, our God once was; as God now is, so man may be, and thus unfolds our destiny."[2]

Prophet Brigham Young said, "How many Gods there are, I do not know. But there never was a time when there were not Gods and worlds...."[3]

And prophet Joseph Smith made these remarks in his infamous King Follet funeral sermon:[4]

Refute the Idea that God was God from all Eternity....You have got to *learn how to make yourselves God*...by going from a small to a great capacity till...able to dwell in everlasting burning and everlasting power. How consoling when called to part with a dear friend to know their very being will rise to dwell in everlasting burning...and *ascend [to] a throne as those who have gone before (emphasis added).*[5]

And, just 11 days before his death, Smith said,

...if Joseph Smith says there are Gods many and Lords many, they cry, "Away with him! Crucify him! Crucify him!" Mankind verily say that the scriptures are with them...Paul, if Joseph Smith is a blasphemer, you are. I say there are Gods many and Lords many....Some say I do not interpret the Scripture the same as they do. They say it means the heathen's gods. Paul says there are Gods many and Lords many; and that makes a plurality of gods, in spite of the whims of all men....You know and I testify that Paul had no allusion to the heathen gods. I have it from God, and get over it if you can.[6]

Even in the Mormon scripture, *Doctrine and Covenants,* (revelations given to Joseph Smith from Jesus Christ) we can read,

Abraham...as Isaac also and Jacob did none other things than that which they were commanded....they have entered into their exaltation, according to the promises, and sit upon thrones, and are not angels but are gods (D&C 132: 37).

We can also read what a faithful Mormon could look forward to:

after the first resurrection, in the next resurrection; and shall inherit thrones, kingdoms, principalities, and powers, dominions, all heights and depths—then shall it be written in the Lamb's Book of Life...and they shall "pass by the angels, and the gods, which are set there, to their exaltation and glory in all things, as hath been sealed upon their heads, which glory shall be a fullness and a continuation of the seeds forever and ever. Then *shall they be gods,* because they have no end; therefore they shall be from everlasting to everlasting...*all things are subject unto them. Then they shall be gods, because they have*

all power, and the angels are subject unto them (D&C
132: 19-20)

The above are promises of not only becoming a god, but having
all things (including angels) subject to the faithful Mormon. The
less faithful Mormon man who had married "him a wife in the
world" will not be able to become a god. He will only be an angel,
to minister to those "who are worthy of a far more and an
exceeding, and an eternal weight of glory" (D&C 132:16, also see
D&C 132:15-17).

Before you assume that modern-day Mormons no longer hold to
these teachings, think again. Mormons are taught in the book
Articles of Faith that "the doctrines taught by Joseph Smith, and by
the church today, are true and scriptural."[7]

So, how do Mormons defend the godhood doctrine scripturally?
They believe the Bible supports their view, but a closer look at the
Scriptures reveals some misunderstandings on their part.

A Mormon Misunderstanding of John 10:34

One day while sharing with two Mormon missionaries, Elders
Appel and Victor, I asked the question, "Why do Mormons say they
can become gods?"   Elder Victor responded, "Because the Bible
says we can become gods." Turning to his Bible, Victor read aloud
John 10:34: "Jesus answered them, Is it not written in your law, I
said, Ye are gods?"

If your friend or the missionary at your door brings up this verse,
don't be intimidated. It's easy to explain the truth of this verse
(and keep in mind your Fact Sheet at the end of this book). Let's
turn the page and take a look.

Mormon Friend, Please Consider:

Before we can interpret John 10:34, we need to look at the *full* context of the passage.

1. Read John 10:33. Here, the Jews accuse Christ of making Himself out to be God.

2. Now read John 10:34. This is Christ's reply to the Jews, which *He quotes from Psalm 82:6.*

3. Read Psalm 82:1-8. Note that Psalm 82 is about unjust judges. God *sarcastically* calls the judges "gods" (Psalm 82:6). Why? Because they were supposed to be His representatives (2 Chronicles 19:6-7) and they failed terribly (Psalm 82:2-4). Because of their failure, they would endure God's wrath (Psalm 82:7) and they will perish (Jeremiah 10:11).

Mormon friend: How could a "god" endure God's wrath? If he's "perfect," why the damnation?

4. Take a look, once again, at John 10:34. Jesus' response, taken from Psalm 82, proves that the word "god" can be legitimately used to refer to others than God Himself, and that the term, in this case, was being used to refer to unjust judges.

The missionaries seemed quite bothered about this, but they didn't give up. Elder Appel then referred me to 1 Corinthians 8:5.

What Does 1 Corinthians 8:5 Really Say?

Appel read aloud: "For though there be that are called gods, whether in heaven or in earth (as there be gods many, and lords many)…" (KJV).

When the missionary read this verse, I could easily tell it was referring to false gods, and I told him so. He chuckled a bit and brushed my comment aside. I then realized I needed to give a step-by-step explanation, which appears below.   You, too, can show your Mormon friend (or missionary) this verse is clearly speaking about false gods. Let's take a look.

Mormon Friend, Please Consider:

• *Mormon friend, we must look at the full context of 1 Corinthians 8:5:*

1. Read 1 Corinthians 8:4. Consider:

—This verse is talking about the eating of food offered to idols.

—It also tells us that "an idol is nothing in the world" and that "there is none other God but one."

2. In the Bible, we see idols referred to as "gods:" gods of silver and gods of gold, (Exodus 20:23).

—Thus, given the clue in 1 Corinthians 8:4, the mention of "gods many, and lords many," 1 Corinthians 8:5 is clearly a reference to idols.

3. Read 1 Corinthians 8:6. Consider: Paul is saying we don't worship idols or these so-called "gods" because "to us there is but one God, the Father...and one Lord Jesus Christ" (1 Corinthians 8:6).

• **Look at Paul and Barnabas' response when people thought they were gods (Acts 14:11-15).** If it's true we can become gods, then this would have been a great opportunity for Paul and Barnabas to talk about godhood. Instead, they were so upset they tore their clothes and cried out, "We also are men of like passions with you" (verse 15 KJV). They then pointed the people to the "living God" (verse 15).

• **The Bible warns those who seek godhood.** Read Ezekiel 28:2, 6-10. These verses warn the man who attempts to make himself to be a god.

• **Mormon friend,** if you are still unsure about this godhood doctrine, review the following Bible verses: Isaiah 43:10; 44:6,8; 2 Thessalonians 2:3-4, 10-12.

Elder Appel was still persistent: "We can reach godhood; Jesus taught it Himself." He then quoted Matthew 5:48:"Be ye therefore perfect, even as your Father which is in heaven is perfect" (KJV).

I countered, "When will you ever be perfect? When will you ever be without sin? It's impossible. That is why we need God's forgiveness."

Elder Victor said, "Well, then, why would Christ say 'be ye therefore perfect' if He knew we couldn't be perfect?"

I answered, "He never asked us to strive towards perfection so we could become a god or goddess. What He is really saying is that we need to depend upon Him and Him alone."

Also Consider:

• *Nowhere does the Bible say that perfection leads to godhood.*

• *Perfection comes from Christ.* Perfection is impossible for us to attain. If we could become perfect, then we would not have needed Jesus to die on the cross to pay the penalty for our sins and be our Savior. Jesus is the *perfecter* of our faith (see Hebrews 12:2).

1. The Bible says that our righteousness is like a "filthy garment" (Isaiah 64:6).

2. Jesus, who knew no sin, became sin for us "so that we might become the righteousness of God in Him" (2 Corinthians 5:21).

3. Again, it is clearly *Jesus* who does the work of perfecting His followers. We don't do it ourselves. Read *Hebrews 10:14* (KJV), below:

> **For by one offering He hath perfected for ever**
> **Them that are sanctified.**

As the missionaries left my house I saw them literally wipe the dust off their feet. The following day, I saw Elder Victor at the local market. I went up to him and, in a cheerful voice, said, "Hi, remember me? You came by my house yesterday."

Elder Victor didn't say a word. He just stood stiff as a board and looked straight ahead even though I was standing 12 inches from his face.   Waving my hands in front of him, I repeated myself, "Hello!"

Still not a word. I   realized then that Elder Victor was treating me as if I were a "son of perdition" even though I had never been a Mormon. I walked away with a sort of bittersweet feeling. The sour part of that encounter was experiencing a small taste of the rejection a Mormon gets when he or she leaves the Mormon church and comes to Christ. It must be painful to be ignored by the people whom one loves. But then, in an odd sort of way, there was a sweet taste as well. I walked away thinking, *Is it possible that I shared something with Elder Victor that is penetrating his soul? Is he refusing to face the truth? Oh Lord, please work in his heart, soul, and mind!*

Sadly, Elder Victor's perspective was most likely affected by the fact that Mormon theology *elevates* man and *lowers* God.

Being Coequal with God

In *Doctrine and Covenants,* Joseph Smith gave the revelation that Mormons are "gods, even the sons of God" (76:58) and that "saints shall be filled with his [The Lamb of God] glory...and be made equal with him" (88:106-107). Brigham Young added that these saints "will wear a celestial crown and have dominion.... They shall reign over kingdoms, and have power to be Gods...."[8]

And in *Doctrines of Salvation,* Joseph Fielding Smith quoted Joseph Smith, Jr., asking rhetorically if he had not said:

God himself was once as we are now, and is an exalted man...that he was once a man like us; yea, that God himself, the Father of us all, dwelt on an earth, the same as Jesus Christ himself did? [9]

We can show our Mormon friend how horribly wrong Joseph Smith and the rest of the Mormon church leaders have been.

Mormon Friend, Please Consider:

• *God did not evolve from manhood to godhood.*

—God is the everlasting Father; He has been the Father for eternity" (Isaiah 9:6; Micah 5:2).

—God has been God since the beginning (John 1:1, 14).

—Before Abraham, God already existed (John 8:58).

—Being pre-existent, God created all things (Colossians 1:16).

—God doesn't change (Malachi 3:6), therefore He could never have been a man.

• *Mankind had a beginning, unlike God.*   Scripture tells the story of man's beginning (Genesis 2:7). This alone proves we cannot be co-equal with God, who has always existed as God.

—We are and always will be in subjection to Him.

—We need His grace, His love, His forgiveness, His mercy.

—We need His guidance, His power, and His Word to live out each day.

Who can even come close to God's greatness?

Turning to the True God

While there are a good number of Mormons who understand what their church teaches about achieving godhood, there are others who don't—at least, not fully. I remember hearing the testimony of one Mormon woman, named Kathy, who was told by her Christian friend, Sarah, about Mormon men becoming gods and women becoming goddesses in the celestial kingdom. She said,

> I had heard about Mormon women being able to attain goddess status in the celestial kingdom, but then I learned that I would be pregnant for the rest of eternity [see note #10 regarding the Mormon view of "spirit babies"[10]]; that me and my husband—and possibly his other wives— would have our own planet just like God the Father and Heavenly Mother [see note #11 regarding the Mormon view of Heavenly Mother[11]] have their own planet. Hearing all this sickened me.

Kathy was equally horrified by Joseph Smith and Brigham Young's teachings about godhood. Kathy talked to her husband, Bob, who said he had never really given much thought to the godhood doctrine until Kathy brought it up. They came to see that the Mormon teaching about godhood wasn't biblical at all.

As a result, Bob, Kathy, and their seven children left the Mormon church and found Jesus Christ.   Let's pray that, like Bob, Kathy, and their children (as well as Kurt, whom we met at the beginning of this chapter), our Mormon friends (and missionaries) will see the problems with pursuing heavenly exaltation and instead will come to pursue the only exalted One. Let's ask the Spirit to open their eyes to what Jesus did on their behalf. He left His throne, came to earth, and "humbled Himself [rather than exalting Himself]....to the point of death, even death on a cross" (Philippians 2:8) that they might be saved.

Let's pray that one day they will lean solely upon Jesus, confessing Him as "Lord, to the glory of God the Father" (Philippians 2:11).

> *My hope is built on nothing less*
> *Than Jesus' blood and righteousness*
> *I dare not trust the sweetest frame,*
> *But wholly lean on Jesus' name.*
> —Edward Mote (1797–1874)

Thinking It Over

1. Mormons believe John 10:34 supports the idea we can become gods and goddesses. How can you respond?

2. Mormons also use 1 Corinthians 8:5 to say there are "gods many, and lords many." What can we share with them about this verse?

3. Mormons believe Jesus affirmed we can achieve godhood because He said, "Be ye therefore perfect, even as your Father which is in heaven is perfect" (Matthew 5:48). What truth can we share in response?

4. Mormons are taught that God evolved from manhood and that we are pre-existent, like God. What can we say to them?

Pray also for me,
that whenever
I open my mouth,
words may be given me
so that I will fearlessly
make known the mystery of
the gospel.

Ephesians 6:19

CHAPTER 12

WHAT DO YOU BELIEVE ABOUT THE TRINITY?

I have always declared God to be a distinct personage, Jesus Christ a separate and distinct personage from God the Father, and the Holy Ghost was a distinct personage and a Spirit: and these three constitute three distinct personages and three Gods.

Joseph Smith

(Joseph Fielding Smith, *Teachings of Prophet Joseph Smith,* p. 370).

One day my friend Mary was sharing with me about a conversation she had with two Mormon missionaries who came to her door. She said, "I had always thought the Mormons rejected the Trinity. But these missionaries told me they wholeheartedly embrace it."

I questioned Mary, " Did you ask them what their definition of the Trinity was?"

Mary replied, "Well, I just assumed that they believed the same as we do."

At one time I made the same assumption as Mary. But I've come to find out that the Mormon Trinity is completely different. Their Trinity is made up of *three separate Gods*—God the Father (whom Joseph Smith has called Ahman[1]), God the Son, and God the Holy Ghost. Now, before we take a look at this Mormon Trinity, it's important to take a look at what Mormons say about the Father, the Son, and the Holy Spirit.

The Mormon Views

THE HOLY SPIRIT

Our Mormon friends are taught that the Holy Spirit and the Holy Ghost are different. *They are not the same person.* If you were to talk to your Mormon friend about the Holy Spirit and the Holy Ghost as the same, there is a good chance she would become confused. Let's seek to understand what she's been taught. The Mormon church teaches that the Holy Spirit is only an "influence" from the Father.[2]

He's generally not personal, although the *Book of Mormon* shows that on one occasion the Holy Spirit came to Nephi "in the form of a man" (1 Nephi 11:11). Still, the Holy Spirit isn't God. You will *never* hear your Mormon friend refer to their "three-god" Trinity as God the Father, God the Son, and God the Holy Spirit. Rejecting the Holy Spirit as God, Mormons believe that only the Holy Ghost is god—and only "a god" at that.   So, how can we get our friends to clearly see that the Holy Spirit and the Holy Ghost are the same person? Simply by turning to First Corinthians.

Mormon Friend, Please Consider:

• *Compare 1 Corinthians 3:16 and 6:19:*
—1 Corinthians 3:16 says "the *Spirit* of God dwelleth *in you*" (KJV).
—1 Corinthians 6:19 refers to, "the *Holy Ghost* which is *in you*" (KJV).

Mormon friend: If the Spirit is only an "influence from the Father," then how can the Spirit dwell in a true believer? And, do you notice that according to the above First Corinthian verses, both the Holy Spirit and the Holy Ghost dwell in you?

• *In both 1 Corinthians 3:16 and 6:19, "Ghost" and "Spirit" are the same Greek word (pneuma[3]). Clearly, then, both refer to the same entity. The Spirit, therefore, is God. (See also Act 5:3-4.)*

What about the Mormon view of Jesus in relation to the Trinity? Let's examine a few of the erroneous ideas they have about Him.

JESUS

In the last few chapters we discovered that your friend is taught that Christ was "begotten of his Father,"[4] that He and Lucifer are spirit brothers,[5] that His death on the cross only allows everyone to be resurrected (they can still go to hell), that He is only the god of this earth, and that we are coequal with Him (D&C 88:106-107).

By contrast, the Bible teaches Jesus was conceived by the Holy Ghost (Matthew 1:18,20; Luke 1:34-35), He is not Lucifer's spirit brother (Colossians 1:16 shows Christ *created* Lucifer), and He is God from all eternity (Isaiah 41:4; John 1:1; 8:58; Revelation 1:8; 21:6).

Through His death we have forgiveness (Hebrews 9:22), redemption (1 Peter 1:18-19), are relieved of judgment (Hebrews 9:27-28) have the very righteousness of God (2 Corinthians 5:21), and have reconciliation with God (2 Corinthians 5:18; Hebrews 2:17). Christ, the sinless One (1 Peter 2:22), is God who dwelt among us as a man (John 1:1,14) to save us (John 3:16). It is absolutely impossible, then, for us to be co-equal with Him.

THE FATHER

Brigham Young told a group of Sunday school children, "Now, children, remember this. We teach you that our Father in heaven is a personage of tabernacle, just as much as I am who stand before you to-day, [sic] and he has all parts and passions of a perfect man, and his body is composed of flesh and bones, but not of blood...."[6]

Children weren't the only ones taught that God has a material body. All Mormons were and continue to be taught this in *Doctrine and Covenants* (130:22) and other church writings. [7] Actually, the Mormon church has officially stated that "to deny the materiality of

God's person is to deny God…an immaterial body cannot exist. The Church of Jesus Christ of Latter-day Saints proclaims against the incomprehensible God, devoid of body, parts, or passions."[8]

When a Methodist minister was sharing with the Mormon Elder Noble about the God he worships, Noble told the minister that his God was "the Mormon's devil" because his God didn't have a body, "whereas our God has body, parts and passions."[9]

Mormon leader Erastus Snow said, "We are asked to believe in, render obedience to and worship this being. The careful thinker says, 'I cannot; it is impossible for me to believe in a being that has neither body parts nor passions, and that is located nowhere; I cannot conceive of him.'"[10]

Along with their scriptures and comments from church leaders, Mormons believe that the Father has flesh and bones because:
1) Joseph Smith said he *saw* the Father with flesh and bones in his First Vision; 2) mankind was created after God's own image and likeness (D&C 20:18), so it goes without saying that the Father has a body of flesh and bones as tangible as man's (D&C 130:22);[11]
3) there are passages in the Bible that refer to God as having eyes (Proverbs 15:3), a mouth (Isaiah 55:11); nostrils (Exodus 15:8), lips and tongue (Isaiah 30:27), a hand and arm (Jeremiah 21:5), fingers (Psalm 8:3), a face (Isaiah 54:8), and even that God spoke to Moses face to face (Exodus 33:11).   How should we respond?

Mormon Friend, Please Consider:

• *The biblical references to God's body parts are figurative.*

1. If the references to body parts were literal, then God would also have feathers and wings (Psalm 91:4).

2. By the same token, Jesus would literally be a "vine" (John 15:1), a "door" (John 10:9), "bread" (John 6:35), and a "lamb" (John 1:29; Revelation 5:6,8).

3. If we take Proverbs 15:3 literally (about God having eyes), for instance, then we must say that God has many eyes. How could only two eyes be in every place?

• *Jesus said the Father "is Spirit" (John 4:24).* Who are we to question Jesus? The Old Testament says that the Father fills "the heavens and the earth" (Jeremiah 23:24). How could the Father fill "the heavens and the earth" if He had a body?

Jesus said that true worshipers "worship the Father in spirit and truth; for such people the Father seeks to be His worshipers" (John 4:23). Wanting to emphasize this truth, Jesus elaborated, saying that those who worship the Father "*must* worship in spirit and in truth" (John 4:24, emphasis added).

The English word *worship* was originally spelled *worth*ship. It means to acknowledge the worth of the object worshiped. Theologian Charles Ryrie says, "We should acknowledge God's worth *in spirit* (in contrast to material ways) and *in truth* (in contrast to falsehood)."[12]

Most Mormons are very sincere in their worship of God; we don't doubt that. But, according to Jesus, their worship isn't acceptable because their worship isn't in truth. True worship corresponds to God's nature. He is a Spirit, *without* body or body parts. And, contrary to what the Mormon church says, we *do* believe the Father has passions. For instance, He demonstrates His love (Jeremiah 31:3; John 3:16), His compassion (Isaiah 25:8), His sorrow (Genesis 6:6), and His righteous anger (Numbers 11:1; 14:18). But again, He is without flesh and bones. He's free from all limitations of time and space. "Behold, heaven and the highest heaven cannot contain You" (1 Kings 8:27). Not only must our Mormon friends worship God according to His true nature, but they must worship Him as *one*, not three.

The Mormon Challenge

Joseph Smith firmly refused to accept the idea of one God in three persons. In his sermon titled "The Christian Godhead— Plurality of Gods," he said, "...we have three Gods anyhow, and they are plural: and who can contradict it?"[13] "Many men say there is one God; the Father, the Son and the Holy Ghost are only one God! I say that is a strange God anyhow—three in one, and one in three!"[14]

Anyone who disagrees with Smith's "plurality of gods" concept is given a challenge by the prophet himself: "I want the apostates and learned men to come here and prove to the contrary, if they can."[15] Let's take up Smith's challenge. It's quite simple to "prove to the contrary" to our Mormon friend and the missionary at our door.

The Christian Response

Proving the Triune God

One day while teaching a group of women about witnessing to Mormons, I said, "A great way to show Mormons that *God is One* is by using their own weapon—the *Book of Mormon*." From the group I heard a gasp of surprise. I was able to understand the reaction. Because we don't recognize the *Book of Mormon* as God's Word, we would not normally expect to use it to defend biblical truth. But because Mormons view the *Book of Mormon* as true, we can use its statements to support our points if those statements happen to agree with biblical truth and contradict Mormon teaching. Like Paul the apostle, who witnessed to ancient philosophers by referring to their own poets (see Acts 17:28), we can refer the Mormons to their own book. In it there is something quite revealing they need to see. With the *Book of Mormon* in their hand, ask them to read aloud the last line of the "Testimony of the Witnesses" (found in the first few pages of the BOM). It reads, "And the honor be to the

Father and to the Son, and to the Holy Ghost, *which is one God*" (emphasis added).

Next, take them to other *Book of Mormon* references that say there is only one God (Mosiah 15:2-4; Alma 11:26-29). As well, *Doctrine and Covenants* speaks of the Trinity as one: "...Father, Son, and Holy Ghost are *one God*" (D&C 20:28, emphasis added).

Now, while you are directing the Mormons to their scripture, they might ask *you* to read from Matthew 3:16-17. These two verses take us to that moment when Christ was being baptized. Your Mormon friends will point out the fact that not only is Christ present, but also the Spirit and the Father, all appearing as separate individuals—three persons, not one!

Let's take a look at the response we can give our Mormon friends.

Mormon Friend, Please Consider:

• *There is only one God.* While Scripture clearly shows that the Father, the Son, and the Spirit are equally God, Scripture confirms that "there is no God but one" (1 Corinthians 8:4).

• *Old Testament proof of the Trinity.* While the Old Testament doesn't reveal the Trinity, it does allow for the later revelation of it. For instance, there are passages that use the plural word *Elohim* and plural pronouns referring to God (see Genesis 1:1, 26; Isaiah 6:8; [16] also see Isaiah 48:12, 16).

• *New Testament confirmation of the Trinity.* In the New Testament there is a clear revelation that the Father, Son, and Spirit are all God, thus a three-in-one Trinity.

The Trinity has the same divine attributes. To name only a few:

—**Life** (Joshua 3:10; John 1:4; Romans 8:2)
—**Omniscience** (Psalm 139:1-6; John 4:17-18; 1 Cor. 2:10-12)
—**Omnipotence** (Genesis 1:1; John 1:3; Job 33:4)
—**Omnipresence** Jeremiah 23:23-24; Mt. 28:20; Ps. 139:7-10)
—**Eternity** (Psalm 90:2, John 1:1, Hebrews 9:14)
—**Holiness** (Leviticus 11:44, Acts 3:14, Matthew 12:32)
—**Truth** John 3:33, 14:6, 14:17).
—**Authority:** We are to be baptized in the **name** of all three, showing equal authority (Mt. 28:19). Also see 2 Cor. 13:14.

— *The Father is God* (John 6:27; Ephesians 4:6).

— *Jesus is God* (John 20:28). The Father says of the Son, "Thy throne, O God, is for ever and ever" (Hebrews 1:8).[17]

— *The Spirit is God* (Acts 5:3-4; 1 Corinthians 12:3).

—The three persons are associated equally and as one (Matthew 28:19; 2 Corinthians 13:14—*Note:* the word "name in Matthew 28:19 is singular, not plural).

If you have been able to get this far with your Mormon friends, then they are truly at a crossroad.

Accepting the Triune God

All of us know who King David was. Through the Spirit, he wrote most of the psalms that appear in the Bible. What many of us don't realize is that he lived in a day and age when belief in the reality of many gods was very strong (see Psalm 86:8). The majority of the people in the nations surrounding Israel believed in many powerful deities and that to deny their existence was absurd. Despite what the majority believed, David (and his fellow Jews) stood firm in the belief that there was only one God (Psalm 86:10). David's steadfastness in this truth certainly went against the grain of popular culture. He was probably ostracized for his view.

Our Mormon friends must make a decision one way or the other. Will they agree with David and the Bible that there is only one true God, and that no one can become a god? Or will they continue to believe there are many gods (including dead friends and relatives, who are believed to be on their way to becoming gods)?

If our Mormon friends are coming to understand that there is only one God, we can gently encourage them that it's not enough to merely know there is one God. Eternal life comes only when we enter into a personal relationship with Him by accepting Christ as our Savior and His atoning sacrifice for our sins. The Lord promises that "you will find Him if you search for Him with all your heart and all your soul" (Deuteronomy 4:29).

And finally, in your Mormon friends' search for the truth, we can calm their fear of the consequences that will come from the Mormon church should they decide to deny Mormon doctrine. How? First, by telling them you will be praying for them—fervently. And second, by encouraging them to pray as David prayed:

Preserve me, O God, for I take refuge in You.
—PSALM 16:1

Thinking It Over

1. How can we explain to a Mormon that the Holy Ghost and the Holy Spirit are the same person?

2. Mormons say God the Father has flesh and bones. They can "prove" it, showing from Scripture that He has eyes, a nose, a tongue, fingers, and so on. How can we respond and explain a correct view of the Father?

3. What do Mormons believe about the Trinity? How can we show them the truth that God is one?

CHAPTER 13

WHAT DO YOU BELIEVE
ABOUT HEAVEN?

In the heaven where our spirits were born, there are many GOD'S, each of who has his own wife or wives which were given to him previous to his redemption while yet in his mortal state.

> Apostle Orson Pratt,
> The Seer, 1:37

Recently I read an intriguing article in *U.S. News & World Report*. It stated that the Mormon doctrine of heaven is "attractive to potential converts." Why? Because:

> In most branches of Christianity, anyone who does not embrace the Gospel and accept Jesus as Savior risks eternity in hell. But in Mormonism, only "sons of perdition"—former believers who betray the church—are destined for eternal punishment. All others are assured at least entry into the *"telestial kingdom"*—a sort of lesser Paradise where one spends eternity apart from God. The most faithful attain the *"celestial kingdom,"* where they commune directly with God and eventually may themselves become gods and populate new universes with their own spiritual offspring[1] (emphasis added).

For those of us who know what the Scriptures say, these comments about various kingdoms may boggle the mind. But, certainly not your Mormon friend's mind. She has been taught that there is the *celestial*, the *terrestrial* (not mentioned in the above paragraph), and the *telestial* heaven. There is also the *outer darkness*, which is reserved only for the "sons of perdition." Sound confusing? Let's look at each Mormon destiny and try to understand why our friends believe the way they do.

The Different Mormon Heavens

Outer Darkness—for the "Most Wicked"

Sadly, an ex-Mormon is called a "son of perdition" (remember, Satan is Perdition) and is thought to be the "most wicked" individual on earth.[2] Why? Because he has committed "the unpardonable sin,"[3] denying "the plan of salvation with his eyes open to the truth of it; and on earth.[2] Why? Because he has committed "the unpardonable sin,"[3] denying "the plan of salvation with his eyes open to the truth of it; and from that time he begins to be an enemy." [4]

Joseph Smith said of Mormon apostates,

> When a man begins to be an enemy of this work, he hunts me, he seeks to kill me, and never ceases to thirst for my blood. He gets the spirit of the devil—the same spirit that they had who crucified the Lord of Life—the same spirit that sins against the Holy Ghost. You cannot save such persons, you cannot bring them to repentance; they make open war, like the devil, and awful is the consequence.[5]

So what are the consequences for apostates? They are temporarily "sent to hell [also called 'spirit prison' [6]] where their suffering begins and continues beyond the time when they are finally resurrected and sent into outer darkness."[7] Once in outer darkness, they shall inherit "the darkest chaos and torment for their eternal reward: They shall go away into everlasting punishment…to reign with the devil and his angels in eternity, where their worm dieth not, and the fire is not quenched, which is their torment.…"

(D&C 76:44-45).[8] They will never be redeemed because they "loved Satan more than God."[9]

That is the terrible news for the apostates who are thrown into outer darkness—"the final and eternal hell."[10] But the Mormon church also professes to have good news for others who are said to be on their way to spirit prison.[11] (The Mormon church doesn't teach that there is just one hell. To believe in one hell is "false teaching."[12]) Spirit prison is for anyone but the apostates (except for a temporary stay) and is said to be an agreeable place.

Hell—An Agreeable Place

Joseph Smith once said,

> We will all go to hell together and convert it into a heaven by casting the Devil out; hell is by no means the place this world of fools supposes it to be, but on the contrary, it is quite an agreeable place.[13]

What makes hell so agreeable? Unlike the sons of perdition, a less wicked group, namely the "liars, and sorcerers, and adulterers and whoremongers, and whosoever loves and make a lie" (D&C 76:103)[14] will be able to get out. Like the jail in the game Monopoly, from which you can be released, these people aren't stuck in spirit prison forever.

Here's how it works: These wicked are first "thrust down to hell where they will be required to pay the uttermost farthing before their redemption comes."[15] Eventually, "they will obtain a kingdom of glory but only after they have suffered during a long sojourn in spirit prison for their sins of the flesh…after their sufferings, will inherit the telestial kingdom…."[16]

So, the Mormon church teaches that after a period of suffering, the people in hell will be released. But that isn't what the Word of God says. The Bible describes hell as a frightening place from which there is no escape—*ever*.

Mormon Friend, Please Consider:

• *The Bible speaks of only one hell.*

• *No one gets out of hell—it's eternal* (Matthew 25:41, 46; Mark 9:48; Luke 16:23-26; Revelation 14:11).

• *Hell is not an agreeable place.* Jesus said of hell:

1. The "cursed" go there (Matthew 25:41).

2. There is "wailing and gnashing of teeth" (Matthew 13:42).

3. It's a place of everlasting fire and punishment (Matthew 25:41, 46).

4. It's a place of torment no one can leave (Luke 16:22-24).

5. The unrighteous can't escape hell (Matthew 23:33).

While the Bible makes it clear that hell is a horrible place that no one can escape, the Mormon church goes so far as to say there's a kind of glory awaiting those who finally get out of hell.

Telestial Glory—for the Wicked

Once the wicked have paid their debt in hell through suffering, they will be released and will be permitted to make their new home in the telestial kingdom. They will be glad to see that they are "governed by the Holy Ghost, with rulers and administrators gathered from the terrestrial worlds" (see D&C 76:86, 88).[17]

Although these citizens of the telestial kingdom are "living in the least of the resurrected states of glory,"[18] the Mormon church guarantees that "they will enjoy an existence of far greater comfort and enjoyment than is now experienced by any mortal on this earth.... In their own way, they will be 'servants of the Most High; but where God and Christ dwell *they cannot come*'" (D&C 76:112, emphasis added).[19]

So, while the inhabitants of the telestial kingdom are no longer in hell, they're also not able to enter Christ's presence.

Christians, by contrast, are assured through God's Word, the Bible, of eternity in the presence of God the Father and God the Son no matter what (John 14:2-3). The next Mormon "heaven" we want to look at is the terrestrial kingdom.

Terrestrial Glory—for the Honorable

The terrestrial kingdom is for "the honorable men of the earth" (D&C 76:75),[20] who are said to be good, moral people. They care about others and try to make the world a better place.[21]

Your Mormon friend would probably place you in this category. She believes that for eternity you will "enjoy the association with more pleasant, honorable, decent people."[22] But before you begin to think perhaps it's a compliment to be called "honorable," think again. The Mormon church says the honorable people in the terrestrial kingdom are "blinded by the craftiness [or philosophies] of men they remain—however just, good, and ethical...[they are] uncommitted to becoming Christ's disciples and progressing towards saintliness or godhood" (D&C 76:75).[23]

Despite the fact these honorable people are uncommitted toward the things of God, they at least have "mansions and worlds prepared for them...[they] are governed by Christ with assistance from the Holy Ghost and other celestial beings" (D&C 76:77,87).[24] They "will be of service in administering God's kingdoms, they can also assist in governing telestial worlds" (D&C 76:88).[25] But sadly, "the glory of their existence and the intensity of their service appear dim and weak in comparison to what is enjoyed by celestial beings residing in God's presence."[26]

Celestial Glory—for God's Children

While those who go to the terrestrial place may be "nice people,"[27] admission to the celestial kingdom is only for God's true children—the Mormons. That's because, according to their theology, they have "completely reconciled themselves with God by accepting Christ and the saving ordinances.... They inherit 'thrones, kingdoms, principalities, and powers' (D&C 132:19) from Heavenly Father in part *because they assisted in bringing to pass the immortality and eternal life of other individuals*" (see D&C 76:54-70; 132:19-20; Moses 1:39, emphasis added).[28]

These celestial citizens "are literally transformed into 'new creatures' and angels on high, some becoming as their heavenly parent, fulfilling their ultimate destiny as gods and goddesses" (2 Corinthians 5:17; D&C 6:58).[29] Mormon theology cites 2 Corinthians 5:17, which talks about being a new creature in Christ, but as you can see from the above quote, the verse is used erroneously. Rather than becoming a god or goddess, when we give our life to Christ, we become new creatures *in this life*. Our old life is gone as we live a new life serving our Lord and Savior Jesus Christ. Our destiny is being the Lord for eternity, singing His praises, giving Him *all the glory*.

In the Mormons' celestial kingdom, men and women not only become gods, but as I mentioned earlier, they are also married and they can have spirit babies (D&C 132:19-20). Joseph Smith says that in the celestial kingdom, "dominion and power in the 'great future' would be commensurate with the number of 'wives, children and friends that we inherit here....'"[30]

By now, you might be scratching your head while reading all this, saying, "But what about Christ's statement that there wouldn't be marriage in heaven…at least in the real heaven?" (see Matthew 22:30).

Mormon tenth prophet Joseph Fielding Smith had an answer to that:

> Why did Jesus teach the doctrine that there was no marrying nor giving in marriage in the other world?….[because] they did not understand the principle of sealing for time and for all eternity; that what God hath joined together neither man nor death can put asunder….[31]

Joseph Fielding Smith also said that because Christ's listeners didn't understand the principle of eternal marriage, he responded to them by saying, "Ye do err, not knowing the Scriptures, nor the power of God."[32]

After reading about the telestial, terrestrial, and celestial kingdoms, you might be wondering, "Why don't the Mormons simply believe in just one heaven?"

The One Biblical Heaven

Our Mormon friends refuse to believe in just one heaven for two reasons: First, they are taught that the doctrine of only one heaven is "false,"[33] and second, they believe their three heavens, or the "three degrees of glory," are mentioned in the Bible. They will refer you to First Corinthians 15:40-42 and Second Corinthians 12:2. Let's go to the following page to read these verses and see what they say.

1 Corinthians 15:40-42

> There are also celestial bodies, and bodies terrestrial: but the glory of the celestial is one, and the glory of the terrestrial is another. There is one glory of the sun, and another glory of the moon, and another glory of the stars: for one star differeth from another star in glory. So also is the resurrection of the dead. It is sown in corruption; it is raised in incorruption (KJV, emphasis added).

At first glance, it may appear these words do support the Mormon teaching that there are multiple heavens. How can we respond? Very simply. Let's take a look:

Mormon Friend, Please Consider:

• *Point One:* Where are the three heavens? I only see *two*.

> **Mormon Friend, take note:** The *telestial* heaven is missing in First Corinthians 15:40-42. Only *terrestrial* and *celestial* are mentioned. **Consider:** This alone discredits the teaching that there are three glories.

• *Point Two: Terrestrial* means "things of earth." Paul says in verse 39 (a verse the Mormons skip over) that the terrestrial things are the flesh of men, of beasts, of birds, and of fish. **Consider:** We can see from Paul's description that the word "terrestrial" in 1 Corinthians refers not to heaven but to earthly things.

• *Point Three:* "Celestial bodies" means "heavenly bodies." Look closely at the verse. Paul clearly states these bodies are the sun, moon, and stars. **Consider:** The sun, moon, and stars are in space, and Paul isn't talking about a type of heaven.

• *Point Four:* In context, we can see that Paul is contrasting only two kinds of things, not three. He is contrasting the earthly with the heavenly—he contrasts the earthly body, which is "sown in corruption," to the resurrected body, which is "sown in incorruption."

Now let's move on to...

2 Corinthians 12:2:

> I knew a man in Christ about fourteen years ago (whether in the body, I cannot tell; or whether out of the body, I cannot tell: God knoweth;) such a one caught up to the third heaven (KJV).

Second Corinthians 12:2, which mentions "the third heaven," is also easy to explain to our Mormon friend. Let's take a look at all three heavens:

Mormon Friend, Please Consider:

• *There is the atmospheric heaven.* The phenomena of weather occurs in the atmospheric heaven. This includes rain (Deuteronomy 11:11; Acts 14:17), snow (Isaiah 55:10), dew (Daniel 4:23), frost (Job 38:29), clouds (Psalm 147:8), and thunder (1 Samuel 2:10).[34]

Mormon friend: Doesn't the atmospheric heaven describe the atmosphere in which the "birds of the heaven" fly? (1 Kings 21:24).

• *The starry heaven.* This refers to space (the expanse of the sky)—the place of all heavenly light, the sun, the moon, and the stars (see Genesis 1:14-17; Nahum 3:16).[35]

Mormon friend: Might the atmospheric heaven **and** starry heaven be for the earth's use, for our enjoyment while on earth, and for declaring God's glory? The Bible says, "The heavens are telling of the glory of God; and their expanse is declaring the work of His hands" (Psalm 19:1; see also Romans 1:19-20).

• *The highest heaven.* This is the third heaven, from which God looks down to see us on earth (Isaiah 63:15), and it's where Paul speaks of a man being taken up to (2 Corinthians 12:2). In this heaven there is a complete acknowledgment of God's glory (Psalm 29:9).[36] This is the one and only heaven (Revelation 5:13).

While you will have clearly shown that the phrase "third heaven" in Second Corinthians 12:2 doesn't mean there are three glories in the hereafter, your Mormon friend or missionary will have one last point to make. They will say that throughout the Bible, we can clearly see there is more than one heaven. For instance, they might quote, "God created the *heavens* and the earth" (Genesis 1:1, emphasis added). By the way, the King James Version (the version the Mormon church uses) renders the word *heaven* in singular form: "God created *the heaven* and the earth" (emphasis added). A missionary especially would quote to you 2 Peter 3:13: "We...look for new *heavens* and a new earth, wherein dwelleth righteousness" (KJV, emphasis added).   Let's once again take our friends and the missionaries to God's Word.

Also Consider:

- *The plural form "heavens" does not refer to multiple heavenly kingdoms.* The heavens are the "clouds" (Job 35:5), "birds" (Job 12:7), lights that separate night and day (Genesis 1:14-17).
- *There is one heaven.* Jesus says, "Our Father which art in heaven" (Matthew 6:9).

   Mormon Friend: Although not true scripture, take a look at your *Book of Mormon. It* gives indication of only one heaven (1 Nephi 15:35).

- *Jesus was taken up into heaven.* There is no mention of other heavens at Christ's ascension (Luke 24:51).
- *Our citizenship is in heaven* (Philippians 3:20). Those who belong to the Lord look forward to their home—heaven, where Christ reigns. Paul didn't talk about three heavens here when he spoke of our destiny.
- *The apostle John wrote about only one heaven.* If the "three glories" are real, John would very likely have written about them in the book of Revelation. But he didn't.

Considering Our Own Destiny
Confronted with a Choice

There is an old legend about a swan and long-necked bird called a crane. The beautiful swan was swimming near the shore of a lake, where the crane was wading about seeking snails. For a few moments the crane viewed the swan in curious wonder and then asked, "Where did you come from?"

"I came from heaven!" replied the swan.

"And where is heaven?" asked the crane.

"Heaven!" said the swan. "Heaven! Have you never heard of heaven?"

The delicate swan went on to describe the grandeur of the eternal city. She told of the streets of gold and the gates and walls of precious stones, of the river of life, pure as crystal, upon whose banks is the tree whose leaves shall be for the healing of all nations. In eloquent terms the swan sought to describe the hosts who live in the other world, but in doing so she was unable to arouse even the slightest interest on the part of the crane.

Finally, the crane asked, "Are there any snails there?"

"Snails?" echoed the swan. "No of course there are not."

"Then," said the crane as it continued its search along the slimy banks, "you can have your heaven. I want snails!"[37]

We must pray fervently for our Mormon friends. You see, like the crane who didn't want heaven because there were no snails, our friends will be tempted to reject the heaven described in the Bible because their scriptures won't be there, their doctrine won't be there, and most of all, their celestial kingdom won't be there.

Let's encourage Mormons to seek what *is* in heaven—truth.

Confronted with Our Helplessness

If your Mormon friend or missionaries have been trusting in their church and their good works to save them, we can only hope that the biblical truths provided in this book will lead them to the blameless One who endured a death reserved for the worst criminals; to the exalted One who sat on a heavenly throne and came to earth to be nailed to a torturous cross; to the holy One who on that cross carried your sins, my sins, and the sins of our Mormon friends that we may be cleansed. *In peace let me resign my breath, And thy salvation see—My sins deserve eternal death, but Jesus died for me.*[38]

Mormon Friend, Please Consider:

If you have reached the point of recognizing your sinfulness and your need for the Lord and Savior, Jesus Christ, I encourage you to go to prayer right now.   If you need assistance, you might want to pray something like this:

Dear Jesus,*
I realize that I am a sinner in need of forgiveness. I ask You for your everlasting forgiveness. From this moment on, I turn from putting the Mormon church first in my life instead of You. I turn from believing in Mormon prophets instead of You. I turn from trusting in the church ordinances and my own works to save me instead of You. I now relinquish all these things and surrender my life completely to You alone. I am turning to You, through repentance, knowing that it's You who cleanses my soul, rather than baptism. Thank You for not only Your forgiveness, but for Your love, and for dying for me that I may have life with You forever. From this point on, I will trust you, rather than the Mormon church for my salvation. Most of all, thank You for coming into my heart and being my Lord and Savior. Amen.

*Note: You may feel uncomfortable praying to Jesus, since you've been taught that you can't pray to Him. Just keep something in mind. While the *Book of Mormon* is not the Word of God, it does say in 3 Nephi 19:18, 25, 26:
> And behold, they began to pray; and *they did pray unto Jesus,* calling him their Lord and their God....And it came to pass that Jesus blessed them *as they did pray unto him....*And Jesus said unto them: *Pray on;* nevertheless they did not cease to pray.

Let's continue to pray that our Mormon friend will seek forgiveness and turn his or her life to Christ. Imagine what a day it will be if your friend embraces the *real* Jesus and all the glorious truths that come from Him! Your friend will no longer be part of the 200 year (plus) Mormon saga. He or she will be living a new story, and the closing line of his or her life will be the echoing words of Jesus:

I will come again

and receive you to Myself,

that where I am,

there you may be also.

John 14:3

Thinking It Over

1. Who are the "sons of perdition" and where do they go?

2. What do Mormons believe about hell? What does the Bible say?

3. What are the three heavens in Mormon theology? What types of people are said to inhabit these different heavens?

4. Mormons use 1 Corinthians 15:40-42 to defend their view that there are three heavens. What can we share with them regarding these verses?

5. What do Mormons believe 2 Corinthians 12:2 says? What truth can we show them?

6. When Mormons tell you that Scripture clearly shows there are "heavens" (for example, as in Genesis 1:1; 2 Peter 3:13), what can we say to show them what is truly meant by the use of the plural form of *heaven*?

7. Go to the Fact Sheet at the end of this book. Photocopy it (and laminate it, if you desire) and insert in your Bible. This will enable you to be prepared at all times when the opportunity arises to share with a Mormon.

8. Get together with a Christian friend so you can practice using your Fact Sheet. Through role-playing, have one person defend the Mormon view and the other oppose it. Then reverse roles.

A COMPARISON BETWEEN
MORMONISM AND THE BIBLE

Take up the Bible,
compare the religion of the Latter-day Saints with it
and see if it will stand the test.

Prophet Brigham Young
Journal of Discourses 16:46

SCRIPTURE

Mormonism: Scripture consists of the Bible (insofar as it is accurately translated[1]), the *Book of Mormon, Doctrine and Covenants*, and the *Pearl of Great Price*.

The Bible: The Bible is sufficient to give us truth. We aren't to add to the Bible (Revelation 22:18).We were given the truth once and for all, no other truth was to be given to the saints (Jude 3). Jesus defends the Bible, not the Mormon scriptures (John 17:17).

BORN AGAIN

Mormonism: You become born again when baptized in the Mormon church. [2]

The Bible: We become born again when we give up our sinful rebellion, receive Christ as our Savior, and thus become reconciled to God and His Word (2 Corinthians 5:17-21; 1 Peter 1:23).

KNOWLEDGE OF GOD

Mormonism: We cannot have knowledge of God without the priesthood. Because the Mormon church has the priesthood, only Mormons can know God. [3]

The Bible: The priesthood we have today (versus Old Testament times) consists of *every single* true believer in Jesus Christ. As a Group, born-again Christians are "a royal priesthood" (1 Peter 2:9). We not only have the knowledge of God, we also know His voice (John 10:14).

GOSPEL

Mormonism: The true gospel is what has been revealed to Joseph Smith.[4] It is the message of the Mormon church's ordinances, doctrines, and scriptures.[5]

The Bible: The Bible tells us that the true gospel is of Jesus Christ (Mark 1:1). It is the good news of God's grace in Christ, who gave Himself for our sins (1 Corinthians 15:1-4; Galatians 1:4). It's message is one of repentance (Luke 24:47) and that *only* through Jesus can we be saved (John 14:6; Acts 4:12; 16:30-31).

THE PRIESTHOOD

Mormonism: The Mormon church is the true church because it holds the keys to the Melchizedek and Aaronic priesthoods.[6]

The Bible: Christ brought an end to the Aaronic priesthood. He is the only High Priest, according to the "order of Melchizedek" (Hebrews 5:10). He holds the priesthood forever and doesn't need a successor (Hebrews 7:23-24).

BAPTISM

Mormonism: Baptism is valid only in the Mormon church because they have the priesthood.[7] Baptism is necessary for salvation;[8] therefore, we must baptize for the dead who were not baptized in this life.[9]

The Bible: You don't need a priest to be baptized. The apostles, John the Baptist, and Philip weren't priests, yet baptized others (John 3:22-23; 4:2; Acts 8:38). All that is necessary before baptism is to "believe with all your heart...that Jesus Christ is the Son of God" (Acts 8:37). Baptism doesn't save, only Jesus saves (John 3:15; 5:24; Acts 16:31; Hebrews 5:9).

THE FALL AND SIN

Mormonism: The fall brought physical death only,[10] not a sinful nature. We are responsible for our own sin—not that of Adam and Eve.[11]

The Bible: "Through one man sin entered into the world and death through sin" (Romans 5:12); therefore, "in Adam all die" (1 Corinthians 15:22). Because of the Fall, mankind's basic nature was affected by sin; everyone is a sinner (Romans 8:5-8).Wrath and condemnation come to all except for those who have been reconciled to God through Jesus Christ (John 14:6; Romans 5:6-11; Ephesians 2:3-5). Once reconciled, they live in the Spirit (see Romans 8:9-11). Therefore, all in Adam die, and all in Christ live (1 Corinthians 15:22).

REPENTANCE

Mormonism: The doctrine of original sin is a false doctrine.[12] We are to repent only of the sins we have committed—not an inherent, sinful nature.[13]

The Bible: The natural condition of mankind is "more deceitful than all else and is desperately sick" (Jeremiah 17:9). Jesus calls "sinners to repentance" (Luke 5:32).

SALVATION BY GRACE

Mormonism: God's grace allows everyone to be resurrected, though you can still end up in hell. You must *work* your way into heaven.[14]

The Bible: God's grace provides salvation, which is a free gift; therefore, it's impossible to use good works as a way to get into heaven (Ephesians 2:8-9).

THE TRINITY

Mormonism: The Father, the Son, and the Holy Ghost are three separate Gods.[15]

The Bible: There is only one God (1 Corinthians 8:4). In the New Testament there is clear revelation that the Father, Son, and Spirit are all God, thus a Trinity.

• The Father is God (John 6:27; Ephesians 4:6).
• Jesus is God (affirmed by the Father, Hebrews 1:8; [16] John 20:28; Col. 2:9).
• The Spirit is God (Acts 5:3-4).

THE FATHER

Mormonism: "God himself was once as we are now, and is an exalted man...the Father of us all, dwelt on an earth, the same as Jesus Christ himself did."[17] "The Father has a body of flesh and bones" (D&C 130:22). He too is a "resurrected, immortal Being."[18] He frequently came to earth to visit Adam.[19]

The Bible: The Father is not a man (Numbers 23:19).He fills "the heavens and the earth" (Jeremiah 23:24). Jesus said the Father "is spirit" (John 4:24).

THE SON

Mormonism: Jesus was "begotten of his Father."[20] He and Lucifer are spirit brothers.[21] We are co-equal with Him (D&C 88:106-107). We can become a god just like Him (D&C 132:20). "Christ alone cannot save you."[22]

The Bible: Jesus was conceived by the Holy Ghost (Matthew 1:18,20; Luke 1:34-35). Because He created everything in heaven and earth (Colossians 1:16), he could not possibly be Lucifer's brother. He is God from all eternity (Isaiah 41:4; John 1:1; 8:58; Revelation 1:8; 21:6). It's impossible for us to be co-equal with God. Jesus Himself said belief in Him *alone* brings salvation (John 3:15; 5:24; 14:6).

THE HOLY SPIRIT

Mormonism: The Holy Spirit is only an influence from the Father.[23] He's not personal, and isn't God. He is different from the Holy Ghost.[24] The Holy Ghost is only *a god*.[25]

The Bible: See 1 Corinthians 3:16 and 6:19 KJV, where "Ghost" and "Spirit" have the same meaning (the Greek word is *pneuma* [26]). Scripture clearly shows the Holy Ghost and Holy Spirit to be the same person: God.

THE VIRGIN BIRTH

Mormonism: Jesus "was begotten of his Father, as we were of our fathers."[27] "...Jesus Christ our elder brother was begotten by the Father in Heaven...He was begotten by the Father and not by the Holy Ghost."[28]

The Bible: Jesus was conceived by the Holy Spirit (Matthew 1:18, 20; Luke 1:34-35).

CHRIST'S SACRIFICE

Mormonism: "All who believe and obey his [Christ's] laws would be cleansed from sin through his blood."[29] "Through the blood of Christ" we shall be resurrected[30] (we can still go to hell or one of the three heavens). Also, Christ's blood does not atone for serious sins—"men must then have their own blood shed to atone for their sin."[31]

The Bible: Christ's death brings forgiveness (Ephesians 1:7; Hebrews 9:22; 1 Peter 1:18-19) and relieves us of judgment (Romans 8:1; Hebrews 9:26-28). Christ's death allows us to have the very righteousness of God (2 Corinthians 5:21). Christ's sacrifice removes sin and restores our relationship with God (Romans 5:1; Hebrews 2:17).

CHILDREN OF GOD

Mormonism: The desire of every Mormon is to become a heavenly son or daughter of God. In order to be a son of God, a Mormon must hold the priesthood and/or, along with the women who want to be daughters of God, must keep the commandments, the covenants, accept the ordinances of the church, and hold to the principles of the gospel (the Mormon gospel) "to the end."[32]

The Bible: All who receive Jesus have been given the right to become children of God (John 1:12). Christ came that "He might redeem those who were under the Law, that we might receive the adoption as sons. Because you are sons, God has sent forth the Spirit of His Son into our hearts, crying, 'Abba! Father!'" (Galatians 4:5-6).

PRE-EXISTENCE

Mormonism: We all pre-existed.[33] We lived in the presence of the Father, we were not like Him, and we were just spirits. We did not have bodies of flesh and bones, but He did.[34] "We sang together with the heavenly hosts for joy when the foundations of the earth were laid....We were present when Satan offered himself as a savior of the world...."[35] We are the spirit children of the Father.[36] We have a Father (Heavenly Father) and a Mother in heaven, just as we have a material father and mother on earth.[37]When found worthy, our spirits were sent to earth to receive a body.[38]

The Bible: There is no evidence that we pre-existed. The Bible says that Jesus alone pre-existed (John 8:58, see also Colossians 1:17). The Bible also tells us that in regard to human beings, the natural (meaning our body, verse 44) comes first, then the spiritual (1 Corinthians 15:46).[39]

HEAVEN

Mormonism: There are three heavens (celestial, terrestrial, telestial). While Christ governs the citizens of the terrestrial kingdom, God the Father is in the celestial kingdom. (Neither the Father or the Son are in the telestial.) Only faithful Mormons are allowed to be with the Father in the celestial. Only they will become gods (D&C 132:19-20).[40] Most of these celestial citizens will be married. They will have their earthly children with them, but they will also have "spirit babies" that will be sent to an earth over which they will be gods.

The Bible: There is only one heaven (Matthew 6:9), where the true saints will live (Philippians 3:20). All who go to heaven will be in the presence of the Father and the Son (Matthew 13:43; Revelation 21:1-6). There will be no marriage (Matthew 22:30), nor the exaltation of individual people to godhood. See Paul and Barnabas's response when people thought they were gods (Acts 14:11-15). God warns those who seek godhood (Ezekiel 28:2,6-10).

HELL

Mormonism: Hell is a temporary "spirit prison."[41] Except for the apostate who will go to "the final and eternal hell" (outer darkness),[42] everyone else can get out of hell and receive redemption only after they have paid "the full price for their wickedness."[43]

The Bible: The Bible speaks of only one hell, and no one will escape this place of torment (Luke 16:22-24). The unrighteous can't get out of hell (Matthew 23:33). Hell is eternal (Matthew 25:41, 46; Mark 9:48; Luke 16:23-26; Revelation 14:11). Jesus said of hell that the "cursed" go there (Matthew 25:41), where there is "weeping and gnashing of teeth" (Matthew 13:42), and everlasting fire and punishment (Matthew 25:41, 46).

THE TRUE CHURCH

Mormonism: The true church was destroyed, or taken away, from this earth. Men had departed from the gospel, ignoring, changing, or misapplying sacraments, ordinances, and God's authority. Men corrupted the Church, and "all their creeds were an abomination in his sight" (*Pearl of Great Price*, J.S.2:19). Therefore, a new dispensation of the gospel was necessary. To restore the gospel, Jesus (and the angel Moroni), came to Joseph Smith to re-establish the true church, here on earth, which includes the priesthood. Thus, the Mormon Church is the true "Church of Christ in its fulness" because it has the Melchizedek and Aaronic priesthood.[44]

The Bible: The true church could not have been taken from the earth because God promises that His truth will be revealed to every generation (Psalm 100:5 KJV; 1 Peter 1:24-25). The true church consists of Christ, who holds the priesthood forever (Hebrews 7:23-24). The true church consists of born-again believers who are part of "a royal priesthood" (1 Peter 2:9). The true church began the day of Pentecost (Acts 2). Since Pentecost it has been devoted to the apostles' teaching, to the breaking of bread, and to prayer (Acts 2:42), and continues to send out missionaries (Acts 13:1-14). Jesus said, *"I will build my church; and the gates of Hades will not overpower it"* (Matthew 16:18).

And there is salvation in
no one else;
for there is no other name
under heaven that has
been given among men,
by which we must be saved.

Acts 4:12

LDS PHOTO ALBUM

Church history can be so interesting and so inspiring as to be a very powerful tool indeed for building faith. If not properly written or properly taught, it may be a faith destroyer. There is a temptation for the writer or the teacher of Church history to want to tell everything, whether it is worthy or faith promoting or not. Some things that are true are not very useful. Historians seem to take great pride in publishing something new, particularly if it illustrates a weakness of a prominent historical figure. For some reason, historians and novelists seem to savor such things. If it related to a living person, it would come under the heading of gossip. History can be misleading as gossip and much more difficult often impossible to verify. That historian or scholar who delights in pointing out the weaknesses and frailties of present or past leaders destroys faith. A destroyer of faith — particularly one within the Church, and more particularly one who is employed specifically to build faith — places himself in great spiritual jeopardy. He is serving the wrong master, and unless he repents, he will not be among the faithful in the eternities.

Apostle Boyd K. Packer
"The Mantle Is Far, Far Greater Than The Intellect"
Journal: 21:3/BYU Studies, Byu.edu. Quoted from pages 5, 7

History is important. *If not manipulated,* it reveals truth. And, if we're truly seeking the truth above all else, we need not fear the results of an honest investigation.

Donna Morley

The Smith Family

Below are just a few family members

The first photo is of Joseph Smith, Jr., (December 23-1805—June 27, 1844), the Founder and first Prophet of Mormonism.

Next, is Joseph's older brother, Hyrum Smith (February 9, 1800—June 27, 1844). He was very much a part of the new religious movement and some believe he died with Joseph because of it.

The third photo is of Joseph and Hyrum's father, Joseph Smith, Sr., (July 12, 1771—September 14, 1840). From all accounts it seems Joseph was greatly influenced by his father.

It may be admitted that some of them [Smith's ancestors] believed in fortune telling, in warlocks and witches.

—B. H. Roberts
Mormon historian

Lastly, here is a picture of Joseph and Hyrum's mother, Lucy Mack Smith (July 8, 1775—May 14, 1856). She wrote the book "Biographical Sketches of Joseph Smith...."

Joseph & Moroni

The angel MORONI delivering the plates of the BOOK OF MORMON to JOSEPH SMITH jun.

Library of Congress, Washington D.C.
(June 11, 1886)

Poster says, "The angel Moroni delivering the plates of the Book of Mormon to Joseph Smith, jun." The plates, according to Moroni, were to give an account of the former inhabitants of the Americas (the supposed Jaredites, Lamanites, and Nephites), as well as the fullness of the everlasting Gospel. (Pearl of Great Price, JS, 2:33.)

At length the time arrived for obtaining the plates, the Urim and Thummim, and the breastplate. On the twenty-second day of September, one thousand eight hundred and twenty-seven, having gone as usual at the end of another year to the place where they were deposited, the same heavenly messenger delivered them up to me with this charge: that I should be responsible for them; that if I should let them go carelessly, or through any neglect of mine, I should be cut off....

Pearl of Great Price
Joseph Smith 2:59

Cumorah

HILL CUMORAH. *Photo by Hopkins, Palmyra, N. Y.*

Taken from *Cumorah Revisited.* (The Standard Publishing Co., 1910, page 2.) This book can be read at Faith and Reason Forum (.org)

The above photo is a picture of the Mormon's sacred hill called, "Cumorah" (also called Ramah. BOM. Ether 15:11). It's at this place on the west side, near the peak, that Joseph said he received the golden plates. Also on this hill, as recorded in the Book of Mormon, was a great battle (Mormon 8:2). Thousands upon thousands of people were massacred, leaving behind their swords, breastplates, chariots, coins, and more. Not one item has ever been found.

The Three Witnesses

Oliver Cowdery (1806-1850)

David Whitmer (1805-1888)

Martin Harris
(1783-1875)

An angel of God came down from heaven, and he brought and laid before our eyes, that we beheld and saw the plates.

—The Three Witnesses

**Cowdery was kicked out of the Church for a variety of reasons, including that he insinuated that Joseph Smith was guilty of adultery.

**Whitmer was accused of many things. He, therefore, left the Church, believing God wanted him to "separate" from the Latter Day Saints.

**Harris was unofficially kicked out of the church because of conflicts with Sidney Rigdon and his refusal to join the bank that Joseph Smith started—which was illegally issuing paper money.

Jesus, Joseph and Oliver

The Youthful Prophet, Joseph Smith, Jr., and Oliver Cowdery, Receiving the Aaronic Priesthood under the hands of John the Baptist, May 15, 1829.

"Upon you my fellow servants, in the name of Messiah I confer the Priesthood of Aaron, which holds the keys of the ministering of angels, and of the gospel of repentance, and of baptism by immersion for the remission of sins; and this shall never be taken from the earth, until the sons of Levi do offer again an offering unto the Lord in righteousness."
—John the Baptist
D&C 13:1

Library of Congress, Washington, D.C.

Poster says, "The youthful prophet, Joseph Smith, Jr., and Oliver Cowdery, receiving the Aaronic priesthood under the hands of John the Baptist, May 15, 1829." Mormons firmly believe that the Mormon church is the one and only true church because of the restoration of the priesthood. For those who want to understand the true development of the Mormon priesthood, read: From Cumorah to the Celestial Kingdom.

The First Mormon Temples

Joseph Smith's Original Temple, Nauvoo, Ills.

The week after the dedication, Joseph Smith and Oliver Cowdery received the following visions, at the pulpit: First Jesus appeared to them, then Moses, then Elisas, and then Elijah (D&C 110:1-13).

-Kirtland Temple: Utah State Historical Society, all rights reserved. --Nauvoo Temple. The Library of Congress.

**The first picture, to the left, is the Kirtland Temple (Kirtland, Ohio). On April 3ᵈ, 1836, the week after the temple's dedication, Joseph Smith and Oliver Cowdery received some visions (read the left corner, below). On the day of the Dedication (March 27, 1836), "very many became drunk. Jo Smith and Hyrum vomited in the pulpit, others vomited in the pews. The Mormon leaders would stand up to prophesy and were so drunk they said they could not get it out, and would call for another drink. Over a barrel of liquor was used at the service" (Affidavit signed by Eliza Morley, wife of Mormon leader, Alfred Morley; another affidavit was given by Mormon, Isaac Aldrich, testifying of this same occurrence.)

**The second temple is in Nauvoo, Illinois, also built under the direction of Joseph. Despite Smith having this temple built, he married the pregnant (8 months) Mrs. Mary Lightner at the Nauvoo Masonic Hall.

Orrin Porter Rockwell

June 25 or 28, 1813 – June 9, 1878

Used by permission, Utah State Historical Society all rights reserved. (Picture, circa 1865-1870)

Mormon Orrin Porter Rockwell was a great asset to Joseph Smith and then (after Smith's death) to Brigham Young, serving as their body guard. Rockwell was one of the leaders of the Danite group (pgs. 28-30), and was known as the Destroying Angel of Mormondom. He spent eight months in jail for the attempt murder of Missouri Governor Lilburn Boggs. He had been suspected of successfully killing many others (some speculate up to 100). Rockwell died of natural causes while awaiting trial for the murder of John and William Aiken.

Porter Rockwell was yesterday afternoon ushered into Heaven clothed with immortality and eternal life, and crowned with all glory which belongs to a departed saint. He has his little faults but Porter's life on earth, taken altogether, was one worthy of example, and reflected honor upon the church. Through all his trials he had never once forgotten his obligations to his brethren and his God.

They say he was a murderer; if he was he was the friend of Joseph Smith and Brigham Young, and he was faithful to them, and to his covenants, and he has gone to Heaven and apostates can go to Hell…

—Joseph F. Smith.
Sixth president and prophet
Spoken at Rockwell's funeral
Salt Lake Tribune
June 13 (p. 4), and 18 (p. 3),
1878

Death of Porter Rockwell
A "Tribute" From the Salt Lake Tribune

Porter Rockwell is another of the long list of Mormon criminals whose deeds of treachery and blood have reddened the soil of Utah, and who have paid no forfeit to offended law. When he was commissioned by the Prophet Joseph Smith, avenger-in-chief for the Lord, the Latter-day Saints were having a troublous life on the border, and it was give and take between the elect and their unconverted enemies. Wherever the former settled, they stirred up strife with their neighbors, until they became so generally hated that they were compelled to seek a home in the inaccessible wilderness in order to get away from the human race.

Arrived in this Territory with the savage Indian only to dispute possession with them, and escape from these rocky fastnesses almost an impossibility, the fanatical hate of inspired leaders of the Church suffered no restraint, and the avenging angels were made bloody instruments of these holy men's will. Porter Rockwell was chosen as a fitting agent to lead in these scenes of blood. Brutal in his instincts, lawless in his habits, and a fanatical devotee of the Prophet, the commands of this gloomy despot he received as the will of the Lord, and with the ferocity born of mistaken zeal, he grew to believe that the most acceptable service he could render the Almighty, was as Lear expresses it, to "kill, kill, kill, kill, kill." He killed unsuspecting travelers, whose booty was coveted by his prophet-master. He killed fellow Saints who held secrets that menaced the safety of their fellow criminals in the priesthood. He killed Apostates who dared to wag their tongues about the wrongs they had endured. And he killed sojourners in Zion merely to keep his hand in.

When the railroad was opened to Utah and the officers began to make their weight felt, murder was no longer practiced as a fine art, and those who had followed the profession sought other avenues of usefulness.

The Danite Rockwell retired from the avenging business, and for some years past has been extensively engaged in raising horses and cattle. But the recollection of his evil deeds haunted him, and conscience preyed upon his soul like the undying worm. To gain escape from this fiery torment he sought the intoxicating bowl, and whenever he appeared in the streets of Salt Lake, it was generally in the character of a vociferating maniac. He died in time to escape the hand of the law. Being indicted in the First District for participation in the Askin murder, District Attorney Van Zile was gathering together evidence which must have convicted him of the crime charged, and brought him to the same fate as was visited upon the 'butcher Lee.'

Death steps in to save these destroyers of their race from the penalty they so richly deserve, but their evil deeds live after them....

(*Salt Lake Tribune*, June 11, 1878, page 2).

The Anti-Banking Company

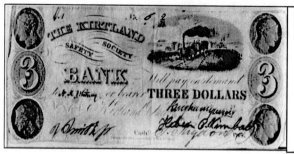

…the Kirtland Safety Society shall become the greatest of all institutions on earth.

...the Kirtland Safety Society shall become the greatest of all institutions on earth.

Part of Wilford Woodruff's Prayer taken from his personal journal January 6, 1837.

The above $3.00 bill, and other currency, was created by Joseph Smith for his new illegally organized bank called, Kirtland Safety Society—later renamed, the "Anti-Banking Company" (Nov. 2, 1836). Two years before Joseph started the bank, he said he received the following revelation from the Lord (April 23, 1834): And again, verily I say unto you, concerning your debts—behold it is my will that you shall pay all your debts....I will soften the hearts of those to whom you are in debt, until I shall send means unto you for your deliverance....I give unto you a promise that you shall be delivered this once out of your bondage. (D&C 104:78, 80, 83).

Although there was a boost in the economy when the Kirtland Temple was built, it was very temporary. A little over two years had passed since the revelation and the people had not, as of yet, been "delivered," nor did their creditors have "softened hearts." It's uncertain if the Mormons were thinking of the above revelation when Smith's bank started. Perhaps it was in the back of their minds—after all, it was a revelation. Therefore, could the bank be their deliverance, especially for those who wanted to invest in it? Possibly. Unfortunately, the bank failed and quite a few lost their money. As a result, many left Mormonism questioning if Smith was truly a prophet. Smith wasn't delivered himself. He, too, was in debt. He left Kirtland, for awhile, trying to avoid the many lawsuits against him. (Photo, used by permission, Utah State Historical Society, all rights reserved.)

SUPER HANC PETRAM ÆDIFICABO.

FOR PRESIDENT,
GEN. JOSEPH SMITH,
OF NAUVOO, ILLINOIS.
FOR VICE PRESIDENT,
SIDNEY RIGDON,
OF PENNSYLVANIA.

License: unknown; presumably, in the Public Domain; Source: Mormonhaven.com/jspress. jpg; realmormonhistory.com; timelines.com

Mitt Romney wasn't the first Mormon to run for President of the United States. Smith was the first, in 1844. You might be puzzled about the title, "General," on the poster. Simply put, Joseph had formed a Nauvoo Legion and, as the head of it, he became Lieutenant-General. To the right is a picture of Sidney Rigdon. He assisted Joseph in The Anti-Banking Company.

I would not have suffered my name to have been used by my friends on anywise as President of the United States, or candidate for that office, if I and my friends could have had the privilege of enjoying our religious and civil rights as American citizens, even those rights which the Constitution guarantees unto all her citizens alike. But this as a people we have been denied from the beginning. Persecution has rolled upon our heads from time to time, from portions of the United States, like peals of thunder, because of our religion; and no portion of this Government as yet has stepped forward for our relief. And in view of these things, I feel it to be my right and privilege to obtain what influence and power I can, lawfully, in the United States, for the protection of injured innocence" –

Joseph Smith, Jr.,
History of the Church, 6:210-11.

Sidney Rigdon

Liberty & Carthage Jail

Let thine anger be kindled against our enemies; and, in the fury of thine heart, with thy sword avenge us of our wrongs. (D&C 121:5)

—Joseph Smith wrote the above while in Liberty Jail

The above photo is Liberty Jail in Liberty, Missouri. While in the Liberty prison, for treason (winter 1838-39), the prophet, Joseph Smith, directed the operation of the Church. It was from here that Joseph wrote information to his followers that is now in Doctrine and Covenants 121, 122, and 123.

They were innocent of any crime, as they had often been proved before, and were only confined in jail by the conspiracy of traitors and wicked men; and their *innocent blood* on the floor of Carthage jail is a broad seal affixed to "Mormonism" that cannot be rejected by any court on earth....
(D&C 135:3)

The above Carthage jail (in Illinois) is where Joseph and Hyrum Smith were assassinated by an angry mob.

A Depiction of Joseph's Assassination

ASSASSINATION OF JOSEPH SMITH

When Joseph went to Carthage to deliver himself up to the pretended requirements of the law, two or three days to his assassination, he he said, I am going like a lamb to the slaughter; but I am calm as the summer's morning; I have a conscience void of offense towards God, and towards all men. I shall die innocent, and it shall yet be said of me—He was murdered in cold cold blood."

(D&C 135:4)

While Joseph and Hyrum were in the two-story Carthage jail, some friends smuggled in a six-shooter for Joseph and a single-barrel pistol for Hyrum. It turned out the prisoners would need their guns... an angry mob of 100 to 200 men broke into the jail and began to randomly shoot their pistols. Joseph and his brother naturally got in on the act and started shooting as well. Bullets were flying everywhere. and while Hyrum was shot dead. Joseph continued to fight. He eventually made an attempt to escape by jumping out of the second-story window—it didn't end well for him.

The Widow—Emma Hale Smith
July 10. 1804 – April 30. 1879

And let mine handmaid, Emma Smith, *receive all those that have been given unto my servant Joseph, and who are virtuous and pure before me; and those who are not pure, and have said they were pure, shall be destroyed, saith the Lord....*And I command mine handmaid, Emma Smith, to abide and cleave unto my servant Joseph, and to none else. *But if she will not abide this commandment, she shall be destroyed, saith the Lord thy God, and will destroy her if she abide not in my law.* But if she will abide this commandment, then shall my servant Joseph do all things for her....

(D&C 132:52, 54-55)

(c 1845)

The above photo is of Emma Smith—Joseph Smith's first wife. At the time the picture was taken, it had been a few months after Joseph's death (June. 1844), and the birth of David Hyrum Smith (shown in the photo). Three years later. she married non-Mormon Lewis Bidamon on Joseph's birthday. (1847). Emma never went back to the LDS church when Brigham Young took over. Emma. and others, believed Joseph wanted his son, Joseph III, to be his successor. Thus the first split of the Mormon Church. In 1860, a new church was formed with Joseph III, as prophet. In 1872 the church officially called itself. The Reorganized Church (now the Community of Christ).

Brigham Young

June 1, 1801 – August 29, 1877

As formerly, I presented myself before you this morning in the capacity Providence has lead me to occupy, acknowledged and sustained by you as the dictator, counsellor, advisor of the people of God.

—Brigham Young
Journal of Discourses
9:267, April 6, 1862

(c 1850)

Brigham Young was the second prophet/president of the Mormon Church. He espoused Joseph Smith's doctrines (such as polygamy, plural gods, saving the dead, and becoming a god, yourself) and brought a few doctrines of his own into the Church (such as the Adam-God and Blood Atonement doctrine). A closer look at Young's (and Smith's) doctrines are in the book, *From Cumorah to the Celestial Kingdom: Mormonism's Changing View of Salvation.*

Library of Congress

"The Mormon pioneers advanced company coming over Little Mountain July 1847"

Library of Congress

"Mormon pioneers about to enter Salt Lake Valley. July 24, 1847."

The Word and Will of the Lord, given through President Brigham Young:

Let all the people of the Church of Jesus Christ of Latter-day Saints, and those who journey with them, be organized into companies, with a covenant and promise to keep all the commandments and statutes of the Lord our God.

Let the companies be organized with captains of hundreds, captains of fifties, and captains of tens, with a president and his two counselors at their head, under the direction of the Twelve Apostles.

(D&C 136:2-3)
Jan. 14, 1847

John Doyle Lee

September 12. 1812 – March 23. 1877

Will my death satisfy the nation for all the crimes committed by Mormons, at the command of the Priesthood, who have used and now have deserted me? Time will tell. I believe in a just God, and I know the day will come when others must answer for their acts, as I have had to do.

—John D. Lee
Last Confession and Statement of John D. Lee

Bishop John D. Lee embraced Mormonism after reading the BOM. particularly Moroni 10:4 (refers to asking God if BOM is true). He was influenced by Smith's polygamy doctrine. and ended up having 15 wives. He became Brigham Young's personal assistant (and "adopted son"). He is best known for having been involved in the Mountain Meadows Massacre. which occurred during the first week of September. 1857. The Fancher-Baker emigrant party (120 people) were traveling by a wagon train from Arkansas to California. When they took a break at Mountain Meadows. the people were murdered (not all at once—between the dates of September 7th to the 11th—although most of them were murdered on the 11th). 17 young children were spared (a few of them came close to being killed. like the older children. but were shown mercy).

John D. Lee on Execution Day

The day is March 23, 1877, and Lee's execution is just minutes away. The location is at Mountain Meadows, (originally called, Utah Territory—today, it's Washington County, Utah) where the massacre occurred.

Here is a close up shot of the larger picture. We can see John D. Lee sitting on his coffin awaiting his execution. He had just given his last speech, and had received spiritual advice from Methodist preacher.

Reverend George Stokes. He looked quite calm. sitting on his casket, didn't he? Despite Lee's apparent sense of calm he had just, minutes before, displayed tormenting emotions while giving his speech. Below is a newspaper write-up, from the Bethlehem Daily News, summing up his statement to the crowd:

Lee made a speech denouncing Brigham Young declaring himself a scapegoat for the sins of others, denying that he was guilty of bloodshed, and asserting that he went to the meadows in the interests of mercy. About 75 persons, including the United States Marshal and a guard of soldiers were present. Lee has left a very long confession, giving an account of the massacre, in which he states that he tried to prevent it, and lays the guilt upon Brigham Young, Higbee, Dame, and other Mormon leaders, who, according to his statement were guilty of the vilest hypocrisy, as well as the most atrocious treachery and cruelty. (Taken from the Bethlehem Daily News, March 24, 1877, front page).

Let's keep in mind, the above is simply a reporter's own summary of what Lee said. If you would like to read Lee's exact words go to the Mormon section of Faith and Reason Forum (.org). There you will find his lengthy account of the facts, as he saw them. It's titled, "Last Confession and Statement Of John D. Lee."

For further reading, at the same Faith and Reason Forum website, read "Mountain Meadow Massacre" by Brevet Major J.H. Carleton. (May 25, 1859). Carleton's paper was the first official federal report on the massacre.

The Polygamy Problem

Cartoonist Frank Leslie posed his own solution to the polygamy problem, in his cartoon: "The Mormon Problem Solved."

Showing President Grant the multitude of children and wives, Brigham Young asks Grant, *"I must submit to your laws - but what shall I do with these?"*

Grant replies: *"Do as I do - give them offices."*

When the polygamy problem became a national discussion many cartoonists expressed their own opinions and concerns. The majority of society couldn't understand polygamy, or believe it was truly from God. Despite the Anti-polygamy bills that were passed in Congress (in 1862 and another in 1882. after Young died) many Mormons still continued on with polygamy. It wasn't until Utah was confronted with the decision to become part of the Union that the Mormon church received a new revelation from God (in 1890). This time—to stop polygamy.

> ### *The Empty Pillow :*
> ### In Memoriam Brigham Young
> "And the place which knew him once shall know him no more"
>
> Sept, 1877.

A Few Words From Brigham Young

Brigham Young (at the age of 56): "Do you think I am an old man? *I could prove to this congregation that I am young; for I could find more girls who would choose me for a husband than can any of the young men.*" (*Journal of* Discourses, 5:210, September 6, 1857)

Brigham Young: (age of 59): "Brother Cannon remarked that people wondered how many wives and children I had. He may inform them that *I shall have wives and children by the million, and glory, and riches, and power, and dominion, and kingdom after kingdom, and reign triumphantly.*" (JD 8:178-179, September 9, 1860)

Brigham Young (age 65): "I heard the revelation on polygamy, and I believed it with all my heart, and I know it is from God - I know that he revealed it from heaven; I know that it is true, and understand the bearings of it and why it is. *"Do you think that we shall ever be admitted as a State into the Union without denying the principle of polygamy?" If we are not admitted until then, we shall never be admitted.*" (JD 11:269, Aug 19, 1866; also see JD 13:166)

A Few (of the many) Promoters of Polygamy

Young & Pratt:
Library of Congress.
Kimball & Wilford:
Permission, Utah
State Historical Society

***The first picture is of Brigham Young in his mid-sixties (c 1866). He ignored the law as it pertained to polygamy. In old age he was still marrying more women, several of them in their early 20's. He married his last wife the year of his death (age 76), making the total to be 53 wives and 55 children.

***Next, Apostle Heber C. Kimball, (1801 – 1868) out of his loyalty to Joseph Smith, gave his fourteen year old daughter Helen, as a plural wife, to Joseph (instead of his wife as Joseph requested).

***The third picture (circa 1857) is of Parley Pratt (1807-1857). Parley was murdered at the hands of an enraged husband after Parley took his children and married his wife (making her Parley's 12th wife). Some historians believe that Parley's murder was the catalyst that precipitated the Mountain Meadows Massacre (the area Parley was murdered).

***Lastly, is fourth prophet/president Wilford Woodruff (1807 – 1898). He is best known for writing the 1890 "Official Declaration Manifesto" with the purpose of stopping polygamy in the Mormon church. Woodruff had five wives (possibly six, after the manifesto was written) and thirty-three children.

Ann Eliza Young 1844 – 1925

Ann Eliza Young was Brigham's 49th wife. She wrote the book:

Wife No. 19 or The Story of a Life in Bondage, Being a Complete Expose' of Mormonism and Revealing the Sorrows, Sacrifices and Sufferings of Women in Polygamy.

The title of her book. indicates she was the nineteenth living wife. at the time of her writing the book.

You can read Ann's book at Faith and Reason Forum.org.

"0, mother, I can't, I can't," I cried in a sudden agony, as the thought of all such a marriage involved, rushed across me. ...."

"Why, I belong to you, father. Tell him so, and that you can't give me away to anybody."

My father smiled a little at me, grew grave again, and went away. He told Brigham how averse I was; and he only laughed, and said I should get over it, if I only had time. He would not give me up, but he would not hasten matters; he would leave me in my parents' hands, and he hoped they would induce me to listen favorably to his proposals. The last remark was made with a peculiar emphasis and a sinister smile, which every Saint who had had dealings with him knew very well, and whose meaning they also knew. It meant. "Do as I command you, or suffer the weight of my displeasure." He sent a message to me, which, though seemingly kind, contained a covert threat; and I began to feel the chains tightening around me already. I felt sure that I could not free myself, but I would struggle to the end. Thus began a year of anguish and torture. I fought against my fate in every possible way. Brigham was equally persistent, and he tried in every way to win me, a willing bride, before he attempted to coerce me....Finding that this declaration of affection failed to move me, he tried another tack. He asked my father if a house and a thousand dollars a year would make me comfortable, as he wished to settle something on me when I married him, taking for granted that I should do so. ....Brigham was our spiritual guide; it might be that in refusing him I should lose all hopes of future salvation. That was my mother's plea. My father's was, that Brigham was able to hurt him pecuniarily [meaning, financially]. And then came my oldest brother, who added...Brigham had it in his power to ruin him....

—Ann Eliza Young

Brigham's Favorite Wife

Permission. Utah State Historical Society

Amelia Folsom (given name: Harriet Amelia Folsom) was considered by many, as Young's favorite wife. She was born in 1838, and was wife # 47 when she married in 1863 (6 months after the Anti-Polygamy law was passed). Amelia was 24 yrs old while Brigham was 62. They never had any children. Young had a home built just for Amelia (not to be shared with the other wives).
Oh my...to be a fly on the wall when the other wives heard about that!

THE favorite wife of the Prophet [Brigham Young], Amelia Folsom, is a woman about forty years of age, [at the time of Young writing this account in her book] and was a New England girl.....

He [Young] was a most arduous and enthusiastic lover, and during all the time that his suit [pursuit of Amelia] was in progress, his carnage might be seen standing before the door of her parents' house several hours at a time every day. He evidently did not intend that absence should render her forgetful of him. He promised her anything that she might desire, and also agreed to do everything to advance the family interests. Promises had no weight with her. He then had recourse to "Revelation;" he had been specially told from heaven that she was created especially for him, and if she married anyone else she would be for ever damned.

The poor girl begged, pleaded, protested, and shed most bitter tears, but all to no purpose. His mind was made up, and he would not allow his will to be crossed. She had been converted to believe in special revelation, and to look upon Brigham as the savior of all the Mormon people, and to think that disobedience to him was disobedience to God, since God's commands came through him. In answer to her pleading, he said, "Amelia, you must be my wife; God has revealed it to me. You cannot be saved by anyone else. If you marry me, I will save you, and exalt you to be a queen in the celestial world; but if you refuse, you will be destroyed, both soul and body. This is the same argument he used to win me, and the one he has always in reserve, as the last resort, when everything else fails to secure his victim.   —Ann Eliza Young

Amelia's Palace: The Gardo House

She [Amelia] accompanies him to the theatre, and occupies the box, while the rest of the wives sit in the parquet....She has a beautiful new house, elegantly furnished, and Brigham has very nearly deserted the "Bee-Hive," [the home where the other wives live] except during business hours, and spends most of his time at Amelia's residence.

–Ann Eliza Young

This house was officially called the Gardo House, and unofficially everyone called it "Amelia's Palace." It was named "Gardo" because the house towered above all the other neighboring houses. Located on the southwest corner of South Temple and State Street, in Utah, it was demolished in 1927 (present site of Zion's Bank). Young thought that the house could be used as a Governor's Mansion, when he would entertain state functions and visiting notables. He wanted only Amelia to live in the home and be his hostess whenever guests arrived. Yet, Young's dreams for himself and Amelia didn't come to full fruition. He died before the house was entirely complete and Amelia only spent a few years in the house, if that. John Taylor (see the "Reward" sign, following page), moved into the house on January 2, 1882 when he became the Mormon President. He would use it, for awhile, as a hiding place when authorities were looking to arrest him for polygamy (his son lied to authorities, otherwise he would have been found in the room he was hiding in). Taylor died elsewhere before getting caught. In 1900 the house was purchased by Col. Edwin F. Holmes. Mrs. Holmes entertained elaborately and the fame of the house spread far and wide. It was used by the Red Cross during the First World War.

$800 Reward:
John Taylor and George Q. Cannon

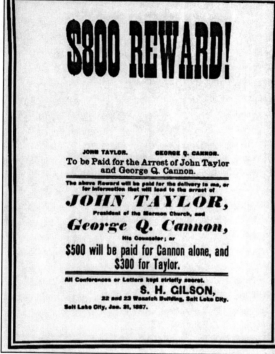

$800 REWARD!

JOHN TAYLOR.   GEORGE Q. CANNON.

To be Paid for the Arrest of John Taylor and George Q. Cannon.

The above Reward will be paid for the delivery to me, or for information that will lead to the arrest of

JOHN TAYLOR,

President of the Mormon Church, and

George Q. Cannon,

His Counselor; or

$500 will be paid for Cannon alone, and $300 for Taylor.

All Conferences or Letters kept strictly secret.

S. H. GILSON,

22 and 23 Wasatch Building, Salt Lake City.

Salt Lake City, Jan. 31, 1887.

Permission, J. Willard Marriott Library, The University of Utah

Thus saith the Lord...I have not revoked this law [plural wives doctrine] nor will I for it is everlasting & those who will enter into my glory must obey the conditions thereof, even so Amen.

—John Taylor
3rd Prophet & President

Now, I want to say for myself personally, if I had not obeyed that command of God, concerning plural marriage, I believe that I would have been damned.

—George Q. Cannon
Counselor

On January 31, 1887, authorities were looking for Mormon president John Taylor and Church counselor, George Cannon, on polygamy charges. Because both men were in hiding, Cannon was unable to see his 30th child after his birth, nor was he around for another child soon to be born by another wife. Wanted: $300 for Taylor and $500 for Cannon. Why the higher price for Cannon? There was a public perception that with Brigham Young dead, Cannon became the brains behind the Mormon organization. He was the church's chief political strategist, labeled by the press as the "Mormon premier," and the Mormon Richelieu (Richelieu was a French clergyman); and he was a five-time congressional delegate representing Utah, and yet, still disobeying the law.

George Quayle Cannon (1827-1901)

Cannon is in stripes, holding a bouquet of flowers (seated at the second row, center, bright white beard). Officials caught him on a train heading out of Utah. He and many other Mormon men (not just those pictured) were assigned to the Utah State Penitentiary for having gone against "The Edmunds Anti-Polygamy Act of 1882." These men proudly called themselves the "Prisoners of Conscience."

"It is a fact worthy of note that the shortest lived nations of which we have record have been monogamic. *Rome...was a monogamic nation and the numerous evils attending that system early laid the foundation for that ruin which eventually overtook her.*" (JD 13:202, October 9, 1869)

Cannon (to the right) in his early 30's.

The Reed Smoot Case 1904

Library of Congress. Washington, D.C.
Originally in Frank Leslie's Illustrated Newspaper (March 17, 1904), 245.

The inscription below the drawing reads:

Shall Reed Smoot, a Mormon, hold a seat in the United States Senate? President Smith [Joseph F. Smith], of the Mormon Church, at the Senate Committee's hearing in the case of Reed Smoot, boldly confessing the practice of polygamy by himself and associates.

The U.S. Senate's Committee on Privileges and Elections is discussed on page 86. Joseph F. Smith (depicted in the above drawing) is pictured on the following page with his family.

Library of Congress

The picture to the left was taken between 1918–1920. It's of new Church president Heber J. Grant (left, 1856-1945) and Reed Smoot (1862-1941). Grant was one of the last LDS presidents to practice plural marriage. Grant's father was Jedediah M. Grant, who preached that Jesus Christ believed in the plurality of wives doctrine (Journal of Discourses 1:346).

Joseph F. Smith & Family

(1901)

This photo shows the sixth Mormon president/prophet Joseph F. Smith (1838-1918). He's situated at the center of the second row, wearing a long white beard. He's with his 6 wives and forty-eight children. One of his many sons, is the well-known Mormon leader Joseph Fielding Smith, (1876-1972). He's at the top row, center—a straight line up from his father. He would become the church's tenth president/prophet.

Elderly Joseph F. Smith wrote the book, _Gospel Doctrine_. Joseph Fielding Smith (the son) wrote the book, _Doctrines of Salvation_. Both books are treasured by Mormons.

Salt Lake City Temple

Library of Congress (1896)

The above Temple is 385,000 square feet. Clearly, there are many rooms. One of the rooms is the Ordinance room. This is where the Endowment is administered.

Other rooms are: the Sealing room; the Creation room (represents the Creation story); the Garden room (represents the Garden of Eden, prior to the Fall); and the World room (represents the world after the Fall). There is also the Terrestial room; and the Celestial room—that represents the Celestial Kingdom of God.

There is one extra room in the SLC Temple that no other Mormon temple has. It's called the Holy of Holies. In this room the Church's

President—acting as the presiding High Priest of the church—performs as High Priest of Israel in direct relationship to God.

Mormon temples are what link the Mormon to godhood. For obvious reasons, then, every worthy Mormon wants a "Temple Recommend" to enter the temple.

To get a Temple Recommend Mormon candidates are asked several questions, such as on morality (making sure they are not involved in adultery or fornication); if they are keeping the Word of Wisdom (not drinking coffee, tea, liquor, or taking tobacco); if they are a tithe-payer (Mormons can be kicked out of the Church for not paying their tithes); if they "attend their sacrament, priesthood, and other meetings; and obey the rules, laws, and commandments of the gospel."

Mormons must also have a clear testimony of the restored gospel; acknowledge that the President of the Church is the prophet, seer, and revelator and recognize him as the "only person on earth able to exercise priesthood keys." They must also agree to sustain other leaders such as General Authorities and local authorities of the Church.

Also, they are asked if their family relations are in harmony. This ensures they are worthy to enter the temple and participate in temple ordinances.

Lastly, Mormons are asked the following question—which may help us understand why they can't have a close relationship with us, even if we're a non-Mormon family member:

Do you affiliate with any group or individual whose teachings or practices are contrary to or oppose those accepted by The Church of Jesus Christ of Latter-day Saints, or do you sympathize with the precepts of any such group or individual?

Mormons use to be asked if they wear their "authorized garments both day and night." It's only speculation, but perhaps the question is no longer asked because it's just assumed they wear their garments. Or, perhaps it was too much of an embarrassing question for some people— especially for women. What woman wants to be asked by a man, not to mention a church leader, if she's wearing her underwear?

The Celestial Room (SLC Temple)

Library of Congress (1912)

Today, Mormons will tell you that the Celestial Room is one way to depict the Mormon heaven, not so much in decoration, but as a reminder of what's ahead: peace, tranquility, and rest. Yet, it's more than that. The Celestial Room has its past in Joseph Smith's polygamy doctrine. It was created to reinforce the doctrine that the Mormon men will be with all their polygamous wives in the Mormon heaven (the Celestial Kingdom). While the Mormon church is no longer involved in polygamy, there are some Mormon men who are sealed to more than one woman for all eternity. Regardless, one wife or more, the Mormon men impregnate their wife (wives) throughout eternity. The babies the women give birth to are "spirit babies." The babies await a body that will be supplied by a woman, not on this earth, but on the earth ruled by the Mormon man and woman, as god and goddess. (D&C 132:19-20; JD 3:26; 1:62-63).

Several approaches to eternal marriage may be made: Two living persons may be sealed to each other for time and eternity. A living man may be sealed for eternity to a dead woman; or a living woman to a dead man. Two dead persons may be sealed to each other. It is also possible, though the church does not now permit it, to seal two living people for eternity only, with no association on earth... Further, under divine command to the Prophet Joseph Smith, it was possible for one man to be sealed to more than one woman for time and for eternity. Thus, came plural marriage among the Latter-day Saints.

—Apostle John Widtsoe *Evidences and Reconciliations,* p. 340.

Notes

Note to the reader: Quotes excerpted from the *Journal of Discourses* (1854-1886) were taken from the *LDS Historical Library CD ROM*, 2nd ed. (Salt Lake City, UT: Infobases International Incorporated, 3/24/93). Some additional references are excerpted from the *Gospel Infobase Library CD ROM*, which is cited in the notes.

Part One—What Is Mormonism All About?
1. Joseph Fielding Smith, *Doctrines of Salvation* (Salt Lake City, UT: Bookcraft, 1954), 1:188.

Chapter 1—Who Was Joseph Smith?
1. Lucy Mack Smith, *Joseph Smith's History by His Mother*, photomechanical reprint of the original 1853 edition. Original title *Biographical Sketches or Joseph Smith the Prophet, and His Progenitors for Many Generations* (Salt Lake City, UT: Utah Lighthouse Ministry), 60.
2. Ibid., 65.
3. Pomeroy Tucker, *Origin, Rise, and Progress of Mormonism* (New York: D. Appleton, 1867), 12-18, cited in Robert D. Anderson, *Inside the Mind of Joseph Smith* (Salt Lake City, UT: Signature Books, 1999), 55.
4. Henry and Elizabeth Stommel, "The Year Without a Summer," *Scientific American* 240 (June 1979), 176-86; quoted in Dan Vogel, *Lucy Smith History* (Salt Lake City, UT: Signature Books), 269-70.
5. Lucy Mack Smith, 87-90. Mormon historian B.H. Roberts said that Alvin didn't die of bilious colic, which he was stricken with, but an overdose of calomel, which lodged in the upper intestines, gangrened, and produced death. Cited in B.H. Roberts, *A Comprehensive History of the Church of Jesus Christ of Latter-day Saints* (Provo, UT: Brigham Young University, 1965; Church of Jesus Christ of Latter-day Saints, 1957), 1:32. (Hereafter shall be referred to as *A Comprehensive History of the Church*).
6. Ibid., 90.
7. Fawn M. Brodie, *No Man Knows My History* (New York: Alfred A. Knopf, Inc., 1945, 1971), 1
8. Robert N. Hullinger, *Joseph Smith's Response to Skepticism* (SLC, UT: Signature Books, 1992), 167.
9. D. Michael Quinn, *Early Mormonism and the Magic World View* (Salt Lake City, UT: Signature Books, 1998), 31.
10. *A Comprehensive History of the Church*, 1:26.
11. Ronald Vern Jackson and Gary Ronald Teeples, eds., *New York 1830 Index* (Bountiful, UT: Accelerated Indexing Systems, 1977), 397; Fayette Lapham, "Interview with the Father of Joseph Smith, the Mormon Prophet, Forty Years Ago: His Account of the Finding of the Secret Plates," *World View Historical Magazine* (May 1870): 306 (for quote); in Quinn, *Early Mormonism and the Magic,* 31. Quinn adds that Joseph Smith, Jr. expressed his belief in witches while he was the LDS church president.
12. Anderson, 55.
13. Ibid., 21, 27.
14. Dan Vogel, ed., *Early Mormon Documents* (Salt Lake City, UT: Signature Books, 1996), 1:652; Vermont Supreme Court Records, 1807 (IV.C.5, Joel K. Noble to Jonathan B. Turner, 8 Mar. 1842, 1).
15. Lucy Mack Smith, 37.
16. Statement made by Anna Ruth Eaton, May 27, 1881, Buffalo, New York at the Union Home missionary meeting, also in Anna Ruth Eaton's *The Origin of Mormonism* (New York: Woman's Executive Committee of Home Missions, 1881), 4; quoted in Vogel, *Early Mormon Documents* (Salt Lake City, UT: Signature Books, 2000), 3:147.
17. Brodie, 5.
18. E.D.Howe (contemporary of Smith's), *Mormonism Unveiled* (Zanesville, OH: printed and published by the author, 1834), 261; a photomechanical reprint (Salt Lake City, UT: Utah Lighthouse Ministry). **Note to reader:** E.D. Howe's book *Mormonism Unveiled* is quite controversial in Mormon circles. It contains negative testimonials about the Smith family and those associated with the Smiths. The affidavits were collected by D.P. Hurlbut and others. Mormon writer Richard Lloyd Anderson (professor of history and religion at Brigham Young University) wrote in his article, "Joseph Smith's New York Reputation Reappraised" (*Brigham Young University Studies*, 10, Spring 1970) that we can't take "at full value the statement of a contemporary" without looking at issues such as: "1) Verification of person...2) Accuracy of reporting...Opportunity for observation.... 4) Bias of the source...." (p. 284). Anderson also explained that "Hurlbut heavily influenced the individual statements.... His language evidently appears in two community affidavits.... When Hurlbut appeared in the Manchester schoolhouse, he undoubtedly had penned the statement that eleven rather nonliterary farmers signed. One would envision the same procedure as inevitable for the fifty-one signers from Palmyra. *Someone authored the general statements, and Hurlbut is the best candidate*" (p. 286, emphasis added).

In response to Richard Anderson's article as well as a book by Hugh Nibley (*The Myth Makers*) that discredit the Smith family neighbors and their affidavits, Roger I. Anderson (not to be confused with Richard Anderson) wrote the book *Joseph Smith's New York Reputation Reexamined* (Salt Lake City, UT: Signature Books, 1990). Roger Anderson said of Richard Anderson's article, "Superior as it is to Nibley's analysis in method and scholarly apparatus, Anderson's article still falls short on several counts. Its errors may be summarized under three main headings: misrepresentation of the contents and circumstances surrounding the compilation of the affidavits; failure to consider alternative interpretations for the evidence; and invalid conclusions based on faulty premises. In Anderson's analysis these errors recur regularly and sometimes flagrantly" (pp. 27-28). Roger Anderson defends what Richard Anderson debunks by explaining: "Hurlbut's witnesses may not have left history 'of the purest ray serene,' but there can be no doubt that these reports, in early twentieth-century German historian Eduard Meyer's words, 'give us the general opinion of his [Smith's] neighbors in their true, essential form' (p. 7). Roger Anderson gives several points in his conclusion, one of which is: "I can find no evidence that the primary source affidavits and other documents collected by Philastus Hurlbut, Eber D. Howe and Arthur B. Deming are other than what they purported to be. The men and women whose names they bear either wrote them or authorized them to be written. Ghost-writing may have colored some of the testimony, but there is no evidence that the vast majority of testators did not write or dictate their own statements or share the attitudes attributed to them (p. 113, emphasis added). The rest of Roger Anderson's concluding remarks can be found on pages 113-116. Anderson's book not only discusses the reliability of the Hurlbut, Deming, Kelly, and Howe affidavits, but also provides the actual affidavits, statements, and interviews; as well as recollections of Lucy Mack Smith and William Smith.

19. Wesley P. Walters, *Joseph Smith's Bainbridge, N.Y. Court Trials* (Salt Lake City, UT: Utah Lighthouse Ministry), 148-49.

20. Ibid., Part 2, 122. According to Walters, "Mormon writers like Francis Kirckham and Dr. Hugh Nibley vigorously denied that their prophet could have participated in such a superstitious practice, or had ever been found guilty in a court of law" (p. 122). In 1971 a bundle of Bainbridge court bills were discovered. Two bills drew plenty of interest and on February 25, 1972, were placed in the custody of the county historian. The bills are those of Constable Philip DeZeng and Justice Neeley. Constable Philip M. DeZeng's 1826 bill has the following charges written: "Serving Warrant on Joseph Smith & travel...1.25; subpoening 12 witnesses & travel...2.50 (3.50?0; Attendance with Prisoner two days & 1 night...1.75; Notifying two Justices...1.—; 10 miles travel with Mittimus to take him...1.— (copy of document in *Joseph Smith's Bainbridge, N.Y. Court Trials*, p. 155, also see p. 130). Justice Neeley's bill shows a list of some of his 1826 court cases. Along with the fees is a description of the cases. In Neeley's own riting, the fifth court case reads: "same [i.e. The People] vs. Joseph Smith, The Glass looker, March 20, 1826;Misdemeanor; To my fees in examination of the above cause 2.68" (p. 129). (copy of document can be found in Jerald and Sandra Tanner, *Mormonism: Shadow or Reality?* 5th ed. (Salt Lake City, UT: Utah Lighthouse Ministry, 1987), 33.

21. Ibid., Part 2, 124.

22. *Early Mormon Documents,* 1:540, Emma Smith Bidamon interview with Joseph Smith III, February 1879.

23. E.D. Howe, 263.

24. Ibid., 234.

25. Ibid., 264.

26. Ibid.27. Ibid.

28. Dan Vogel, ed., *Early Mormon Documents* (Salt Lake City,UT: Signature Books, 2000), 3:391, Sara Melissa Ingersoll Reminiscence, November 27, 1899.

29. Joseph Smith, *History of the Church of Jesus Christ of Latter Day Saints,* 7 vols. (Salt Lake City, UT: Deseret Book Co., 1978), 1:78. (Hereafter shall be referred to as *History of the Church*).

30. Charles Dickens, *In the Name of the Prophet—Smith!* (July 19, 1851), 385; quoted in Hugh Nibley, *Collected Works*

32. *History of the Church,* 1:142.

33. John Whitmer, *John Whitmer's History,* 5; a photomechanical reprint (Salt Lake City, UT: Utah Lighthouse Ministry). Also in *History of the Church,* 1:216, footnote.

34. William Swartzell, (A Danite) daily journal, July 14 1838 and July 21, 1838 in his *Mormonism Exposed, Being a Journal of a Residence in Missouri From the 28th of May to the 20th of August, 1838* (Pittsburgh: A. Ingrim Jr., printer, 1840), 18, 22; a photomechanical reprint (Salt Lake City, UT: Utah Lighthouse Ministry).

35. John D. Lee (contemporary of Smith's and a Mormon bishop), *Confessions of John D. Lee* (Salt Lake City, UT: Utah Lighthouse Ministry), 158. Photomechanical reprint of the original 1877 edition of *Mormonism Unveiled; or The Life and Confessions of the Late Mormon Bishop, John D. Lee.*

36. *History of the Church,* 3:167, footnotes; Thomas Marsh affidavit, October 24, 1838.

37. William Swartzell journal, July 19, 1838, in his *Mormonism Exposed,* 23.

38. Lee, 284. Lee also said he knew of "many a man who was quietly put out of the way by the orders of Joseph and his Apostles."

39. *The Reed Peck Manuscript: Concerning the Mormon War in Missouri and the Danite Band,* 10; a photomechanical 1839 reprint (Salt Lake City, UT: Utah Lightouse Ministry).

40. John C. Bennett, *The History of the Saints; or An Exposé of Joe Smith and Mormonism* (Boston, MA: 1842), 302; a photomechanical reprint (Salt Lake City, UT: Utah Lightouse Ministry).

41. Stephen C. LeSueur, *The 1838 Mormon War in Missouri* (Columbia, MO: University of Missouri Press, 1987), 75.

42. Ibid., 135.

43. Ibid.

44. *Reed Peck Manuscript,* 35.

45. LeSueur, 117.

46. Ibid., 136.

47. Ibid., 124.

48. Ibid., 135.

49. Ibid., 124.

50. *Reed Peck Manuscript,* 20.

51. Bennett, 278. John Bennett said that "when Joe is in want of funds for the Temple, Nauvoo House, or *private use,* he commissions some of his satellites of the illuminati..and sends them out, all panoplied with Mormon glory, to *milk the Gentiles!* (emphasis in Bennett), p. 278.

52. *John Whitmer's History,* 22. Also repeated on page 23, including, "God has said by the mouths of the Prophets that he would consecrate the riches of

the Gentiles to the house of Israel, and we are the house of Israel...God is not intending to give it himself, but you are agents, and these things are before you, go and help yourselves."

53. LeSueur, 214-15.

54. *Whitmer's History,* 22.

55. Ibid., 20.

56. Ibid.

57. Ibid.

58. Bennett, 85. Joseph was released from jail on June 9, 1837.

59. D.Michael Quinn, *The Mormon Hierarchy: Origins of Power* (Salt Lake City, UT: Signature Books in association with Smith Research Associates, 1994), Appendix 7, 639, August 1, 1843.

60. Edwin Brown Firmage and Richard Collin Mangrum, *Zion in the Courts: A Legal History of the Church of Jesus Christ of Latter-day Saints 1830-1900* (Chicago: University of Illinois Press, 1988), 54.

61. Smith had prophesied that "Lilburn Boggs would die by violent hands within a year. And in a fit of pique he added that Governor Carlin would die in a ditch"—quoted in Mormon writer Harold Shindler's *Orrin Porter Rockwell: Man of God/Son of Thunder,* 2nd ed. (Salt Lake City, UT: University of Utah Press, 1983), 64. Shortly after that prophecy, Smith hired Orrin Porter Rockwell to murder the former governor of Missouri, Lilburn Boggs, cited in *John Whitmer's History,* 23. You can also read about the attempted murder of Governor Boggs in Bennett, *History of the Saints,* 281-86; and a note to Smith by Governor Thomas Carlin regarding the Boggs affair in *History of the Church,* 5:50, June 30, 1842.

62. According to Firmage and Mangrum, on November 2, 1836 Smith started a bank for the church called the "Kirtland Safety Society Bank" (November 2, 1836). The Ohio state legislature denied the church's request for starting the bank. "Rather than scrapping the 'bank' for lack of legislative authority," Smith organized the bank but called it the "Kirtland Safety Society Anti-Banking Company.... Because the society had no state charter, notes were consistently rejected by merchants in New York, Pittsburgh, and Cleveland, where large quantities of merchandise had been purchased on credit for use in Kirtland. Newspapers of the day sensationalized the 'worthless paper' that was being circulated by the Kirtland Safety Society. Within six months the financial "panic of 1837" swept the entire nation, taking down the Kirtland Society along with thousands of other over-subscribed banks and institutions. Firmage and Mangrum, 54-55. There was an early Mormon belief (and possibly there still is today) that the reason Joseph Smith was denied the opportunity to start a legal bank was simply because Smith and his followers were "Mormons." Therefore the "legislature raised some frivolous excuse on which they refused to grant us those banking privileges they so freely granted to others." *History of the Church* 1836-

1844 (Reorganized Church of Jesus Christ of Latter Day Saints), 2:83.

63. Firmage and Mangrum, 54-57. Firmage and Mangrum, both professors of law, wrote that the cases in Ohio against Joseph and other Mormons "suggest that the Saints generally received fair treatment in the Ohio courts" (54).

64. Ibid., 56-57.

65. Ibid., 58.

66. William Law diary, 13 May 1844, in Cook, *William Law,* 52-53; quoted in Quinn, *The Mormon Hierarchy: Origins of Power,* 138.

67. Francis M. Higbee to Thomas Gregg, [torn] May 1844, Mormon Collection, Chicago Historical Society, quoted in Quinn, *The Mormon Hierarchy: Origins of Power,* 139.

68. Ibid.

69. *History of the Church,* 6:534, a letter from Governor Ford to "Mayor and Council of the City of Nauvoo," June 22, 1844.

70. June 12, 1844, Squire Thomas Morrison sent a constable with a writ to Nauvoo to arrest Joseph. John E. Hallwas and Roger D. Launius, *Cultures in Conflict: A Documentary History of the Mormon War in Illinois* (Logan, UT: Utah State University Press, 1995), 195.

71. William Law diary, 10 June 1844, in Cook, *William Law,* 55; quoted in Quinn, *Origins of Power,* 139.

72. Firmage and Mangrum, 114. Also quoted was, "It is not surprising that the Missourians were raised to madness and drove them from the state."

73. *History of the Church,* 6:534; letter dated June 22, 1844 from Governor Ford to Smith.

74. Ibid., 6:534.

75. Ibid., 6:537.

76. *The Quincy Whig,* May 6,1846. Harold Shindler, *Orrin Porter Rockwell: Sons of God/Sons of Thunder* (Salt Lake City, UT: University of Utah Press, 1983), 146.

77. *History of the Church,* 6:548, June 22, 1844.

78. Ibid., 6:548, June 22-23, 1844.

79. Ibid., 6:548, June 23, 1844.

80. Ibid., 6:549, June 23, 1844.

81. Wandle Mace, "Journal," p. 144, Utah State Historical Society, Salt Lake City, Utah. Also cited in Hallwas and Launius, 178.

82. *History of the Church,* 6:549, June 23, 1844.

83. Ibid., 6:561, June 25, 1844.

84. There are conflicting reports as to whether Smith and his brother were kept in jail or released. John E. Hallwas and Roger D. Launius say that Smith and his brother were released from the riot charge on June 25, 1844 by voluntarily posting bail to guarantee their appearance at the circuit court. Immediately thereafter, the two brothers were arrested for treason against the State of Illinois. Hallwas and Launius, 178. Writer Fawn Brodie states that all men with Smith were released on bail except for Joseph and his brother Hyrum. They were kept in custody. Brodie, 388.

85. Brodie, 393.

86. *History of the Church,* 6:622.

87. Two other Mormons were with Joseph and Hyrum in jail. They were John Taylor and Dr. Williard Richards. Richards escaped without being hurt, but Taylor was hit four times. He survived. William Clayton diary, in George D Smith ed. *An Intimate Chronicle: The Journals of William Clayton* (Salt Lake City, UT: Signature Books in association with Smith Research Associates, 1995), 542-43.

88. The diary of William Clayton, account written between January 15–October 15, 1886, in George D. Smith, ed., *An Intimate Chronicle,* 542,

89. *Times and Seasons,* July 1, 1844, vol. V, no. 12, whole no. 96.

90. Tanner and Tanner, *Mormonism: Shadow or Reality?* 259. It's important to note that most Mormons consider Jerald and Sandra Tanner to be "anti-Mormon" (the Tanners vehemently deny they are anti-Mormon). Despite the Mormon feeling about the Tanners, they do have credibility within Mormon circles. In *Mormon America: The Power and the Promise* by Richard N. Ostling and Joan K. Ostling (New York, NY: HarperCollins Publishers Inc., 1999), it is stated that the Tanners' work (especially in regard to their writings on Masonry and Mormon ritual) is "generally acknowledged to be factually accurate and honest" (page 193). When the "discovery" in 1984 of a document (called the "salamander letter") gained credibility even by the Mormon church's experts, "judging the document to be genuine" (page 348), Jerald Tanner boldly came forward and exposed the document as a fraud. This document could have been used as "juicy propaganda for attackers of the Book of Mormon" (page 348), yet the Tanners' honesty and integrity kept that from happening.

91. *Bloomington Herald,* July 5, 1844,Vol. IV, No. 35,Whole No. 191, p. 2.

92. This statement was in a written letter from David Wells Kilbourne to a Reverend T. Dent dated June 29, 1844. Found in the David Wells Kilbourne Papers, State Historical Society of Iowa, Des Moines, quoted in Hallwas and Launius, 227.

93. Anna Ruth Eaton, *The Origin of Mormonism* (New York: Woman's Executive Committee of Home Missions, 1881), 4. Also published in *Wayne County Journal*, 28 July 1881; and John McCutchen Coyner, *Hand-Book on Mormonism* (Salt Lake City, UT: Hand-Book Publishing Co., 1882), 1-4; quoted in *Early Mormon Documents* 3:150-51.

Chapter 2—Why Is Joseph's First Vision So Important?

1. In the Mormon church, "elder" is in the Melchizedek Priesthood. Daniel H. Ludlow, ed., *Encyclopedia of Mormonism: The History, Scripture, Doctrine, and Procedure of the Church of Jesus Christ of Latter-day Saints*, 4 vols. (New York: Macmillan Publishing Co., 1992), 2:447.

2. *Pearl of Great Price* (Salt Lake City, UT: Church of Jesus Christ of Latter-day Saints, 1921, 1948), (Joseph Smith 2:15-16), 48.

3. *Dialogue: A Journal of Mormon Thought*, Autumn, 1966, p. 29; quoted in Jerald and Sandra Tanner, *Mormonism: Shadow or Reality?*5th ed. (Salt Lake City, UT: Utah Lighthouse Ministry, 1987), 143.

4. Lavina Fielding Anderson ed., *Lucy's Book* (Salt Lake City, UT: Signature Books, 2001), 170.

5. Wesley P. Walters, *New Light on Mormon Origins from the Palmyra (N.Y.) Revival* (Salt Lake City, UT: Utah Christian Tract Society, 1967), 5; quoted in Tanner and Tanner, *Mormonism: Shadow or Reality?* 156.

6. Ibid, Forward, quoted in Tanner and Tanner, 156.

7. Letter of Rev. James Murdock, dated New Haven, 19 June 1841, to the *Congregational Observer*, Hartford and New-Haven, Connecticut, 2 (3 July 1841): Interview of William Smith aboard an Ohio River boat on 18 April 1841. Original of *The Congregational Observer* is located in the Connecticut State Historical Society, Hartford. This interview was republished in the *Peoria Register and North-Western Gazette* 5 (3 Sept. 1841). H. Michael Marquet and Wesley P. Walters, *Inventing Mormonism: Tradition and Historical Record* (Salt Lake City, UT: 1994), 19.

8. Dan Vogel, *Early Mormon Documents* (Salt Lake City, UT: Signature Books, 1996), 1:513. William Smith interview with E.C. Briggs. Interview took place at William Smith's residence at Osterdock, Clay County, Iowa shortly before his death on November 13, 1893.

9. Ibid.

10. *Latter-Day Saints' Messenger and Advocate*, Vol. 1,No. 3,Whole No. 3,December 1834.

11. Lucy Mack Smith, *Joseph Smith's History by His Mother*, photomechanical reprint of the original 1853 edition. Original title *Biographical Sketches or Joseph Smith the Prophet, and His Progenitors for Many Generations* (Salt Lake City, UT: Utah Lighthouse Ministry), 78.

12. Fawn M. Brodie, *No Man Knows My History* (New York: Alfred A. Knopf, Inc., 1945, 1971), 24.

13. Ibid.

14. *Improvement Era*, July 1961, 490. Joseph Smith published his story in the Mormon publication *Times and Seasons*, 1842,Vol. 3, pp. 727, 748; quoted in *Tanner and Tanner, Mormonism: Shadow or Reality?* 143.

15. *Early Mormon Documents*, 1:512 (footnote 8), William Smith interview with E.C. Briggs, November 13, 1893.

16. Brodie, 24, 410.

17. Tanner and Tanner, *Mormonism: Shadow or Reality?* 162-C.

18. "Mormon History," *Amboy [Illinois] Journal*, 30 Mar. 1879, 30 Apr. 1879, 21 May 1879, and 11 June 1879. Also cited in the *Utah Christian Tract Society Newsletter* (La Mesa, CA), July-Aug. 1971. Also, in Linda King Newell and Valeen Tippetts Avery, *Mormon Enigma* (New York: Doubleday, 1984), 25. Quoted in Robert D. Anderson, *Inside the Mind of Joseph Smith* (Salt Lake City, UT: Signature Books, 1999), 91.

19. "Mormon History," *Amboy [Illinois] Journal*, 30 Mar. 1879, 30 Apr. 1879, 21 May 1879, and 11 June 1879, quoted in Robert D. Anderson, 91.

20. See E.D. Howe (contemporary of Smith's), *Mormonism Unveiled* (Zanesville, OH: printed and published by the author, 1834), 261; a
photomechanical reprint (Salt Lake City, UT: Utah Lighthouse Ministry).

21. Preston Nibley, *Joseph Smith the Prophet* (1944), 30; quoted in Tanner and Tanner, *Mormonism: Shadow or Reality?* 145.

22. *Dialogue: A Journal of Mormon Thought*, Autumn 1966, 38-39; quoted in Tanner and Tanner, *Mormonism: Shadow or Reality?* 155.

23. Joseph Fielding Smith, *Doctrines of Salvation* (Salt Lake City,UT: Bookcraft, 1954), 1:2.

24. Tanner and Tanner, 147. A written document by Joseph Smith referring to only Christ coming to him has been proven genuine by Professor James B. Allen, assistant church historian. Also confirming its authenticity is Dean C. Jessee, on staff at the LDS church historian's office in Salt Lake City. Jessee claims the document was written in 1831 or 1832. Smith's comments first appeared in Mormon Paul R. Cheesman's thesis, "An Analysis of the Accounts relating Joseph Smith's Early Visions." Tanner and and Tanner, 145-46.

25. *Deseret News*, Saturday, May 20, 1852,Vol. 2, No. 15. Photocopy of the *Deseret News* article can be found in Tanner and Tanner, *Mormonism: Shadow or Reality?* 149-50.
Although Joseph Smith died in 1844, he was quoted in 1852 because the *Deseret News* was publishing *Joseph Smith's History.*

26. *Journal of Discourses*, 26 volumes (London: Latter-day Saints Book Depot, 1854-1886), 2:171, February 18, 1855, Brigham Young.

27. *Journal of Discourses*, 20:167,March 2, 1879, John Taylor.

28. *William Smith on Mormonism* (Lamoni, IA, 1883) as quoted in *A New Witness for Christ in America* 2:414-15. Also in *The Saints Herald*, Vol. 31,No. 40, p. 643, cited in Tanner and Tanner, *Mormonism: Shadow or Reality?* 154.

29. Joseph Smith, *History of the Church of Jesus Christ of Latter Day Saints*, 7 vols. (Salt Lake City, UT: Deseret Book Co., 1978), 2:312, November 14, 1835. (Hereafter shall be referred to as *History of the Church*). The comparison between two *History of the Church* editions was taken from Tanner and Tanner, *Mormonism: Shadow or Reality?* 150.

30. Wesley P. Walters, "New Light on Mormon Origins from the Palmyra (N.Y.) Revival," *Journal of the Evangelical Theological Society* 10 (Fall 1967): 227-44; *New Light on Mormon Origins* (La Mesa, CA; Utah Christian Tract Society, 1967); quoted in Edmond C. Gruss' *Cults and the Occult*, 4th ed. (Phillipsburg, NJ: P&R Publishers, 1974), 37.

31. Adapted from Fanny Crosby's *Tell Me the Story of Jesus*, as appears in *The New Church Hymnal* (Lexicon Music, Inc., 1976), 139.

Chapter 3—What Is the *Book of Mormon* About?

1. Joseph originally wrote on the manuscript that the angel's name was Nephi—*Times and Seasons,* vol. 3, no. 12, p. 753, April 15, 1843. Smith never made a retraction. The name *Nephi* was even in the 1851 edition of the *Pearl of Great Price.* Cited in Tanner & Tanner, *Major Problems of Mormonism* (Salt Lake City, UT: Utah Lighthouse Ministry, n.d.), 82-84. Lucy Mack Smith said in her book *Joseph Smith's History by His Mother* (Salt Lake City, UT: Utah Lighthouse Ministry) that Joseph was approached by the angel "Nephi," 79.

2. Joseph F. Smith, *Gospel Doctrine* (Salt Lake City, UT: Deseret Book Co., 1977), 483.

3. Moroni blowing the horn is "a symbol of the restoration of the gospel through divine messengers," quoted in Daniel H. Ludlow, ed., *Encyclopedia of Mormonism: The History, Scripture, Doctrine, and Procedure of the Church of Jesus Christ of Latter-day Saints*, 4 vols. (New York: Macmillan Publishing Co., 1992), 2:953.

4. *Pearl of Great Price* (Salt Lake City, UT: The Church of Jesus Christ of Latter-day Saints 1921, 1948), Joseph Smith 2:34.

5. James E. Talmage, *The Articles of Faith* (Salt Lake City, UT: The Church of Latter-day Saints, 1977), 251.

6. In 1981 the *Book of Mormon* (and since then) changed the word from "white" to "pure."

7. D. Michael Quinn, *The Mormon Hierarchy: Extensions of Power* (Salt Lake City, UT: Signature Books, 1997), 878-79.

8. This quote was written in a letter from the LDS church to its members, May 3, 1936. It was duplicated and distributed again to leaders in Cleveland, Ohio in 1959; quoted in Tanner and Tanner, *Mormonism: Shadow or Reality?* 5th ed. (Salt Lake City, UT: Utah Lighthouse Ministry, 1987), 97.

 9. Jerald and Sandra Tanner, *Mormonism: Shadow or Reality?* 97.

10. Ibid., 98.

11. *The Book of Mormon* (Salt Lake City, UT: The Church of Jesus Christ of Latter-day Saints, 1978. See the commentary at the beginning of Ether, chapter 15. In the 1990 reprint, the commentary is changed to: "Millions of the Jaredites are slain in battle."

12. *Salt Lake Tribune*, November 30, 2000, Science and Medicine, B-3, "Gene Data May Shed Light on Origin of Book of Mormon's Lamanites."

13. Ibid.

14. Ibid.

15. Ibid.

16. Ibid., B-1.

17. Ibid., B-3.

18. Ibid.

19. Ibid.

20. Ibid.

21. Lucy Mack Smith, 85.

22. *The Saints' Herald,* August 24, 1868,Vol. 14, p. 92. Also cited in *History of the Church of Jesus Christ of Latter Day Saints 1844-1872* (Lamoni, IA: Reorganized Church of Jesus Christ of Latter Day Saints, 1908), 3:502.

23. Lavina Fielding Anderson, ed., *Lucy's Book: A Critical Edition of Lucy Mack Smith's Family Memoir* (Salt Lake City, UT: Signature Books, 2001), 110.

24. Ibid., 111.

25. Ibid., 110-11.

26. Dan Vogel, *Early Mormon Documents* (Salt Lake City, UT: Signature Books, 1996), 1:227, "Lucy Smith History," 1845.

27. Pamphlets by Orson Pratt (photomechanical reprint of eight pamplets by Orson Pratt, Salt Lake City, UT: Utah Lighthouse Ministry), "Spiritual Gifts," 65.

28. Ibid., 75.

29. Ibid.

30. E.D. Howe (contemporary of Smith's), *Mormonism Unveiled* (Zanesville, OH: printed and published by the author, 1834), 241; a photomechanical reprint (Salt Lake City, UT: Utah Lighthouse Ministry).

31. Ibid., 241.

32. Ibid.

33. Ibid.

34. Ibid., 242.

35. Ibid., 247.

36. Ibid., 246.

37. John A. Widtsoe, *Joseph Smith—Seeker After Truth* (Salt Lake City, UT: 1951), 338-39; quoted in Tanner and Tanner, *Mormonism: Shadow or Reality?* 52.

38. *The Book of Mormon,* Testimony of the Three Witnesses.

39. Ibid. The Testimony of Eight Witnesses.

40. Joseph Smith, *History of the Church of Jesus Christ of Latter-day Saints,* 7 vols. (Salt Lake City, UT: Deseret Book Co., 1978), 3:16. (Hereafter will be referred to as *History of the Church.*)

41. Dan Vogel, ed., *Early Mormon Documents* (Salt Lake City, UT: Signature Books, 1998), 2:506, "G.J. Keen Statement," April 14, 1885.

42. Ibid.

43. *Senate Document* 189, pages 6-9, February 15, 1841; quoted in Tanner and Tanner, *Mormonism: Shadow or Reality?* 53-54.

44. David Whitmer, *An Address to All Believers in Christ* (Richmond, Missouri, 1887, 27; reprinted in Salt Lake City, UT: Utah Lighthouse Ministry). In his defense David Whitmer said, "In the spring of 1838, the heads of the church and many of the members had gone deep into error and blindness. I had been striving with them for a long time to show them the errors into which they were drifting, and for my labors I received only persecutions."

45. Smith, *History of the Church* 3:19,April 13, 1833, in Whitmer's letter to John Murdock, the president of the High Council.

46. David Whitmer, *An Address to All Believers in Christ*, 27.

47. E.D. Howe, 252.

48. *Early Mormon Documents,* 2:31. Abigail's husband Peter Harris is the brother of Martin Harris' wife, Lucy Harris. Martin Harris is Peter and Lucy's first cousin. *Early Mormon Documents,* 2:31, 34.

49. E.D. Howe, 254. Statement made November 11, 1833. Lucy Harris corroborated this claim (Howe, 256), "realizing that I must give an account at the bar of God what what I say" (Howe, 254, "Lucy Harris Statement," 29 November 1833). See also, *Early Mormon Documents,* 3:116 regarding Pomeroy Tucker's own testimony of the money Harris felt he could make off the sales of the *Book of Mormon.*

50. Daniel H. Ludlow, ed., *Encyclopedia of Mormonism: The History, Scripture, Doctrine, and Procedure of the Church of Jesus Christ of Latter-day Saints,* 4 vols. (New York: Macmillan Publishing Co., 1992), 2:576.

51. *Millennial Star,* Vol. 8, November 15, 1846, 124-28; quoted in Tanner and Tanner, *Mormonism: Shadow or Reality?* 56.

52. Joseph Smith diary, December 16, 1838, Scott H. Faulring, ed., *An American Prophet's Record: The Diaries and Journals of Joseph Smith* (Salt Lake City, UT: Signature Books in association with Smith Research Associates, 1989), 223.

53. *Early Mormon Documents,* 2:288, Stephen Brunett to Br. [Lyman E.] Johnson, 15 April 1838, in Joseph Smith Letter Book, 2; archives Church of Jesus Christ of Latter-day Saints, Salt Lake City, Utah.

54. *Tiffany's Monthly*, 1859, 166. Interview with Martin Harris, quoted in *Revealing Statements by the Three Witnesses to the Book of Mormon*, 166; a photomechanical reprint (Salt Lake City, UT: Utah Lighthouse Ministry).

55. Ibid. Also see an account in *Early Mormon Documents* 2:255. John H. Gilbert memorandum, 8 September 1892, Martin Harris saw the plates "with a spir[i]tual eye."

56. Dean C. Jessee, ed., *The Papers of Joseph Smith* (Salt Lake City, UT: Deseret Book Co., 1989), 1:471.

57. B.H. Roberts, *Comprehensive History of the Church of the Church of Jesus Christ of Latter-day Saints* (Salt Lake City, UT: Church of Jesus Christ of Latter-day Saints, 1957), 1:104.

58. Ibid.

59. Ibid.

60. Ibid.

61. *Times and Seasons*, Vol. 2, no. 18, whole no. 30, p. 482, Nauvoo, Illinois, November 1, 1840, "Poetry."

62. E.D. Howe, 252.

63. *Early Mormon Documents*, 1:541-42. Emma Smith Bidamon interview with Joseph Smith III, February 1879.

64. *Early Mormon Documents*, 1:510, 517.William Smith interview with E.C. Briggs, 1893, the Introduction to Katharine Smith Collection.

65. Lucy Mack Smith, 107.

66. Noel B. Reynolds, ed., *Book of Mormon Authorship Revisited: The Evidence for Ancient Origins* (Provo, UT: Foundation for Ancient Research and Mormon Studies, 1997), 163. Chapter 6, "Is the Book of Mormon True? Notes on the Debate," written by Daniel C. Peterson.

67. John C. Bennett, *The History of the Saints; or An Exposé of Joe Smith and Mormonism* (Boston, MA: 1842), 175; a photomechanical reprint (Salt Lake City, UT: Modern Microfilm Co.).

68. Testimony by GB Frost before justice of the peace (Bradford Sumner) on September 19, 1842; quoted in John C. Bennet, *The History of the Saints;or An Expose' of Joe Smith and Mormonism* (Boston, MA: 1842), 87; a photomechanical reprint (Salt Lake City, UT: Modern Microfilm Co.).

69. Hugh Nibley, *Lehi in the Desert,* 123; quoted in Reynolds, 163.

70. *History of the Church,* 2:470, footnotes.

71. Dan Vogel, ed., *Early Mormon Documents* (Salt Lake City, UT: Signature Books, 2000), 3:115. Pomeroy Tucker Account, 1867.

72. Robert D. Anderson, *Inside the Mind of Joseph Smith* (Salt Lake City, UT: Signature Books, 1999), 17. A partial account is in Lucy Mack Smith, *Joseph Smith's History by His Mother*, 15-20.

73. For more comparisons, see Tanner and Tanner, *Mormonism: Shadow or Reality?* 86-87.

74. For more detailed information about the King James influence, the apocryphal influence, the Old and New Testament influence, along with a list of parallels, see Tanner and Tanner, *Mormonism: Shadow or Reality?* 72-81.

75. B.H. Roberts, *Studies of the Book of Mormon,* Brigham D. Madsen, ed. (Salt Lake City, UT: Signature Books, 1992), A Biographical Essay, xix, quoted by Sterling McMurrin.

76. B.H. Roberts, *Studies of the Book of Mormon,* 155, 160.

77. Ibid., 30.

78. Ibid., 309-10.

79. Ibid., 323-44, "A Parallel."

80. Ibid., 240.

81. Ibid.

82. Ibid., 173.

83. Ibid., 174.

84. Ibid., 177.

85. Ibid., 271.

86. Ibid., 258.

87. Ibid., 30.

88. Ibid., 29.

89. Ibid., 22-23.

90. Reynolds, 164.

91. Walter B. Knight, *Knight's Treasury of 2,000 Illustrations* (Grand Rapids, MI: William B. Eerdman's Publishing Co., 1963), 209.

Chapter 4—*Doctrine and Covenants*—Revelations from the Lord?

1. Joseph Fielding Smith, *Doctrines of Salvation* (Salt Lake City, UT: Bookcraft, 1956), 3:199.

2. L.G. Otten and C.M. Caldwell, *The Sacred Truths of the Doctrine and Covenants* (Salt Lake City, UT: Lemb, Inc., 1982, Gospel Infobase Library CD ROM, 3rd ed., March 23, 1993, Infobases Inc., 1993), 2:38; quote is in the acknowledgments, titled "Doctrine and Covenants—the Lord's Book.

3. Bruce R. McConkie, *Mormon Doctrine* (Salt Lake City, UT: Bookcraft, 1966, Gospel Infobase Library CD ROM, 3rd ed., 3/24/93, Infobases Inc., 1991, 1992), 206.

4. *Journal of Discourses*, 17:159-161, August 9, 1874, Brigham Young.

5. Scott H. Faulring, ed., *An American Prophet's Record: The Diaries and Journals of Joseph Smith*, (Salt Lake City, UT: Signature Books, 1989), 339. The statement was made on April 2, 1843. Interestingly, this statement was kept out of *History of the Church* (see Volume 5, p. 326).

6. Victor L. Ludlow (Mormon theologian), *Principals and Practices of the Restored Gospel* (Salt Lake City, UT: Deseret Book Co., 1992), 445.

7. *Mormon Doctrine*, 845

8. *Journal of Discourses*, 12:158, Brigham Young, February 8, 1868.

9. *Des Moines Daily News*, October 16, 1886. Taken from Tanner and Tanner, 406.

10. Ibid.

11. *Journal of Discourses*, 2:212, George A. Smith, March 18, 1855.

12. *Doctrines of Salvation* 2:16

13. Joseph F. Smith, *Gospel Doctrine* (Salt Lake City, UT: Deseret Book Co., 1977), 435.

14. Ibid.

15. Ibid.

16. *Journal of Discourses* 21:317-318, October 10, 1880, Wilford Woodruff.

17. Ibid.

18. Ibid., 7:240, September 1, 1859, Brigham Young.

19. Charles Caldwell Ryrie, *The Ryrie Study Bible* (Chicago, IL: Moody Press, 1976, 1978), 1942-43.

20. "Mormon History," *Amboy [Illinois] Journal*, 30 March 1879, 30 April 1879, 21 May 1879, and 11 June 1879. Cited in Robert D. Anderson's *Inside the Mind of Joseph Smith* (Salt Lake City, UT: Signature Books, 1999), 91.

21. Robert D. Anderson, *Inside the Mind of Joseph Smith* (Salt Lake City, UT: Signature Books, 1999), 91.

22. *History of the Church of Jesus Christ of Latter Day Saints: 1844-1872* (Lamoni, IA: Reorganized Church of Jesus Christ of Latter Day Saints, 1908), 3:485-487, footnotes.

23. Ibid., 7:260, August 19, 1844.

24. Ibid., 3:486-87, footnotes.

25. *Journal of Discourses*, 3:116, Brigham Young, October 8, 1855.

26. Joseph Fielding Smith, *Doctrines of Salvation*, 3:191.

27. Ibid. In the *Encyclopedia of Mormonism*, you can find lengthy selections of "The Joseph Smith Translation of the Bible" (JST). The encyclopedia says that the JST "contains several thousand verses that are different from the King James Version. The examples the encyclopedia gives have been "selected for their doctrinal value...." 94:1709). See Mormon writer, Daniel H. Ludlow's, ed., *Encyclopedia of Mormonism: The History, Scripture, Doctrine, and Procedure of the Church of Jesus Christ of Latter-day Saints*, 4 vols. (New York: Macmillan Publishing Co., 1992), 4:1709-23.

28. *History of the Church*, 3:16, April 11, 1838.

29. Richard S. Van Wagoner, *Mormon Polygamy: A History* (Salt Lake City, UT: Signature Books, 1992), pg. 79.

30. William Clayton diary, August 16, 1843, in George D. Smith, ed., *An Intimate Chronicle: The Journals of William Clayton* (Salt Lake City, UT: Signature Books in association with Smith Research Associates, 1995), 117.

31. Ibid.

32. W. Wyle, 62.

33. Dan Vogel, ed., *Early Mormon Documents* (Salt Lake City, UT: Signature Books, 1998), 2:348.

34. Joseph literally "demanded the wives of *all* the twelve [Mormon] apostles," W. Wyle, 70.

35. Joseph Smith's Documented Wives:

Emma Hale (age 22, married Smith in Jan. 1827); Fanny Alger (age 16, married 1833); Lucinda Morgan Harris, (age 37, polyandrous wife of Smith's–legal husband was George W. Harris. Married Smith in 1838); Louisa Beaman (age 26, April 1841); Zina Huntington Jacobs (age 20, polyandrous wife of Smith's–legal husband was Henry Jacobs. Married Smith in Oct. 1841); Presendia Huntington Buell (age 31, polyandrous wife of Smith's–legal husband was Norman Buell. Married Smith in December 1841); Agnes Coolbrith (age 33, married Smith in Jan. 1842); Sylvia Sessions Lyon (age 23, polyandrous wife of Smith's–legal husband was Windsor Lyon. Married Smith in Feb. 1842); Mary Rollins Lightner (age 23, polyandrous wife of Smith's–legal husband was Adam Lightner. Married Smith in Feb. 1842); Patty Bartlett Sessions (age 47, polyandrous wife of Smith's–legal husband was David Sessions. Married Smith in Mar. 1842); Marinda Johnson Hyde (age 27, polyandrous wife of Smith's–legal husband was Orson Hyde. Married Smith in April 1842); Elizabeth Davis Durfee (age 50, polyandrous wife of Smith's—legal husband was Jabez Durfee. Married Smith in June 1842); Sarah Kingsley Cleveland (age 53, polyandrous wife of Smith's–legal husband was John Cleveland. Married Smith in June 1842); Eliza R. Snow (age 48, married Smith in June 1842); Delcena Johnson (age 37, married Smith in Jul. 1842); Sarah Ann Whitney (age 17, married Smith in July 1842); Martha McBride Knight (age 37, married Smith in Aug. 1842); Ruth Vose Sayers (age 33, polyandrous wife of Smith's–legal husband was Edward Sayers. Married Smith in February 1843); Flora Ann Woodworth (age 16, married Smith in the Spring of 1843); Emily Dow Partridge (age 19, married Smith in March 1843); Eliza Maria Partridge (age 22, married Smith in March 1843); Almera Johnson (age 30, married Smith in April 1843); Lucy Walker (age 17, married Smith in May 1843); Sarah Lawrence (age 17, married Smith in May 1843); Maria Lawrence (age 19, married Smith in May 1843); Helen Mar Kimball (age 14, married Smith in May 1843); Hanna Ells (age 29, married Smith in mid 1843); Elvira Cowles Holmes (age 29, polyandrous wife of Smith's–legal husband was Jonathan Holmes. Married Smith in June 1843); Rhoda Richards (age 58, married Smith in June 1843); Desdemona Fullmer (age 32, July 1843); Olive Frost (age 27, married Smith in mid 1843); Melissa Lott (age 19, married Smith in Sept. 1843); Nancy Winchester (age 14, married Smith in 1843); Fanny Young (age 56, November 1843).

Mary Elizabeth Rollins Lightner (age 23) and Smith's ninth wife, claimed that Smith had a private conversation with her in 1831 when she was then just twelve years old:
"[At age 12 in 1831], [Smith] told me about his great vision concerning me. He said I was the first woman God commanded him to take as a plural wife. ... In 1834 he was commanded to take me for a Wife ... [In 1842 age 23] I went forward and was sealed to him. Brigham Young performed the sealing ... for time, and all Eternity. I did just as Joseph told me to do[.] Linda King Newell and Valeen Tippetts Avery, *Mormon Enigma: Emma Hale Smith, Prophet's Wife, "Elect Lady," Polygamy's Foe* (Urbana, IL: University of Illinois Press, 1994), 65.

In regard to 16 year old Marinda Nancy Johnson (Hyde), we have the following account:
"In the summer of 1831 the Johnson family took Joseph and Emma Smith into their home as boarders, and soon thereafter the prophet purportedly bedded young Marinda. Unfortunately, the liaison did not go unnoticed, and a gang of indignant Ohioans—including a number of Mormons—resolved to castrate Joseph so that he would be disinclined to commit such acts of depravity in the future." (Joe Krakauer, *Under the Banner of Heaven: A Story of Violent Faith,* (Doubleday, 2003), 39.

Miranda's older brother Luke Johnson said of the above incident:
"[the mob] had Dr. Dennison there to perform the operation [of castration]; but when he saw the Prophet stripped and stretched on the plank, his heart failed him and he refused to operate." (Joe Krakauer, *Under the Banner of Heaven: A story of Violent Faith* (Doubleday, 2003), 120.

Helen Mar Kimball—Joseph's 14 year old wife made the following comment:
"Without any preliminaries [my father] asked me if I would be sealed to Joseph ... [Smith] said to me, 'If you will take this step, it will ensure your eternal salvation & exaltation and that of your father's household & all of your kindred.['] This promise was so great that I willingly gave myself to purchase so glorious a reward. ... [After the marriage] I felt quite sore over it ... and thought myself an abused child, and that it was pardonable if I did murmur." Cited in Todd Compton's, *In Sacred Loneliness: The Plural Wives of Joseph Smith* (Salt Lake City, Ut: Signature Books, 1997), 497-498.

According to Apostle Orson F. Whitney, we have the following account in regard to the Kimball's situation, which involved their daughter Helen (Helen's testimony above): "Joseph Smith finally demanded the wives of all the twelve apostles that were at home then in Nauvoo...Vilate Kimball, the first wife of Herbert Kimball, ...loved her husband, and he, ...her, hence a reluctance to comply with the Lord's demand that Vilate should be consecrated ... they thought the command of the Lord must be obeyed on some way, and a proxy way suggested itself to their minds. They had a young daughter only getting out of girlhood, and the father apologizing to the prophet for his wife's reluctance to comply with his desires, stating, however, that the act must be right or it would not be counseled — the abject slave of a father asked Joseph Smith if his daughter wouldn't do as well as his wife. Joseph replied that she would do just as well, and the Lord would accept her instead. The half ripe bud of womanhood was delivered over to the prophet." (Mormon Portraits, 1886. pp. 70-72) This testimony was also written in the book The Life of Herbert C. Kimball by Mormon Apostle Orson F.

Whitney pages 333-335. You can download Whitney's book, for free, at http://www.scribd.com/doc/26120004/Download-Free-LDS-Books

Recommended reading for further study:
– *Mormon Polygamy: A History* by Richard S. Van Wagoner, (Salt Lake City, Signature Books, 1992)
–*In Sacred Loneliness: The Plural Wives of Joseph Smith* by Todd Compton
–*Mormon Enigma: Emma Hale Smith, Prophet's Wife, "Elect Lady," Polygamy's Foe* by Linda King Newell and Valeen Tippetts.
–*Under the Banner of Heaven: A Story* of *Violent Faith*, by Joe Krakauer
–*Joseph Smith and Polygamy*, by Stanley S. Ivan

36. Brigham Young's Wives:
  1. Miriam Works 1824 (2 children); 2. Mary A. Angel 1834 (6 children); 3. Lucy A. Decker (Seeley) 1842 (7 children); 4. Harriet E. Cook (Campbell) 1843 (1 child); 5. Lucy Augusta Adams (Cobb) 1843 (no children); 6. Clarissa C. Decker 1844 (5 children); 7. Clarissa Ross-Chase 1844 (4 children); 8. Louisa Beaman (Smith) 1844 (4 children); 9. Zina D. Huntington (Jacobs, Smith) 1844 (1 child, Zina was also plural wife of Joseph Smith); 10. Emily D. Partridge (Smith) 1844 (7 children–Emily, also plural wife of Joseph Smith); 11. Eliza R. Snow (Smith) 1844 (no children–Eliza, also plural wife of Joseph Smith); 12. Elizabeth Fairchild 1844 (no children, divorced young in 1855); 13. Clarissa Blake 1844 (no children); 14. *Rebecca W. Greenleaf Holman 1844 (no children); 15. Diana Chase 1844 (no children, separated from Young around 1844, remarried 1849); 16. Maria Lawrence (Smith) 1844 (no children, also plural wife of Joseph Smith. Maria separated from Young in 1845, remarried in 1846); 17. Susannah Snively 1844 (no children); 18. Olive G. Frost (Smith) 1844 (no children, also plural wife of Joseph Smith); 19. Mary A. Clark (Powers) 1845 (no children, divorced Young in 1851); 20. Mary Harvey Pierce 1845 (no children); 21.. Margrette W. Pierce (Whitesides) 1845 (1 children); 22 Rhoda Richards (Smith) 1845 (no children); 23. Emmeline Free 1845 (10 children); 24. Mary E. Rollins (Lightner, Smith) 1845 (no children, also plural wife of Joseph Smith; while a legal husband of Young, Rollins claims to have been deserted by Young in 1846); 25. Margaret Maria Alley 1845 (2 children): 26. Mary Ann Turley 1845 (no children, divorced in 1851); 27. Olive Andrews (Smith) 1846 (no children, also plural wife of Joseph Smith); 28. Emily Haws (Chesley, Whitmarsh) 1846 (no children, separated from Young in 1848); 29. Ellen A. V. Rockwood 1846 (no children); 30. Abigail Marks (Works) 1846 (no children); 31. Mary E. Nelson (Greene) 1846 (no children); 32. Mary E. de la Montague (Woodward) 1846 (no children, divorced Young and returned to her legal husband in 1847, returned to Young in 1851); 33. Amy C. Cooper 1846 (no children); 34. Julia Foster (Hampton) 1846 (no children, separated from Young in 1846, married another man, returned to Young in 1855, only to leave him, later); 35. Abigail Harback (Hall) 1846 (no children, 1846 she left Young and returned back to legal husband; 36. Naamah K. J. Carter (Twiss) 1846 (no children, canceled sealing with Young in 1871, sealed to deceased first husband); 37. Nancy Cressy (Walker) 1846 (no children); 38. Eliza Babcock 1846-53 (no children; divorced Young in 1853); 39. Jane Terry (Tarbox, Young) 1847; 40. Mary J. Bigelow 1847 (no children, divorced Young in1851); 41. Lucy Bigelow 1847 (3 children); 42. Sarah M. Guckin (Malin) 1848 (no children); 43. Eliza Burgess 1852 (1 child); 44. Mary Oldfield (Kelsey) 1852 (no children); 45. Catherine Resse (Clawson, Egan) 1855 (no children); 46. Harriet E. Barney (Sagers) 1856 (1 child); 47. Harriet Amelia Folsom 1863 (no children); 48. Mary Van Cott (Cobb) 1865 (1 child); 19. Ann Eliza Webb Dee Denning (no children, divorced Young); 50. Ann E. Webb (Dee) 1868 (no child, divorced 1875); 51. Elizabeth Jones (Lewis, Jones) 1869 (no children); 52. Lydia Farnsworth (Mayhew) 1870 (no children); 53. Hannah Tapfield (King) 1872 (no children) Cited in D. Michael Quinn's, The Mormon Hierarchy: Origins of Power, Signature Books, Salt Lake City, 1994, Appendix 6, "Biographical Sketches of Officers of the Church of Jesus Christ of Latter- day Saints, 1830-47" pp. 607-608). **Note:** Quinn had Ann Eliza Webb Dee Young Denning as wife #50. Others refer her to being Young's 52nd wife., still others as her "27th wife." She claimed, in the title of her book, to be wife #19. The reason for this is Because she was the 19th living wife. You can read her story by going to faithandreasonforum.org.

(Mormonism section), "Wife Number 19...."

37. Todd Compton, *In Sacred Loneliness: The Plural Wives of Joseph Smith* (Salt Lake City, UT: Signature Books, 2001), 15.

38. Ibid., 11.

39. The child was born on February 8, 1844. The mother was legally married to Windsor P. Lyon—cited in former Mormon historian, D. Michael Quinn's *The Mormon Hierarchy: Origins of Power* (Salt Lake City, UT: Signature Books in association with Smith Research Associates, 1994), 642, Appendix 7.

One contemporary Mormon woman said, "you hear often that Joseph had no polygamous offspring. The reason of this is very simple. Abortion was practiced on a large scale in Nauvoo. Dr. John C. Bennett, the evil genius of Joseph brought this abomination into a scientific system. He showed to my husband and me the instruments with which he used to 'operate for Joseph.' There was a house in Nauvoo, 'right across the flat'...a kind of hospital. They sent the women there, when they showed signs of celestial consequences. Abortion was practiced regularly in this house" (emphasis in original). W. Wyle, 59.

Heber C. Kimball confirms that abortions were quite prominent. He gives this account: "The priests of the day in the whole world keep women, just the same as the gentlemen of the Legislatures do. The great men of the earth keep from two to three, and perhaps half-a-dozen private women. They are not acknowledged openly, but are kept merely to gratify their lusts; and if they get in the family way, they call for the doctors, and also upon females who practise under the garb of midwives, to kill the children, and thus they are depopulating their own species. {Voice: "And their names shall come to an end."] *Yes, because they shed innocent blood. I knew that before I received "Mormonism." I have known of lots of women calling for a doctor to destroy their children; and there are many of the women in this enlightened age and in the most popular towns and cities in the Union that take a course to get rid of their children. The whole nation is guilty of it. I am telling the truth. I won't call it infanticide. You know I am famous for calling things by their names. I have been taught it, and my wife was taught it in our young_days, when she got into the family way, to send for a doctor and get rid of the child, so as to live with me to gratify lust. It is God's truth, and I know the person that did it. This is depopulating the human species; and the curse of God will come upon that man, and upon that woman, and upon those cursed doctors. There is scarcely one of them that is free from the sin. It is just as common as it is for wheat to g grow. Do we take that course here? No. I have buried several children; I have buried them in York State, too, in Monroe county, where I lived all my young days, and where I became acquainted with brother Brigham, which is rising of thirty years that we have been together, about twelve miles from where Joseph Smith lived and found the Book of Mormon. I buried two children there, lawful children, born to me by my first wife; and then I have buried some ten children here, born to me by my lawful wives; and I have had altogether about fifty children; and one hundred years won't pass away before my posterity will out-number the present inhabitants of the State of New York, because I do not destroy my offspring...."(Journal of Discourses, 5:91, July 26, 1857).*

Additional note: In the Mormon's, *History of the Church* 5:71, there is confirmation (by Hyrum Smith) that Dr. Bennett was willing to perform an abortion for any woman who became pregnant (especially the women that he would personally seduce). He would give a type of "medicine" to the pregnant woman, which would assist in the abortion.

40. Donny Osmond, *Life is Just What You Make It* (New York: Hyperion, 1999), 13.

41. Contributor, 5:259; quoted in Ogden Kraut's *The Church and the Gospel* (Salt Lake City, UT: Pioneer Press, 1993), 186.

42. *Millennial Star*, Vol. 27:673; quoted in Kraut, 186-87.

43. *Salt Lake City Tribune*, January 6, 1880; quoted in Kraut, 187.

44. Revelation given by John Taylor, dated September 27, 1886; photocopy of the original appears in *1886 Revelation—A Revelation of the Lord to John Taylor.* Published by the "Fundamentalists," quoted in Tanner and Tanner, *Mormonism: Shadow or Reality?* 242.

45. *Journal of Discourses*, 13:166, Wilford Woodruff, December 12, 1869.

46. Wilford Woodruff, OFFICIAL DECLARATION (1), Doctrine and Covenants, (copyright, 1921, 1949), 256-257.

47. *Reed Smoot Case* 4:476. The Congressional Committee gave a long list of cases of plural marriages by the apostles of the church—after the Manifesto.

48. For example, in 1896 Mormon apostle Abraham H. Cannon took a plural wife by the name of Lillian Hamlin. President Joseph F. Smith performed the ceremony and "obtained the acquiescence of President Woodruff [who wrote the manifesto], on the plea that it wasn't an ordinary case of polygamy but merely a fulfilment of the biblical instruction that a man should take his dead brother's wife..." *Daily Journal of*

Abraham H. Cannon, April 5, 1894, Vol. 18, 70; quoted in Tanner and Tanner, *Mormonism: Shadow or Reality?* 244-A

49 According to the Tanners, the "apostle Abraham H,. Cannon's journal not only reveals that the Mormon leaders approved of polygamy after the manifesto [Official Declaration], but it shows they were considering the idea of a secret system of concubinage: George Q. Cannon said, "I believe in concubinage, or some plan whereby men and women can live together under sacred ordinances and vows until they can married. . .such a condition would have to be kept secret. . . " President Snow said, "I have no doubt but concubinage will yet be practiced in this church. . .when the nations are troubled good women will come here for safety and blessing, and men will accept them as concubines." President Woodruff (author of the Manifesto) said, "If men enter into some practice of this character to raise a righteous posterity, they will be justified in it. . . ." Ibid., 244-B.

50. *Dialogue: A Journal of Mormon Thought* (Salt Lake City, UT: Dialogue Foundation, 1994), Vol. 27, No. 1, Spring 1994, 36.

51. Walter B. Knight, *Knight's Master Book of 4,000 Illustrations* (Grand Rapids, MI: William Eerdman's Publishing Co., 1956), 704.

Chapter 5—What Do I Need to Know About Other Mormon Scriptures?

1. Joseph Smith, *History of the Church of Jesus Christ of Latter Day Saints*, 7 vols. (Salt Lake City, UT: Deseret Book Co., 1978), 2:235, 348, 350 (footnotes). (Hereafter, referred to as *History of the Church*.)

2. *Gospel Principles* (Salt Lake City, UT: The Church of Jesus Christ of Latter-day Saints, 1992), 379, "*Pearl of Great Price*: One of the standard works, including ancient and modern scripture."

3. *History of the Church*, 2:238, July 1835.

4. Ibid., 2:329, December 12, 1835.

5. Ibid., 2:330, December 12, 1835.

6. Jerald and Sandra Tanner, *The Case Against Mormonism* (Salt Lake City, UT: Utah Lighthouse Ministry, 1968), 2:125. (For a list of these world-renowned scholars and some of their comments, refer to pages 124-26 of this book.)

7. Jerald and Sandra Tanner, *Mormonism: Shadow or Reality?* 5th ed. (Salt Lake City, UT: Utah Lighthouse Ministry, 1987), 332.

8. *Improvement Era,* 16:615; quoted in Tanner and Tanner, *The Case Against Mormonism*, 2:164.

9. Ibid.

10. *History of the Church*, 1:20.

11. Dean C. Jessee, ed., *The Papers of Joseph Smith: Autobiographical and Historical Writings* (Salt Lake City, UT: Deseret Book Co., 1989), 1:471.

12. E.D. Howe (contemporary of Smith's),*Mormonism Unveiled* (Zanesville, OH: printed and published by the author, 1834), 270; a photomechanical reprint (Salt Lake City, UT: Utah Lighthouse Ministry). A large portion of this letter can also be found in B.H. Roberts, *A Comprehensive History of the Church of Jesus Christ of Latter-day Saints* (Salt Lake City, UT: Church of Jesus Christ of Latter-day Saints, 1957), 1:102-04. (Hereafter will be referred to as *A Comprehensive History of the Church*.)

13. E.D. Howe, 270. Professor Anthon did not know Martin Harris's name. Throughout his testimony, Anthon referred to this individual as "the farmer." There is no question that "the farmer" was Martin Harris. Harris's own testimony of his visit with Anthon can be found in *History of the Church*, 1:20.

14. Ibid., 271-72. The only portion of this paragraph in *A Comprehensive History of the Church* is "the paper contained any thing else but Egyptian Hieroglyphics" (103). Also is the following quote, "Upon examining the paper in question, I soon came to the conclusion that it was all a trick—perhaps a hoax," 103.

15. *Dialogue: A Journal of Mormon Thought,* vol. 33, no 4,Winter 2000, 123, "Ashment: Joseph Smith's Identification of Abraham in Papyrus JS 1."

16. Ibid., 126.

17. *History of the Church*, 4:501, January 25, 1842.

18. John J. Steward and William E. Berrett, *Mormonism and the Negro*, Part 2, 19; quoted in Tanner and Tanner, *The Case Against Mormonism*, 2:172.

19. Joseph Fielding Smith, *Doctrines of Salvation* (Salt Lake City, UT: Bookcraft, 1955), 2:55.

20. Bruce R. McConkie, *Mormon Doctrine* (Salt Lake City, UT: Bookcraft, 1966, Gospel Infobase Library CD ROM, 3rd ed., 3/24/93, Infobases Inc., 1991, 1992), 527-28.

21. *Salt Lake Tribune*, October 25, 1969; quoted in Ogden Kraut's *The Church and the Gospel* (Salt Lake City, Pioneer Press, 1993), 186-87.

22. *Deseret News*, October 5, 1963; quoted in Kraut, 206.

23. The deacons (organized into quorums of 12 or fewer members) are usually 12-year olds, continuing in that priesthood office until age 14. In each quorum there is one deacon called president, two as counselors, and another as secretary. The bishopric is assigned to an adult to teach and train the deacons. Daniel H. Ludlow, ed., *Encyclopedia of Mormonism* (New York: Macmillan Publishing Company, 1992), 1:361.

24. Kraut, 208.

25. *Ensign*, November 1974, p. 35; quoted in Kraut, 208.

26. *Deseret News*, September 10, 1977; quoted in Kraut, 209.

27. *Mormon Doctrine*, 527, "Negroes."

28. Kraut, 212.

29. Tanner and Tanner, *Mormonism: Shadow or Reality?* 332.

30. *Dialogue: A Journal of Mormon Thought*, Autumn 1970, 96; quoted in Tanner and Tanner, *Mormonism: Shadow or Reality?* 332.

31. *History of the Church*, 6:12, important Conference of the Twelve, held at Boylston Hall, Boston, September 9, 1843.

32. *Gospel Principles* (Salt Lake City, UT: The Church of Jesus Christ of Latter-day Saints, 1992), 49-50.

33. *October 1963 Conference Report of the Church of Jesus Christ of Latter-day Saints* (Salt Lake City, UT: Church of Jesus Christ of Latter-day Saints, 1963, Gospel Infobase Library CD ROM, 3rd ed., 3/24/93), 17, Ezra Taft Benson. Also see *Conference Report*, October 1897, 18-19, Brigham Young.

34. Ezra Taft Benson, *Teachings of Ezra Taft Benson* (Salt Lake City, UT: Bookcraft, 1966, Gospel Infobase Library CD ROM, 3rd ed., 3/24/93, Infobases Inc., 1991, 1992), 137. Formerly the words of President Heber J. Grant.

35. *Mormon Doctrine*, 416, "Kingdom of God."

36. *Journal of Discourses*, 26 volumes (London: Latter-day Saints Book Depot, 1854-1886), 3:262, June 10, 1855, Heber C. Kimball.

37. L.G. Otten and C.M. Caldwell, *The Sacred Truths of the Doctrine and Covenants* (Salt Lake City, UT: Lemb, Inc., 1982, Gospel Infobase Library CD ROM, 3rd ed., 3/24/93, Infobases Inc., 1993), 1:94. Warning given by Mormon apostle and later president Harold Lee.

38. *Journal of Discourses*, 3:335, April 24, 1870, Brigham Young.

Part Two—Questions to Ask Our Mormon Friends

1. W.Wyle, *Joseph Smith the Prophet: His Family and Friends* (Salt Lake City, UT: Tribune Printing and Publishing Company, 1886); a photomechanical reprint (Salt Lake City, UT: Utah Lighthouse Ministry), 265.

Chapter 6—Why Don't You Believe the Bible Alone Is Sufficient?

1. Joseph Fielding Smith, *Doctrines of Salvation* (Salt Lake City, UT: Bookcraft, 1956), 3:190.

2. Ibid.

3. Bruce R. McConkie, *Mormon Doctrine* (Salt Lake City, UT: Bookcraft, 1966, Gospel Infobase Library CD ROM, 3rd ed., 3/24/93, Infobases Inc., 1991, 1992), 99. McConkie was quoting the words of Joseph Smith. See *The Teachings of Joseph Smith* (Salt Lake City, UT: Deseret Books, 1976), 71.

4. *Doctrines of Salvation*, 3:191.

5. *The Pearl of Great Price* (Salt Lake City, UT: The Church of Jesus Christ of Latter-day Saints, 1921, 1948), 67, "The Articles of Faith," number 8.

6. Joseph Smith, *History of the Church of Jesus Christ of Latter Day Saints*, 7 vols. (Salt Lake City, UT: Deseret Book Co., 1978), 4:461. (Hereafter shall be referred to as *History of the Church*.)

7. Charles Caldwell Ryrie, *The Ryrie Study Bible* (Chicago, IL: Moody Press, 1976, 1978), 1053.

8. John MacArthur, *The MacArthur Study Bible* (Nashville: Word Publishing, 1997), 1205.

9. Jerald and Sandra Tanner, *3,913 Changes in the Book of Mormon* (Salt Lake City, UT: Utah Lighthouse Ministry), 6. This book is a photo reprint of the *original 1830 edition* of the *Book of Mormon* with all the changes marked.

10. Ibid., 5.

11. Ibid., 6.

12. Ibid.

13. *History of the Church*, 4:461, November 28, 1841. Other Mormon leaders have quoted this same statement, for instance—see *Mormon Doctrine*, 99.

Chapter 7—Why Do You Trust in Joseph Smith for Your Salvation?
1. *Journal of Discourses*, 26 volumes (London: Latter-day Saints Book Depot, 1854-1886), 6:229, July 26, 1857, Joseph Young.
2. Joseph Fielding Smith, *Doctrines of Salvation* (Salt Lake City, UT: Bookcraft, 1954), 1:189-90.
3. According to Chawkat Moucarry in *The Prophet and the Messiah: An Arab Christian's Perspective on Islam and Christianity* (Downers Grove, IL: InterVarsity Press, 2001), 176, Muslims point to Deuteronomy 18:15-18 and apply these prophetic verses to Muhammad rather than to Jesus. What's important to know is that the apostle Peter in Acts 3:22 is repeating what Moses said of Jesus in Deuteronomy 18:15.
4. Daniel H. Ludlow, ed., *Encyclopedia of Mormonism: The History, Scripture, Doctrine, and Procedure of the Church of Jesus Christ of Latter-day Saints*, 4 vols. (New York: Macmillan Publishing Company, 1992), 4:1692.
5. Ibid., 4:1695.
6. *Gospel Principles* (Salt Lake City, UT: The Church of Jesus Christ of Latter-day Saints, 1992), 358-59.
7. Joseph Smith's diary, January 20, 1836, Scott H. Faulring, ed., *An American Prophet's Record: The Diaries and Journals of Joseph Smith* (Salt Lake City, UT: Signature Books in association with Smith Research Associates, 1989), 117. In the diary there is a thin line through the words "cheerful and."
8. Ibid., 294. Prophecy would never be fulfilled, January 20, 1843.
9. Ibid., 486, June 1, 1844.
10. Ibid., 329, March 10, 1843.
11. Joseph Smith, *History of the Church of Jesus Christ of Latter Day Saints*, 7 vols. (Salt Lake City, UT: Deseret Book Co., 1978), 6:111, December 12, 1843. Joseph Smith at this time was the mayor of Nauvoo. (Hereafter shall be referred to as *History of the Church*.)
12. Harold Schindler, *Orrin Porter Rockwell: Man of God/Son of Thunder* (Salt Lake City, UT: University of Utah Press, 1966), 104. This incident is described in detail by the eldest son of the prophet, Joseph Smith III, who witnessed the argument between his parents. See *Joseph Smith III and the Restoration*, edited by Mary Audentia Smith Anderson and condensed by Bertha Audentia Anderson Holmes (Independence, Missouri, 1952), 74-76.
13. On October 7, 1873, George Albert Smith remarked, "We are doing a great business in tea, coffee and tobacco in the Co-operative Store," quoted in *Journal of Discourses*, 16:238. On December 22, 1841 eight years after Word of Wisdom was put in place, Joseph records that 13 wagons of groceries arrived at the new store, delivering, among other things, tea and coffee. Cited in *History of the Church*, 4:483.
14. Robert Bruce Flanders, *Nauvoo Kingdom on the Mississippi* (Urbana, IL: University of Illinois Press, 1965), 248.
15. *History of the Church*, 7:559. "Dialogue Between Joseph Smith and the Devil," which first appeared in the *New York Herald* by Mormon Elder Parley P. Pratt. Mormon apostate Ezra Booth reported that Smith described an angel "as having the appearance of 'a tall, slim, well built, handsome man, with a bright pillar upon his head.'" The Devil, he said, once "appeared to him in the same form, excepting upon his head he had a 'black pillar,' and by this mark he was able to distinguish him from the former." E.D. Howe (contemporary of Smith's),*Mormonism Unveiled* (Zanesville, OH: printed and published by the author, 1834), 187; a photomechanical reprint (Salt Lake City, UT: Utah Lighthouse Ministry).
16. John Whitmer, *John Whitmer's History*, a hotomechanical reproduction (Salt Lake City, UT: Modern Microfilm Co.), 22. While Sidney Rigdon preached the sermon, Joseph and his brothers were instigators. Whitmer credits these three as being involved. John Whitmer's exact wording was "Thus, on the 19th of June, 1838, they preached a sermon called the salt sermon, in which these Gideonites understood that they should drive the dissenters, as they termed those who believed not in their secret bands, in fornication, adultery or midnight machinations" (22). It seems likely that it was this sermon Joseph Smith referred to in his diary in June 1838. Faulring, ed., *An American Prophet's Record*, 187.
17. Facts surrounding the Mormons in Missouri are in William Swartzell's daily journal from May 28 to August 20, 1838. See William Swartzell's *Mormonism Exposed, Being a Journal of a Residence in Missouri From the 28th of May to the 20th of August, 1838* (Pittsburgh: A. Ingrim Jr., printer, 1840); a photomechanical reprint (Salt Lake City, UT: Utah Lighthouse Ministry).
18. David Whitmer, *An Address to All Believers in Christ* (Richmond, MO: 1887), 31; reprint (Salt Lake City, UT: Utah Lighthouse Ministry).
19. Ibid.
20. Bruce McConkie, *The Millennial Messiah*, book six of the "Messiah Series" (Salt Lake City, UT: Deseret Book Co., 1982, Gospel Infobase Library CD ROM, 3rd. ed., 3/24/93, Infobases Inc., 1991, 1992), 281.
21. E.D. Howe, 177, September 1831.
22. Ibid.
23. Bruce McConkie, *A New Witness for the Articles of the Faith* (Salt Lake City, UT: Deseret Book Co., 1985, Gospel Infobase Library CD ROM, 3rd ed., 3/24/93, Infobases, Inc., 1991, 1992), 603.

24. Ibid., 590.

25. Bruce McConkie, *The Millennial Messiah*, 285-86.

26. Prophecy found in *History of the Church*, 1:301-02; D&C 87:1-8. Mormons didn't know of this prophecy until years later. Mormon historian B.H. Roberts admits that this prophecy was never put in print until the *Millennial Star*, Vol. XIII, 1851, 216-17 advertised the church publication of the *Pearl of Great Price*, in which this 1832 revelation would be told. B.H. Roberts, *A Comprehensive History of the Church of Jesus Christ of Latter-day Saints* (Salt Lake City, UT: Church of Jesus Christ of Latter-day Saints, 1957), 1:294. (Hereafter will be referred to as *A Comprehensive History of the Church*.)

27. Joseph F. Smith, *Gospel Doctrine* (Salt Lake City, UT: Deseret Book Company, 1977), 486.

28. *A Comprehensive History of the Church*, 1:294.

29. Jerald and Sandra Tanner, *Mormonism: Shadow or Reality?* 5th ed. (Salt Lake City ,UT: Utah Lighthouse Ministry, 1987), 191; for more details on the Civil War see 190-92.

30. *History of the Church*, 5:394, May 18, 1843.

31. Ibid., 6:116, December 16, 1843.

32. See the William Swartzell (A Danite) daily journal in his *Mormonism Exposed, Being a Journal of a Residence in Missouri From the 28th of May to the 20th of August, 1838* (Pittsburgh: A. Ingrim Jr., printer, 1840), 18, 22; a photomechanical reprint (Salt Lake City, UT: Utah Lighthouse Ministry).

33. Joseph Smith's diary, April 6, 1843, Scott H. Faulring, ed., *An American Prophet's Record: The Diaries and Journals of Joseph Smith* (Salt Lake City, UT: Signature Books in association with Smith Research Associates, 1989), 349.

34. William Clayton diary, August 27, 1843, in George D. Smith, ed., *An Intimate Chronicle: The Journals of William Clayton* (Salt Lake City, UT: Signature Books in association with Smith Research Associates, 1995), 119.

35. Sarah Hall Scott to Calvin and Abigail Hall, 22 July 1844, quoted in D. Michael Quinn's *The Mormon Hierarchy: Origins of Power* (Salt Lake City, UT: Signature Books in association with Smith Research Associates, 1994), 144.

36. Erastus Snow sermon in *Deseret Evening News*, 9 October 1882, [2] quoted in Quinn, *Mormon Hierarchy: Origins of Power*, 144. Snow was a member of Smith's Council of Fifty in 1844.

37. Quinn, *The Mormon Hierarchy: Origins of Power*, 101.

38. Joseph's fears resulted from being accused of attempted murder on Missouri's governor, Lilburn Boggs. Smith had prophesied that "Lilburn Boggs would 'die by violent hands within a year'" and that Illinois Governor Thomas "Carlin would die in a ditch." Smith was accused of hiring Orrin Porter Rockwell to kill Boggs. See Harold Schindler's *Orrin Porter Rockwell: Man of God/Son of Thunder* (Salt Lake City, UT: University of Utah Press, 1966), 64-65. A copy of the letter from Thomas Carlin to Joseph Smith can be found in Smith's diary, August 18, 1843—Scott H. Faulring, ed., *An American Prophet's Record: The Diaries and Journals of Joseph Smith* (Salt Lake City, UT: Signature Books in association with Smith Research Associates, 1989), 410-11.

39. See Joseph Smith's diary, January 29, 1844 in Faulring, *An American Prophet's Record*, 443.

40. Joseph Smith's diary, April 7, 1844, in Faulring, *An American Prophet's Record*, 465.

41. Walter B. Knight, *Knight's Treasury of 2,000 Illustrations* (Grand Rapids, MI: William B. Eerdmans Publishing Co., 1963), 184. Author unknown.

Chapter 8—What Does God's Grace Mean to You?

1. Joseph Fielding Smith, *Doctrines of Salvation* (Salt Lake City, UT: Bookcraft, 1955), 2:310.

2. *Journal of Discourses*, 26 volumes (London: Latter-day Saints Book Depot, 1854-1886), 1:312, February 20, 1853, Brigham Young.

3. Ibid., 2:132, December 18, 1853, Brigham Young.

4. Joseph Fielding Smith, *Doctrines of Salvation*, 3:90.

5. Other verses in the *Book of Mormon* that teach a salvation by works include 2 Nephi 9:23-24; Mosiah 5:5-8; 13:27; Alma 7:16. Also in *Doctrine and Covenants*, 6:37.

6. James E. Talmage, *The Vitality of Mormonism* (Salt Lake City, UT: James E. Talmage, 1919; Gospel Infobase Library CD ROM, 3rd ed., 3/24/93, Infobases, Inc., 1992), 48-49, "The Cooperative Plan of Salvation—Christ Alone Cannot Save You."

7. *Doctrines of Salvation*, 3:91.

8. Charles Caldwell Ryrie, *The Ryrie Study Bible* (Chicago, IL: Moody Press, 1976, 1978), 1792

9. Andrew F. Ehat and Lyndon W. Cook, eds., *The Words of Joseph Smith*, 7 volumes (Provo, UT: Brigham Young University, 1980), May 16, 1841, 6:74. Extracts from William Clayton's private book. Also see Bruce R. McConkie's, *Mormon Doctrine* (Salt Lake City, UT: Bookcraft, 1966, Gospel Infobase Library CD ROM,

3rd ed., 3/24/93, Infobases 1991, 1992), 92, which states that murder is one of those sins that can't be cleansed with the blood of Christ. Mormon theology also says children under eight "cannot sin" (D&C 29:46-47), therefore, they "need no repentance" (*Book of Mormon*, Moroni 8:11,19). See *Mormon Doctrine*, pp. 852-53 for "Years of Accountability." Because Mormon children are baptized at age eight, we can ask Mormons, "Why are Mormon children baptized for their sins [Mormons believe baptism is for cleansing one of sin] if they supposedly haven't sinned?'

10. Walter B. Knight, *Knight's Master Book of 4,000 Illustrations* (Grand Rapids, MI: Eerdman's Publishing Co., 1956), 227.

11. Donna Morley, *A Woman of Significance* (Santa Clarita, CA: Faith & Reason Press, 2001, 2009), 139. Words by minister Joseph Hart engraved on his tombstone in England. Died May 24, 1783.

12. *Doctrines of Salvation*, 2:138.

13. Ibid., 2:139.

14. Ibid., 2:140.

15. LeGrand Richards, *A Marvelous Work and a Wonder* (Salt Lake City, UT: Deseret Book Company, 1977), 24.

16. *Doctrines of Salvation*, 2:138.

17. H.D.M. Spence and Joseph S. Exell, *The Pulpit Commentary: Gospel of John* (Peabody, MA: Hendrickson Publishers, n.d.), 17:444.

Chapter 9—Why Do You Rely on Baptisms for the Living and the Dead?

1. *Journal of Discourses*, 26 volumes (London: Latter-day Saints Book Depot, 1854–1886), 1:239, July 24, 1853, Brigham Young.

2. G. Abbott-Smith, *A Manual Greek Lexicon of the New Testament*, 3rd ed. (Edinburgh: T&T Clark, 1937), 133.

3. "Prepositions with baptizo," *The New International Dictionary of New Testament Theology*, Colin Brown, ed. (Grand Rapids: Zondervan, 1978), 3:1208-09.

4. Gordon R. Lewis and Bruce A. Demarest, ed., *Integrative Theology*, Three Volumes in One (Grand Rapids, MI: Zondervan Publishing House, 1996), 3:285.

5. H.E. Dana and Julius R. Mantey, *A Manual Grammar of the Greek New Testament* (Toronto: Macmillan, 1927), 104.

6. Bruce Demarest, *The Cross and Salvation* (Wheaton, IL: Crossway, 1997), 296. He cites *A Linguistic Key to the Greek New Testament*, Fritz Rienecker and Cleon L. Rogers, Jr., eds. (Grand Rapids, MI: Zondervan, 1982), 324.

7. Joseph Fielding Smith, *Doctrines of Salvation* (Salt Lake City, UT: Bookcraft, 1955), 2:148.

8. *U.S. News & World Report*, Science & Society, "Latter-day struggles." September 28, 1992, 74.

9. Gregory A. Prince, *Power from on High: The Development of Mormon Priesthood* (Salt Lake City, UT: Signature Books, 1995), 181.

10. Andrew F. Ehat and Lyndon W. Cook, *The Words of Joseph Smith* (Provo, UT: Religious Studies Center, Brigham Young University, 1980), 6:77, October 3, 1841.

11. Ibid., 6:318, January 21, 1844.

12. Ibid., 6:353, April 7, 1844. The unedited version reads, "a friend who has got a friend in the world can save him unless he has comd. the unpard sin & so you can see how far you can be Savior...."

13. Ibid., April 7, 1844.

14. Ibid., 6:98. This policy regarding baptisms for the dead was given to the Mormon church by Joseph Smith, on October 3, 1841. According to the editors of *The Words of Joseph Smith* (Ehat and Cook), "subsequent revelation has added to this responsibility,"98.

15. *Doctrines of Salvation*, 2:148.

16. *October 1954 Conference Report of the Church of Jesus Christ of Latter-day Saints* (Salt Lake City: Church of Jesus Christ of Latter-day Saints, 1954, Gospel Infobase Library CD ROM, 3rd ed., 3/24/93), 26, Eldred G. Smith.

17. *U.S. News & World Report*, Science & Society, "Latter-day struggles." September 28, 1992, 74-75.

18. Lucy Mack Smith, *Joseph Smith's History by His Mother*, photomechanical reprint of the original 1853 edition. Original title *Biographical Sketches or Joseph Smith the Prophet, and His Progenitors for Many Generations* (Salt Lake City, UT: Utah Lighthouse Ministry), 265.

19. Ibid., 266.

20. Charles Hodge, *Commentary on the First Epistle to the Corinthians* (Grand Rapids, MI: William B. Eerdman's Publishing Co., 1950, 1980, 1994), 337.

21. Ibid., 339.

Chapter 10—In Your View, Who Is Jesus Christ?

1. *Journal of Discourses*, 26 volumes (London: Latter-day Saints Book Depot, 1854-1886), 8:115, July 8, 1860, Brigham Young.

2. Ibid., 1:50-51,April 9, 1852, Brigham Young. Brigham Young said much more in this sermon. He said that Adam is "Michael, the Archangel, the Ancient of Days...He is our Father and Our God, and the only God with whom we have to do." Young also said that Eve is "one of his wives." The full text of this sermon can be found in *Journal of Discourses*, 1:46-53.

3. Joseph Fielding Smith, *Doctrines of Salvation* (Salt Lake City, UT: Bookcraft, 1954), 1:18.

4. Ibid., 1:19.

5. *Journal of Discourses*, 13:282, October 30, 1870, Brigham Young.

6. Mormons are taught that "the fall of man came as a blessing in disguise, and was a means of furthering the purposes of the Lord in the progress of man, rather than a means of hindering them." *Doctrines of Salvation*, 1:114. Brigham Young said, "Some may regret that our first parents sinned. This is nonsense... I will not blame Adam and Eve. Why? Because it was necessary that sin should enter into the world, no man could under-stand the principle of exaltation without its opposite....The Lord knew they would do this, and he designed that they should...." *Doctrines of Salvation*, 1:112-13. Also refer to the "Beneficent Results of the Fall" found in James E. Talmage's *The Articles of Faith* (Salt Lake City, UT: The Church of Jesus Christ of Latter-day Saints, 1977), 476.

7. Bruce R. McConkie, *Mormon Doctrine* (Salt Lake City, UT: Bookcraft, 1966, Gospel Infobase Library CD ROM, 3rd ed., 3/24/93, Infobases, Inc., 1991, 1992), 92.

8. Ibid., 93.

9. Ibid., 92.

10. *April 1959 Conference Report of the Church of Jesus Christ of Latter-day Saints* (Salt Lake City: Church of Jesus Christ of Latter-day Saints, 1959, Gospel Infobase CD ROM, 3rd ed., 3/24/93), 23, Joseph Fielding Smith.

11. Joseph Fielding Smith, *Doctrines of Salvation* (Salt Lake City, UT: Bookcraft, 1955), 2:310.

12. *Journal of Discourses*, 7:298, December 25, 1859, Amasa M. Lyman.

13. Jerald and Sandra Tanner, *Mormonism: Shadow or Reality?* 5th ed. (Salt Lake City, UT: Utah Lighthouse Ministry, 1987), preface, 2.

14. Joseph Smith, *History of the Church of Jesus Christ of Latter-day Saints*, 7 vols. (Salt Lake City, UT: Deseret Book Co., 1978), 5:296, March 4, 1843.

15. John D. Lee, *Confessions of John D. Lee*, 283; a photomechanical reprint of the original 1877 edition of *Mormonism Unveiled; or the Life and Confessions of the Late Mormon Bishop, John D. Lee* (Salt Lake City, UT: Utah Lighthouse Ministry).

16. Lee, 282-83. Lee gives the account of a Danish man, Rosmos Anderson, who was informed that he had to be killed for his sin of adultery. Both Rosmos and his wife agreed. Lee tells of the gruesome act Anderson went through.

17. In the Mormon Security Forces (1833-1847), it is noted under March 13, 1847 that the response toward a dissenter would be to "cut him off—behind the ears—according to the law of God in such cases;" quoted in D. Michael Quinn, *The Mormon Hierarchy: Origins of Power* (Salt Lake City, UT: Signature Books in association with Smith Research Associates, 1994), 477, Appendix 2.

18. December 13, 1846, Brigham Young said, "When a man is found to be a thief he will be a thief no longer, cut his throat, & thro' him in the River"; quoted in Quinn, *The Mormon Hierarchy: Origins of Power*, 657, Appendix 7.

19. Lee, 284.

20. Ibid., 281.

21. D. Michael Quinn, *The Mormon Hierarchy: Extensions of Power* (Salt Lake City, UT: Signature Books in association with Smith Research Associates, 1997), 246. When informed that a black Mormon in Boston had married a white woman, Brigham Young told "the apostles he would have both killed if he could." Quoted in Quinn, *The Mormon Hierarchy: Origins of Power*, 660, Appendix 7, December 3, 1847.

22. Lee, 283.

23. Not all who confessed were spared. Rosmos Anderson had committed adultery and confessed his sin. Despite this, he was notified that he must die. And he did—the blood-atoning way. Lee, 282-83.

24. Lee, 282.

25. Ibid., 132. Lee said, "My station as a guard was at the Prophet's mansion, during his life, and after his death my post was changed to the residence of Brigham Young."

26. Ibid., 282.

27. Jerald and Sandra Tanner, *Mormonism: Shadow or Reality?* 5th ed. (Salt Lake City, UT: Utah Lighthouse Ministry, 1987), 568-69.

Chapter 11—Why Do You Believe You Can Become a God?

1. Joseph Fielding Smith, _Doctrines of Salvation_ (Salt Lake City, UT: Bookcraft, 1995), 2:43-44, 60-62, 78-79; LeGrand Richard, _A Marvelous Work and a Wonder_ (Salt Lake City, UT: Deseret Book Co., 1976), 190.

2. Andrew F. Ehat and Lyndon W. Cook, _The Words of Joseph Smith_ (Provo, UT: Religious Studies Center, Brigham Young University, 1980), 6:84, January 5, 1841. Editors Ehat and Cook said that "perhaps no one in the history of the Church, except Joseph Smith has popularized this concept [having a body of resurrected flesh and bones] more than Lorenzo Snow," 6:84.

3. _Journal of Discourses_, 26 volumes (London: Latter-day Saints Book Depot, 1854-1886), 7:334, October 8, 1859, Brigham Young.

4. Mormon elder King Follet had been crushed to death in a well by the falling of a tub of rock on him. Cited in Joseph Smith's diary, April 7, 1844, in Scott H. Faulring, ed., _An American Prophet's Record: The Diaries and Journals of Joseph Smith_ (Salt Lake City, UT: Signature Books in association with Smith Research Associates, 1989), 465.

5. Joseph Smith's diary, April 7, 1844, Faulring, _An American Prophet's Record_, 465. See also _History of the Church_ 6:305. For the full sermon, see _Journal of Discourses_ 6:3-4.

6. Joseph Smith, _History of the Church of Jesus Christ of Latter Day Saints_, 7 vols. (Salt Lake City, UT: Deseret Book Co., 1978), 6:474-75, June 16, 1844.

7. James E. Talmage, _The Articles of Faith_ (Salt Lake City, UT: The Church of Jesus Christ of Latter-day Saints, 1977), 28.

8. _Journal of Discourses_, 6:322, April 7, 1852, Brigham Young.

9. Joseph Fielding Smith, _Doctrines of Salvation_ (Salt Lake City, UT: Bookcraft, 1954), 1:11. See also _History of the Church_ 6:305.

10. The Mormon husband and wife (or wives), while in the celestial kingdom, procreate for all eternity. The babies they have are "spirit babies" that await a body that will be supplied by a woman on the earth that is ruled by the god and goddess (see D&C 132: 19-20). Brigham Young said, "Spirits must be borne, even if they have to come to brothels for their fleshly coverings." _Journal of Discourses_, 3:264, July 14, 1855. The "more noble" or choice spirits are to be born as Mormons. _Journal of Discourses_, 1:62-63, August 29, 1852, Orson Pratt.

11. "This doctrine that there is a Mother in Heaven was affirmed in plainness by the First Presidency of the Church...they said that 'man, as a spirit, was begotten and born of heavenly parents, and reared to maturity in the eternal eternal mansions of the Father, that man is the 'offspring of celestial parentage' and that 'all men and women are in the similitude of the universal Father and Mother and are literally the sons and daughters of Deity.'" Bruce R .McConkie, _Mormon Doctrine_ (Salt Lake City, UT: Bookcraft, 1966, Gospel Infobase Library CD ROM, 3rd ed., 3/24/93, Infobases Inc., 1991, 1992), 516,"Mother in Heaven."

Chapter 12—What Do You Believe About the Trinity?

1. Joseph Smith said,"...the Great God has a name by wich [sic] He will be Called which is Ahman" (sic); quoted in Andrew F. Ehat and Lyndon W. Cook, _The Words of Joseph Smith_ (Provo, UT: Religious Studies Center, Brigham Young University, 1980), 6:64, March 9, 1841. _Doctrine and Covenants_ says that Jesus is the "Son of Ahman" (D&C 78:20; 95:17).

2. James E. Talmage, _The Articles of Faith_ (Salt Lake City, UT: The Church of Jesus Christ of Latter-day Saints, 1977), 162.

3. Greek word _pneuma_ (#4151) taken from Robert L. Thomas, ed., _Exhaustive Concordance of the Bible; Hebrew-Aramaic and Greek Dictionaries_ (Anaheim, CA: Foundation Publications, Inc., 1981, 1998), 1558.

4. _Journal of Discourses_, 26 volumes (London: Latter-day Saints Book Depot, 1854-1886), 8:115, July 8, 1860, Brigham Young.

5. Ibid., 13:282, October 30, 1870, Brigham Young.

6. Ibid., 19:65, July 24, 1877, Brigham Young.

7. Ibid., 18:292, November 12, 1876, Orson Pratt.

8. _The Articles of Faith_, 48.

9. _Journal of Discourses_, 5:331-32, October 7, 1857, told by Brigham Young.

10. Ibid., 19:269, March 3, 1878, Erastus Snow.

11. _The Articles of Faith_, 50.

12. Charles Caldwell Ryrie, _The Ryrie Study Bible_ (Chicago, IL: Moody Press, 1976, 1978), 1606.

13. Joseph Smith, _History of the Church of Jesus Christ of Latter Day Saints_, 7 vols. (Salt Lake City, UT: Deseret Book Co., 1978), 6:474, June 16, 1844.

14. Ibid., 6:476, June 16, 1844; _Articles of the Faith_ (pp. 47-48) also disagrees with historic Christianity's position on the Trinity.

15. Ibid., 6:475, June 16, 1844.

16. Ryrie, _The Ryrie Study Bible,_ 1936.

17. In *The MacArthur Study Bible*, Dr. MacArthur confirms it is the Father who is speaking in Hebrews 1:8: "The text is all the more significant since the declaration of the Son's deity is presented as the words of the Father Himself (cf. Isaiah 9:6; Jeremiah 23:5-6; John 5:18; Titus 2:13; 1 John 5:20)." John MacArthur, *The MacArthur Study Bible* (Nashville, TN: Word Publishing, 1997), 1898.

Chapter 13—What Do You Believe About Heaven?
1. *U.S. News & World Report*, Science & Society, "Latter-day struggles." September 28, 1992, 74.

2. Victor Ludlow, (Mormon theologian), *Principles and Practices of the Restored Gospel* (Salt Lake City, UT: Deseret Book Co., 1992), 238.

3. Ibid., 239.

4. Ibid.

5. Joseph Smith, *History of the Church of Jesus Christ of Latter Day Saints*, 7 vols. (Salt Lake City, UT: Deseret Book Co., 1978), 6:314-15.

6. *Principles and Practices of the Restored Gospel*, 223.

7. Ibid., 225.

8. Ibid., 239.

9. Ibid.

10. Ibid., 223.

11. Ibid., 222.

12. LeGrand Richards, *A Marvelous Work and a Wonder* (Salt Lake City,UT: Deseret Book Co., 1977), 25.

13. W. Wyle, *Joseph Smith the Prophet: His Family and Friends* (Salt Lake City, UT: Tribune Printing and Publishing Company, 1886), 2; a photomechanical reprint (Salt Lake City, UT: Utah Lighthouse Ministry).

14. *Principles and Practices of the Restored Gospel*, 240.

15. Joseph Fielding Smith, *Doctrines of Salvation* (Salt Lake City, UT: Bookcraft, 1955), 2:22.

16. *Principles and Practices of the Restored Gospel*, 239-40.

17. Ibid., 240.

18. Ibid.

19. Ibid., 241.

20. Ibid.

21. Ibid.

22. Ibid., 242.

23. Ibid., 241.

24. Ibid.

25. Ibid., 242.

26. Ibid.

27. Ibid.

28. Ibid.

29. Ibid.

30. Benjamin F. Johnson, *My Life's Review* (Independence, MO: Zion's Printing and Publishing Co., 1947), 10; quoted in Donna Hill, *Joseph Smith; The First Mormon* (Garden City, NY: Doubleday and Company, 1977), 342.

31. Joseph F. Smith, *Gospel Doctrine* (Salt Lake City, UT: Deseret Book Co., 1977), 279-80.

32. Ibid., 280.

33. LeGrand Richards, 25.

34. Walter A. Elwell, *Evangelical Dictionary of Biblical Theology* (Grand Rapids, MI: Baker Books, 1996), 332.

35. Ibid.

36. Ibid., 333.

37. Walter B. Knight, *Knight's Master Book of 4,000 Illustrations* (Grand Rapids, MI: Eerdmans Publishing Co., 1956), 277.

38. H.D.M. Spence and Joseph S. Exell, ed., *The Pulpit Commentary: Acts, Romans* (Peabody, MA: Hendrickson Publishers, n.d.), Romans, 143.

Appendix A—A Comparison Between Mormonism and the Bible

1. *Pearl of Great Price*, (Salt Lake City, UT: the Church of Jesus Christ of Latter-day Saints, 1921, 1943), 67, "The Articles of Faith", article number 8.

2. *Gospel Principles* (Salt Lake City, UT: Church of Jesus Christ of Latter-day Saints, 1981), 134.

3. Joseph Fielding Smith, *Doctrines of Salvation* (Salt Lake City, UT: Bookcraft, 1956), 3:142-143.

4. *Doctrines of Salvation*, 2:78.

5. *Gospel Principles*, 113.

6. Joseph F. Smith, *Gospel Doctrine* (Salt Lake City, UT: Deseret Book Co., 1977), 189. See also *Doctrine and Covenants*, 84:35, 42.

7. James E. Talmage, *Jesus the Christ* (Salt Lake City, UT: Deseret Book Co., 1977), 779. See point 5, "Consistency of the Church's Claim to Authority."

8. James E. Talmage, *The Articles of Faith* (Salt Lake City,UT: The Church of Jesus Christ of Latter-day Saints, 1977), 128, "Baptism Essential to Salvation."

9. *The Articles of Faith*, 145 and in *Doctrine and Covenants*, 127:5; 128:1-18.

10. Bruce R. McConkie, *Mormon Doctrine* (Salt Lake City, UT: Bookcraft, 1966, Gospel Infobase Library CD ROM, 3rd ed., 3/24/93, Infobases, Inc., 1991, 1992), 268-69.

11. *Doctrines of Salvation*, 2:9-10. Also see *The Articles of Faith*, "The Fall Foreknown," 476.

12. Ibid., 2:49.

13. Ibid., 2:9-10. Also see *The Articles of Faith*, "The Fall Foreknown," 476.

14. Ibid., 2:310.

15. Joseph Smith, *History of the Church of Jesus Christ of Latter Day Saints*, 7 vols. (Salt Lake City,UT: Deseret Book Co., 1978), 6:474. June 16, 1844, sermon by the prophet: "The Christian Godhead—Plurality of Gods." (Hereafter shall be referred to as *History of the Church*.) See also *The Articles of Faith*, 47-48, which discusses the fallacy of the Christian view of the Trinity.

16. John MacArthur confirms that it is indeed the Father speaking in Hebrews 1:8: "The text is all the more significant since the declaration of the Son's deity is presented as the words of the Father Himself (cf. Isaiah 9:6; Jeremiah 23:5-6; John 5:18; Titus 2:13; 1 John 5:20) ." John MacArthur, *The MacArthur Study Bible* (Nashville, TN: Word Publishing, 1997), 1898.

17. *Doctrines of Salvation*, 1:11.

18. *Mormon Doctrine*, 288.

19. *Journal of Discourses*, 26 volumes (London: Latter-day Saints Book Depot, 1854-1886), 9:149, January 12, 1862, Brigham Young.

20. Ibid., 8:115, July 8, 1860, Brigham Young.

21. Ibid., 13:282, October 30, 1870, Brigham Young.

22. James E. Talmage, *The Vitality of Mormonism* (Salt Lake City, UT: James E. Talmage, Feb. 3, 1919; Gospel Infobase Library CD ROM, 3rd ed., 3/24/93, Infobases, Inc., 1992), 48-49, "The Cooperative Plan of Salvation—Christ Alone Cannot Save You."

23. *The Articles of Faith*, 162-63.

24. The Mormon difference between Ghost and Spirit is found in *Articles of Faith*, 162-63.

25. See Joseph Smith, *History of the Church of Jesus Christ of Latter Day Saints*, 7 vols. (Salt Lake City, UT: Deseret Book Co., 1978), 6:474, 476, June 16, 1844; also *The Articles of Faith*, 47-48 (refutes historic Christianity's position that there is one God in the Trinity).

26. Greek word *pneuma* (#4151) taken from Robert L. Thomas, ed., *Exhaustive Concordance of the Bible: Hebrew-Aramaic and Greek Dictionaries* (Anaheim, CA: Foundation Publications, Inc., 1981, 1998), 1558.

27. *Journal of Discourses*, 8:115, July 8, 1860, Brigham Young. See also *Doctrines of Salvation* 1:18.

28. *Journal of Discourses*, 1:50-51, April 9, 1852, Brigham Young.

29. *Mormon Doctrine*, 92.

30. *Doctrines of Salvation*, 2:310.

31. *Mormon Doctrine*, 92.

32. *Doctrines of Salvation*, 2:37-40.

33. Ibid., 1:56.

34. Ibid., 1:56-57.

35. *Gospel Doctrine*, 92-93

36. *Mormon Doctrine*, 539.

37. "This doctrine that there is a Mother in Heaven was affirmed in plainess by the First Presidency of the Church...they said that man, as a spirit, was begotten and born of heavenly parents, and reared to maturity in the eternal mansions of the Father, that man is the 'offspring of celestial parentage' and that 'all men and women are in the similitude of the universal Father and Mother and are literally the sons and daughters of Deity.'" Bruce R. McConkie, *Mormon Doctrine* (Salt Lake City, UT: Bookcraft, 1966, Gospel Infobase Library CD ROM, 3rd ed., 3/24/93, Infobases Inc., 1991,1992), 516,"Mother in Heaven."

38. *Doctrines of Salvation*, 1:66-68.

39. According to John MacArthur: "In verse 46 Paul points out the obvious: ...*the spiritual is not first, but the natural; then the spiritual.*" MacArthur says that every human being [including Christ when He was man], begins life in a natural, physical body. "Adam, *the first man*, from whom came the natural race, originated on the earth, in fact was created directly *from the earth* (Genesis 2:7)." In every way Adam was earthly. "But Christ, called *the second man* because He has produced a spiritual race, existed eternally before He became a man. He lived on earth in a natural body, but He came *from heaven.*

Adam was tied to earth; Christ was tied to heaven.... *And just as we have born the image of the earthy, [sic] we shall also bear the image of the heavenly. Just as we will exchange Adam's natural body for Christ's spiritual body, we will also exchange Adam's *image* for Christ's. John MacArthur, *The MacArthur New Testament Commentary: 1 Corinthians* (Chicago, IL: Moody Bible Institute, 1984), 439, emphasis in original. According to Gordon R. Lewis and Bruce A. Demarest, "Once the human spirit *exists* it has a *continuous, everlasting identity.* Our spirits have not always existed, for God alone is eternal or 'immortal' in the past, as well as future (1 Timothy 6:16)." Quoted in *Integrative Theology*, Three Volumes in One (Grand Rapids, MI: Zondervan Publishing House, 1996), 14

40. Victor L. 1440. Victor L. Ludlow (Mormon theologian), *Principles and Practices of the Restored Gospel* (Salt Lake City, UT: Deseret Book Co., 1992), 239-40.

41. Ibid., 222. See also *Journal of Discourses*, 15:320-21, January 19, 1873, Orson Pratt.

42. Ibid., 223.While the references support the conclusion, not all apostates are said to go to "outer darkness." Only those who have had their "calling and election made sure," and yet have turned away—will be sent there. That means Christ had to have visited them personally and told them that Mormonism is true and a place is prepared for them in heaven. Then if they turn away after that, they will be sons of perdition. A Mormon who turns away *without* that experience of the Savior's "direct manifestation of his glory" will be sent to the lowest heavenly kingdom. See *Principles and Practices of the Restored Gospel*, 239, and *Mormon Doctrine*, 109-10.

43. Ibid.

44. *Gospel Doctrine*, 189.

FACT SHEET:
YOUR QUICK GUIDE
TO THE TRUTH

I will shew thee
that which is written
in the Scripture of truth.

Daniel 10:21

I have always had a hard time with facts. Throughout high school and college, I hated them. In high school, I felt that memorizing a zillion dates in history was irrelevant to my life. And in college chemistry, memorizing the periodic table not only seemed irrelevant but boring beyond description. Of course, that was then, and this is now. I can now honestly say I love facts—especially facts that can help save a soul. The Fact Sheet on the very last page of this book is filled with scriptures that can help you bring your Mormon friend to Christ. The best part of using this Fact Sheet is you won't have to memorize a thing! Although I couldn't include every scripture verse we've looked at in this book, I am giving you the most pertinent verses to assist you in your witnessing, in season and out (1 Peter 3:15). This Fact Sheet is designed to help you start your discussion in the right place, to focus on the key verses, and to stay on track while addressing the main issues of Mormonism.

Best of all, the Fact Sheet will give you the confidence you need as you share your faith with others. Of course, sharing the good news of Jesus Christ is more than just facts. We are not to be mere fact-givers, but servants of God with a genuine concern for those who aren't Christians and thus don't have eternal life.

This is what I recommend: Photocopy the Fact Sheet pages, trim them down to size, put the pages back to back, then laminate them. By laminating the Fact Sheet you will keep it in usable condition for years to come. Once your Fact Sheet is ready for use, take a good look at it. You will notice there are eight questions. These questions correspond to chapter titles in this book and can be used as questions to your Mormon friend. After reading this book, you will know how your friend is likely to respond to these questions. And, as they respond, all you have to do is refer to this Fact Sheet. It's quite easy!

For example, some time ago my Christian friend Cynthia had a lot of questions about how to share the gospel with someone who grew up Catholic. She knew very little about Catholicism and didn't know what to say. Rather than answer Cynthia's questions right away, I wanted to see how effective a Catholicism Fact Sheet would be for someone like her. Grabbing from my desk my newly made Catholic Fact Sheet, I said, "Let's role play." And so we did. I played the Catholic, and she played herself, the Christian. She asked the first question from the Fact Sheet, and I gave her the Catholic answers. With the help of the Fact Sheet she was able to converse with me, give me appropriate Scripture verses, and show me what God had to say about certain subjects.

Cynthia enjoyed this so much that she wanted to go through the entire Fact Sheet with me. She did a great job of "witnessing" to me, although she admits she now wants to read my book on Catholicism (forthcoming) so she can truly understand the religion and *why* Catholics believe what they do.

By the way, to save space on the Fact Sheet, I abbreviated some references to the books of the Bible. For instance, Genesis is "Gen.," Deuteronomy is "Deut.," Matthew is "Mt.," Hebrews is "Heb.," and so on. "BOM" refers to the *Book of Mormon*.

Before you meet with a Mormon friend, you'll want to review this book and look over the Fact Sheet. In fact, you'll find it helpful to review the book and Fact Sheet periodically so you're also ready for Mormon missionaries who may come knocking at your door!

And in regard to the missionaries, when they are at your door, start out by saying, "Can I ask you some questions about your teachings?" They'll certainly be responsive to your request, but be ready for a few (and I mean just a few) missionaries who might not like seeing you use this Fact Sheet. They may even refuse to answer your questions. If they tell you that they don't want to answer the Fact Sheet questions because "they aren't really *your* questions," you can answer them by saying, "Yes, they are my questions. They are questions that I would like answered. *Besides, does it really matter where the questions come from? Aren't the answers more important?*"

If you want to avoid possible confrontation, you may want to take the time to somewhat memorize the questions and answers. Or, you are welcome to write, *for your own use,* these questions and answers inside your Bible or on another piece of paper.

Faith and Reason Press kindly requests that you make copies of the Fact Sheet for personal use only. If you would like to make copies for others, please obtain our written permission by writing to,

helpdesk @faithandreasonforum.com.

Let us know what use you would like to make of the copies, and the quantity. Please keep in mind that the Fact Sheet is protected by copyright laws.

In ending, whether you use the Fact Sheet, or memorize it, or write the questions and answers in your Bible, this will go a long way toward helping you to be ready to...

Make a defense to everyone

who asks you to give

an account

for the hope

that is in you.

1 Peter 3:15

1. Why don't you believe the Bible alone is sufficient?

• Could the *BOM* be scripture in light of Galatians 1:6-8?
  The Bible doesn't need a second witness—it already has 40 writers as witnesses.
—**Why do we need a restored gospel?**
• The Bible is incorruptible (1 Peter 1:23); will never vanish; shall endure (Ps. 100:5;
  1 Peter 1:25).   • Bible gave us truth once and for all (Jude 3).
—**Bible "prophecies" regarding the *Book of Mormon*:**
• **Isaiah 29:4:** Not about the *BOM*—verses 1-4 show it's a warning of judgment upon
"Ariel" (Jerusalem) because of her hypocrisy.
• **Ezekiel 37:16-17, 22:** It's not about the Bible or the *BOM*. These verses illustrate that God
will re-gather the Israelites to their land and restore union between Israel and Judah in the
Messianic reign. **Show in verse 16** that the 2 sticks refer to the 2 nations that God will
bring together, making them into one nation during His Messianic reign.
—**Book of Mormon "translated by the power of God"?**
• If the *BOM* was translated "by the power of God," then why is there an incorrect
prophecy about Christ's birth? (Contrast Alma 7:10 to Micah 5:2; Mt 2:1)

2. Why do you trust in Joseph Smith for your salvation?

• Bible "prophecy" regarding Smith—Acts 3:22: It's not about Joseph Smith; it's about
Jesus (see Acts 3:14-22).
• Acts 3:22 can't be about Smith—he was a false prophet. Smith said Christ would return
between 1890 and 1891. No one can predict Christ's return—Matthew 24:23, 36-37.
• Salvation in Christ only—John 14:6; Acts 16:30-31; Romans 5:10.

3. What does God's grace mean to you?

• By grace you are saved, not that of yourselves (Ephesians 2:8-9).
• If by works, we eliminate God's grace (Romans 11:5-6).
• If by works, Christ died needlessly (Galatians 2:21).
—**EXPLAINING James 2:20:**
• Yes—faith without works is dead, but genuine faith cannot be dead (James 2:14, 18, 20).
True faith believes what Jesus says (John 11:25; 1 John 5:13), it relies upon His
righteousness (Philippians 3:9). Therefore, works are a *result* of my salvation—not the
cause of salvation (see John 6:28-29).
—**EXPLAINING Philippians 2:12:**
• *Work out your salvation*—Paul is telling the Philippians not to rely on him. They need to
stand on their own feet, knowing God was working in them (see Philippians 2:13).
• *Fear and trembling* refers to having a healthy fear of not wanting to offend God.

4. Why do you rely on baptisms for the living and the dead?

• 1 Corinthians 15:29 is not teaching that we should baptize the dead. This is what you can
explain to your Mormon friend—Show that all verses in chapter 15 (except vs 29) Paul uses
the words "I,""we,""you." In verse 29, Paul uses "they." He is disassociating himself
from this doctrine.   *Bottom Line:* There is no second chance (Heb. 9:27; Ps. 49:7).
Even *BOM* says there's no second chance (Alma 34:32-35)

—**Forgiveness of Sin Doesn't Come Through Baptism:**
• Mormons use Acts 2:38 to show that through baptism you receive forgiveness of sins.
EXPLAIN: Acts 2:38 speaks of repentance and baptism.
ASK: Is it through baptism or repentance that we receive forgiveness?
READ: Acts 3:19--shows repentance leads to salvation. Read Acts 10:43; and 1 John 1:9

5. In your view, who is Jesus Christ? ASK:

- *Did you know your church teaches that Jesus was conceived via physical union between Mary and God the Father?*—The Bible says differently (Mt. 1:18, 20; Luke 1:34-35).
- *Did you know the Mormon church teaches that Jesus and Lucifer are spirit brothers?*
EXPLAIN:—The Bible says Jesus created all things (Colossians 1:16).
—**ASK:** How could they be brothers if Jesus created Lucifer?
- *Did Jesus' death on the cross take away the sins of the world?*
—Christ's death brings forgiveness (Hebrews 9:22).
—Christ's shed blood brought redemption (1 Peter 1:18-19).

6. Why do you believe you can become a god?
—*Mormon defense for becoming a god and how to respond:*

A. EXPLAIN: John 10:34—"ye are gods"
—John 10:33—Jews accuse Jesus of making Himself to be God.
—John 10:34—Christ's reply to the Jews, quoting Psalm 82.
—Read Psalm 82:1-8, which is about the unjust judges who will receive God's wrath.
ASK: How could a "god" receive God's wrath if he's a god?
—Go back to John 10:34. Jesus' argument is that if God can refer to others as a god,"
then why should the Jews object to His statement (Jn 10:36) that He is the Son of God?

B. EXPLAIN: 1 Corinthians 8:5— "many gods...many lords"
—See 1 Corinthians 8:4—This verse is talking about IDOLS yet states: "There is no other God but one." *Important:* The so called many gods and lords in 1 Cor. 8:5 are IDOLS.
—In Scripture idols are referred to as "gods" (Exodus 20:23).
—**Read 1 Corinthians 8:6.** We don't worship idols, only God
  - Paul and Barnabas's reaction (Acts 14:11-15).
  - Warning to those who seek godhood (Ezekiel 28:2, 6-10).

7. What do you believe about the Trinity?

- There is only one God (1 Corinthians 8:4). The Father is God (John 6:27); Jesus is God (Jn 20:28; Heb. 1:8); the Spirit is God (Acts 5:3-4. All are equal and *as one* (Mt. 28:19).
  NOTE: In Mt. 28:19, the word "name" is singular, not plural.
  - God the Father is not flesh and bones but spirit (John 4:24).
  - Holy Ghost, Holy Spirit are the same (1 Corinthians 3:16; 6:19 KJV)
  - Also refer to last line in the *BOM*'s "Testimony of Witnesses" and the *Book of Mormon* text: Alma 11:26-29; 3 Nephi 11:14

8. What do you believe about heaven?

- *Mormons use 1 Corinthians 15:40- 42.* **EXPLAIN:**
** —The *Telestial* glory isn't mentioned in these verses.
**—*Terrestrial* means "things of earth." This is not about heaven (see 1 Cor. 15:39).
    Paul points out terrestrial things such as flesh of men, of beasts, of birds, and of fish.
** —*Celestial* means "heavenly bodies"—the sun, moon, and stars. Paul had been contrasting the earthly body sown in corruption to the heavenly body raised in incorruption.

- *Mormons also use 2 Corinthians 12:2.* **EXPLAIN:**
    —Atmospheric heaven (Deuteronomy 11:11, Isaiah 55:10);
    starry heaven   (Genesis 1:14-17; Nahum 3:16); highest heaven (Isaiah 63:15)
  - "Heavens" in Scripture does not refer to heavenly kingdoms, but to "clouds" (Job 35:5), birds" (Job 12:7),"light" (Genesis 1:14-17). There is only one heaven (Mt. 6:9). John wrote about only one heaven--See the Book of Rev.

BOOKS BY
DONNA MORLEY:

Choices That Lead to Godliness

A Woman of Significance:
Discovering Your Value and Purpose
in the Eyes of God

Becoming A Woman of
Spiritual Passion

What Do I Say to Mormon
Friends and Missionaries?

FORTHCOMING:

From Cumorah to the
Celestial Kingdom:
Mormonism's Changing View of Salvation

What Do I Say to
Jehovah's Witnesses?

Then Agrippa said to Paul,
Do you think that in such
a short time you can persuade me
to be a Christian?

Paul replied,
Short time or long—
I pray to God
that not only you
but all who are listening
to me today
may become what I am . . . .

Acts 26:28-29

CPSIA information can be obtained at www.ICGtesting.com
Printed in the USA
LVOW08s0845020416

481888LV00001B/67/P